Its status as a genre unto itself often disputed, the short story sequence is a hybrid organism which defies the stereotypes imputed to more conventionally recognized forms of narrative, such as the short story and the novel. By resisting precise definition, it lays down a critical challenge to decode its perplexing formal ambiguities. *Modern American Short Story Sequences* meets this challenge by suggesting an entirely new means of inquiry. Gathering together eleven full-length essays, this book is an invitation to reconsider the short story sequence as a tradition proper, one formed in the twentieth-century crucible of American literature and whose very inscrutability continues to provoke intense debate in the realm of fiction studies.

J. Gerald Kennedy's introduction investigates these and other problems of defining the genre, citing notable instances (such as Sherwood Anderson's *Winesburg, Ohio*), and exploring the implications of its modern emergence and popularity. Subsequent essays discuss illustrative works by such figures as Henry James, Jean Toomer, Ernest Hemingway, Richard Wright, William Faulkner, Eudora Welty, J. D. Salinger, John Cheever, John Updike, Louise Erdrich, and Raymond Carver. While examining distinctive thematic concerns, each essay also considers the implications of form and arrangement in the construction of composite fictions that often produce the illusion of a fictive community.

MODERN AMERICAN SHORT STORY SEQUENCES

MODERN AMERICAN SHORT STORY SEQUENCES

Composite Fictions and Fictive Communities

Edited by
J. GERALD KENNEDY
Louisiana State University

CAMBRIDGE
UNIVERSITY PRESS

Published by the Press Syndicate of the University of Cambridge
The Pitt Building, Trumpington Street, Cambridge CB2 IRP
40 West 20th Street, New York, NY 10011–4211, USA
10 Stamford Road, Oakleigh, Melbourne 3166, Australia

First Published 1995

Printed in the United States of America

Library of Congress Cataloging-in-Publication Data

Modern American short story sequences : composite fictions and fictive communities /
edited by J. Gerald Kennedy.

p. cm.

ISBN 0–521–43010–0

1. Short stories, American – History and criticism.   2. American fiction – 20th century –
History and criticism.   3. Community life in literature.   4. Narration (Rhetoric)   5. Cycles
(Literature)   6. Fiction – Technique.   7. Literary form.   I. Kennedy, J. Gerald.
PS648.S5M63   1995

813'.0108 – dc20   94–27032
                                                                                          CIP

A catalog record for this book is available from the British Library.

ISBN 0–521–43010–0 Hardback.

The essays by John Lowe, Susan V. Donaldson, and Robert M. Luscher originally
appeared in the *Journal of the Short Story in English*, vol. 11, 1988. They are reprinted here in
revised form with the kind permission of the Presse Universitaire d'Angers.

Contents

Contributors

Scott Donaldson, *Cooley Professor of English, Emeritus, College of William and Mary*

Susan V. Donaldson, *Associate Professor of English, College of William and Mary*

Richard A. Hocks, *Professor of English, University of Missouri–Columbia*

J. Gerald Kennedy, *Professor of English, Louisiana State University*

John Lowe, *Associate Professor of English, Louisiana State University*

Robert M. Luscher, *Associate Professor of English, Catawbe College*

Ruth Prigozy, *Professor of English, Hofstra University*

Michael Reynolds, *Professor of English, North Carolina State University*

John Carlos Rowe, *Professor of English, University of California–Irvine*

Linda Wagner-Martin, *Hanes Professor of English, University of North Carolina–Chapel Hill*

Hertha D. Wong, *Associate Professor of English, University of California–Berkeley*

Introduction: The American Short Story Sequence – Definitions and Implications

J. GERALD KENNEDY

A literary form at once ancient and avant-garde, the story sequence resists precise definition and occupies an odd, ambiguous place between the short story and the novel. Critics still disagree about what to call it: The genre discussed here as the sequence – to emphasize its progressive unfolding and cumulative effects – has been variously labeled the "short story cycle," the "short story composite," and the "rovelle" (a fusion of *roman* and *nouvelle*). Although such works as Joyce's *Dubliners* and Anderson's *Winesburg, Ohio* epitomize the type and herald a remarkable outpouring of such collections in the twentieth century, the combining of stories to create a linked series dates back from *The Thousand and One Arabian Nights* to Chaucer and Boccaccio and even further to classical antiquity itself. Yet efforts to trace the history of the form at once confront the stark discontinuity of its development. Lacunae of centuries between identifiable story sequences call into question the very notion of a sustained tradition. Meanwhile inquiries into its poetics raise a number of difficult questions: What features of arrangement and emphasis differentiate the sequence from the miscellaneous collection? What measure of coherence must a volume of stories possess to form a sequence? In the twentieth century, what distinguishes a connected set of stories from the multifaceted modern novel? Such questions suggest the complications that beset our understanding of what the story sequence is and how it works.

Readers conversant with twentieth-century fiction will, however, instantly recognize the ubiquity and importance of the form as represented by several collections from the era of high modernism. Gertrude Stein's *Three Lives,* Willa Cather's *The Troll Garden,* Franz Kafka's *Ein Hungerkünstler,* Edith Wharton's *Tales of Men and Ghosts,* Virginia Woolf's *Monday or Tuesday,* Ernest Hemingway's *Men Without Women,* Jean Rhys's *The Left Bank,* and F. Scott Fitzgerald's *Tales of the Jazz Age* chronologically surround the exemplary texts of Joyce and Anderson. As the preceding roster may suggest, American writers have been notably productive in the story sequence. During the century's middle decades, Katherine Ann Porter's *Flowering Judas,* Kay Boyle's *The Smoking Mountain,* Eudora Welty's *The Golden Apples,* Flannery O'Connor's *A Good Man is Hard to Find,* John Steinbeck's *Pastures of Heaven,* James Baldwin's *Going to Meet the Man,* John Barth's *Lost in the Funhouse,* Robert Coover's *Pricksongs and Descants,* and Ernest Gaines's *Bloodline* have underscored American achievement in the genre.

Since 1970, Reynolds Price's *Permanent Errors,* Alice Walker's *In Love and Trouble,* Joyce Carol Oates's *The Goddess and Other Women,* John Updike's *Too Far to Go,* Jayne Anne Phillips's *Black Tickets,* Raymond Carver's *What We Talk About When We Talk About Love,* Charles Johnson's *The Sorcerer's Apprentice,* Bobbie Ann Mason's *Love Life,* Sandra Cisneros's *Woman Hollering Creek,* and Tim O'Brien's *The Things They Carried* have all exemplified the peculiar force of separate, juxtaposed stories linked by common ideas, problems, or themes. To this list of recent American sequences we might add Robert Olen Butler's *A Good Scent from a Strange Mountain,* which garnered the 1993 Pulitzer Prize for fiction, and Edward P. Jones's *Lost in the City,* nominated for the 1992 National Book Award for fiction. Although recent collections by such writers as Alice Munro, Angela Carter, Gabriel Garcia-Marquez, and Italo Calvino remind us that the proliferation of short story sequences is truly a global phenomenon, still the pragmatic affinity for short stories that shaped the literature of the United States decisively in the nineteenth century seems to persist in our national avidity for organized story collections.[1] Perhaps the very determination to build a unified republic out of diverse states, regions, and population groups – to achieve the unity expressed by the motto *e pluribus unum* – helps to account for this continuing passion for sequences.

Although the massing of bibliographical evidence produces the impression of a veritable canon of "major" American texts, such a view proves slightly misleading. The collections cited above display, we should recognize, varying degrees of apparent arrangement and cohesiveness. In some cases, introductions, reiterated themes, or recurrent characters signal a conscious design; in other instances, connections between narratives seem more casual or adventitious. Ever since nineteenth-century writers like Poe, Gogol, Hawthorne, and Turgenev began to gather their own magazine tales into salable volumes, collections by single authors have filled the literary marketplace. But not all such volumes reflect a deliberate ordering of stories to produce a total effect; by their sheer heterogeneity, some betray more commercial than artistic impetus.

Formal organization in a set of stories may, as Susan Garland Mann observes, manifest itself in various ways: through a developing character (as in the *Bildungsroman*), a composite type, or a set of characters; through a dominant, explicit theme, such as isolation or revolt; or through the delineation of a particular locale, milieu, or community.[2] As we see in works such as *Dubliners* and *Lost in the Funhouse*, the title of a volume may likewise indicate an organizing concept that acquires depth and resonance as the collection unfolds. Other signs of orchestration may appear in the sequential ordering: The arrangement can suggest a cyclical process or an incremental action, produce striking juxtapositions of individual texts, or create clusters of closely linked stories within a volume. Organization may range from obvious to subtle; connections between stories may be patent or covert.[3]

Taking for granted the formal unity of the story sequence, Forrest Ingram – applying the term "cycle" – has distinguished three types of collections: the "composed" text, conceived from the outset as a set of related tales and often accompanied by a formal introduction; the "completed" text, generated when an author discovers a connection between two or more narratives already in print and writes additional stories to elaborate a pattern; and the "arranged" text, assembled by an author (often with editorial advice) from separate, previously published pieces to form a recognizably connected volume.[4] But this plausible scheme of classification depends crucially upon details of composition history that may remain ambiguous or even inaccessible to the scholar-critic. Ingram's categories moreover conceal the obstinate fact that no clear distinction exists between the arranged story sequence and the collection of assorted tales. In a sense, every single-author volume of stories manifests certain narrative homologies, commonalities of style or sensibility, that (in the absence of scholarly evidence) might be construed as a predetermined design. Given the ultimate inscrutability – if not irrelevance – of authorial intention, we face the impossibility of distinguishing in certain cases between ordered sequences and mere selections of stories editorially arranged. One must concede at last that textual unity, like beauty, lies mainly in the eye of the beholding reader.

This imponderable problem justifies the broadly inclusive view of the story sequence assumed here, a formal rubric that may be said to include all collections of three or more stories written and arranged by a single author.[5] Such an expansive definition would bracket titles carrying the phrase "and other stories" – volumes that despite their more relaxed organization often cohere thematically around the title story. But it would generally exclude editions designated as an author's "selected" or "collected" stories as well as omnibus editions (like Raymond Carver's *Where I'm Calling From*) that repackage stories from prior collections and lack any semblance of a controlling idea.

Having reached a provisional understanding of certain formal parameters, however, we confront another problem: Sequences also risk confusion with those twentieth-century novels that fragment narrative point of view to project multiple versions of a complex experience. Although such novels as Faulkner's *As I Lay Dying* or Gaines's *A Gathering of Old Men* include relatively few sections that resemble short stories, the generic issue becomes more ambiguous when we consider Faulkner's *The Unvanquished* or Gloria Naylor's *The Women of Brewster Place*. Faulkner stitched together his narrative of the Sartoris family from five independent stories that had first appeared in the *Saturday Evening Post*.[6] But even without this information, one observes that Faulkner's "chapters" depict relatively self-contained and completed actions. Naylor's powerful account of a community of black women has been marketed as "a novel in seven stories" – a designation that flaunts the undecidability of its form – and here too the narratives of Mattie Michael, Etta Mae Johnson, Kiswana Brown, and their sisters seem virtually complete and autonomous. A number of recent "genealogical" novels, such as John Edgar Wideman's *Damballah* and Lee Smith's *Oral History*, stake out an ambiguous middle ground between the novel and the story sequence, unfolding as separate yet intertwined short narratives about different family members. Such strategies accord with the tendency in many twentieth-century novels – such as *The Sound and the Fury*, *To the Lighthouse*, and *U.S.A.* – to renounce the organizing authority of an omniscient narrator, asserting instead a variety of voices or perspectives reflective of the radical subjectivity of modern experience. In its more experimental aspect, then, the novel has for about seventy-five years been veering toward the story sequence as a decentered mode of narrative representation.

Although it may be argued – as Mann does – that the effect of the sequence relies mainly on "the simultaneous independence and interdependence" of its constituent stories, a similar tension also informs such recent works as Amy Tan's *The Joy Luck Club* and James Gordon Bennett's *My Father's Geisha* – two fine volumes that illustrate the pervasive trade practice of configuring novels partly from previously published short stories.[7] Works of this type, which seem increasingly numerous, expose the uselessness of strict generic distinctions and demonstrate the palpable influence of marketing considerations on literary form. Such tactics blur generic boundaries and render precise distinctions between the segmented novel and the story sequence impossible; both contain connecting elements sharpened by the very discontinuities that complicate and enrich the reading experience.

Emerging from the nineteenth-century collection, which often presented a narrative hodgepodge, the story sequence has quietly gained prominence among twentieth-century literary forms. Its sheer proliferation since 1900 suggests an inherent consonance with certain pervasive modes of modernist expression. In the collections mentioned earlier, we routinely encounter such devices as fragmentation (in discrete, discontinuous short narratives), juxtaposition (in the purposive conjoining of complementary texts), and simultaneism (in the theoretically concurrent unfolding of separate actions) – aesthetic strategies which, as Roger Shattuck has shown, have long been used to render the complexity of modern experience.[8] Projecting diverse situations from different perspectives through separate narratives, the story sequence typically assumes a form reflective of the "multiplicity" that Henry Adams identified as the quintessential feature of the new century. Developing a dynamic "theory of history" to account for an accelerating profusion of "forces," Adams anticipated "complexities unimaginable to an earlier mind," the geometrical multiplication of forces, energies, and truths that have indeed determined the cosmopolitan, cultural pluralism of the twentieth century.[9]

The tension between unity and multiplicity foregrounded by Adams has an obvious correlation to the poetics of the story sequence, which relies on a balancing of centrifugal and centripetal impulses and on the ambiguous interplay between its discrete narrative parts and the formal or aesthetic whole. Critical neglect of the genre in recent decades remains almost inexplicable. Perhaps the very ambiguities that complicate formal definition have likewise deterred theoretical reflection. To extend the preliminary inquiries of Ingram and Mann and to initiate a more openly speculative consideration of story sequences, however, the present volume brings together eleven essays on important twentieth-century collections.

Richard A. Hocks leads the way with an account of the tentative formal experiment undertaken late in the career of Henry James in *The Finer*

Grain (1910). Hocks reviews recent critical responses to the volume before tracing the "geographical trajectory" and "patterning of reversals"
that enable us to understand the specific arrangement of the five stories.
He then shows how the collection anticipates "the tangential, fragmentary aspect of modernity itself," especially in its projection of problematic sexual relations between men and women. Linda Wagner-Martin
next examines the "modernist aesthetic" of Jean Toomer's *Cane* (1923)
to clarify issues of race and gender in the embedded "sequential narrative." Comprised of stories, poems, and drama, the collection breaks
down genre distinctions as it embodies Toomer's "multiple, inclusive
aims." Wagner-Martin traces the interplay of eros and violence in a collage of diverse texts that nevertheless define a "linear movement" or
figural journey. Michael Reynolds follows with an account of how Ernest Hemingway composed *In Our Time* (1925) and why that sequence,
with its alternating stories and vignettes, shows the author "at his most
experimental." Reynolds focuses especially on "Big Two-Hearted
River," with its deleted, metafictional conclusion, and explains why
Hemingway replaced "Up in Michigan" with "The Battler." Through
its reiterated themes, Reynolds contends, *In Our Time* offers a "visual
scrapbook" of "an emotionally desperate period" bracketing the First
World War.

After these essays on modernist sequences, John Lowe turns our attention to Southern literature and analyzes the mixture of folklore, religion, and politics in Richard Wright's explosive collection, *Uncle Tom's
Children* (1938). Lowe calls attention to the ideological strategies worked
out in these five stories, emphasizing Wright's "re-historicizing of the
black experience," his use of biblical motifs to advance communist
views, and his "appropriation of the structure and language of torture
rituals." Applying narrative theory, Lowe describes the recurrent design
that underlies these wrenching stories. Issues of race and racism likewise
pervade John Carlos Rowe's discussion of William Faulkner's *Go Down,
Moses* (1942). Challenging traditional readings that foreground Ike
McCaslin's expiatory role as the heir of slaveholders, Rowe focuses on
those stories that show Faulkner's effort to "grant his African-American
characters the independent voices he knows they must have in a truly
'New' South." This bold project fails, Rowe argues, because Faulkner
cannot finally transcend his white, Southern heritage to imagine "an
African-American identity that can govern its own historical representation." In quite different critical terms, Susan V. Donaldson extends the
consideration of Southern short story sequences to Eudora Welty's *The*

Wide Net (1943). Probing the elusive – and perhaps illusory – epiphanies in these stories, Donaldson surprisingly evokes Derrida's critique of "the metaphysics of presence" to show how Welty "exposes the drive for power underlying the desire for illumination." She sees Welty valorizing "questioning, openness, and transformation" in *The Wide Net* – an approach Donaldson ultimately connects with recent feminist aesthetics.

The ensuing three essays focus on writers closely associated with the *New Yorker* magazine and with suburban, middle-class life in the northeast. Taking on the challenge of J. D. Salinger's *Nine Stories* (1953), Ruth Prigozy calls attention to the Zen *koan* epigraph that prefigures the unresolved mysteries in these finely nuanced tales. Prigozy finds subtle thematic and structural parallels throughout the arrangement but shows how unresolved questions persistently undermine narrative closure. She argues that whereas these enigmas generate discontinuity from story to story, they paradoxically also manifest a relatedness through "an ineffable narrative dimension that itself functions much like a Zen *koan*." Scott Donaldson approaches John Cheever's *The Housebreaker of Shady Hill and Other Stories* (1958) as a collective critique of the illusions and hypocrisies of suburban life. Convinced that the short story best represented the "unsettled nature of contemporary existence," Cheever expresses in *Shady Hill* his ambivalence about "the manners and mores of suburbia." Donaldson argues that although Cheever mainly stages the "sorry spectacle" of a community masking its miseries, he also projects in "The Worm in the Apple" the ironic possibility of middle-class contentment. Robert M. Luscher demonstrates that although critics often dismiss John Updike's *Olinger Stories: A Selection* (1963) as an anthology, the collection forms "a unique aesthetic whole" reminiscent of the *Bildungsroman* structure of *Winesburg, Ohio*. Linked by their evocation of place and by a recurring character type (the maturing local boy), these stories suggest through epiphanic moments that the town of Olinger is indeed the "realm of grace." Citing "Packed Dirt, Churchgoing, A Dying Cat, A Traded Car" as a microcosm of Updike's connective scheme, Luscher proposes that *Olinger Stories* embody the double action of recapturing the past while performing "a ceremony of farewell."

Hertha D. Wong then questions the novelistic status of Louise Erdrich's *Love Medicine* (1984), showing how this Native American narrative of community more closely resembles the story sequence. Taking account of the newly revised version of the sequence (1993), she explores Erdrich's polyvocal, intratextual scheme, tracing patterns of imagery and sources of humor while also delineating the "somewhat chiasmic" mirroring effects of the sequential arrangement. Wong also situates *Love Medicine* in the broader contexts of Native American narrative and the fictional tetralogy planned by Erdrich. My own contribution explores ironic analogies between the story sequence and the idea of community, moving from Anderson's *Winesburg* to Raymond Carver's *Cathedral* (1983) to show how discontinuities in both works imply the breakdown of communal relations in ordinary, middle-class experience. Whereas Anderson subtly implies the alienating aspects of modern culture, Carver depicts the virtual end of collective life in the postmodern era. Both works project a residual nostalgia for community that permeates American story sequences.

The attentive reader will discover in many of these essays a recurrent interest in the problem of community and its relation to the fictional form under discussion. Some story collections literally "represent" communities; others imply by an interweaving of voices and narratives a communal consciousness. Whereas ethnic and minority sequences often affirm an ongoing sense of community, collections portraying mainstream, middle-class life typically emphasize the precariousness of local attachments. Perhaps insofar as story sequences present collective or composite narratives, they may all be said to construct tenuous fictive communities. Whether this resemblance is simply analogical or somehow constitutive of the poetics of the modern story sequence, the following essays will suggest various ways of thinking about the invisible community figured in every organized collection.

However one wishes to account for the extraordinary profusion of story sequences in this century, their prominence as a fictional form seems indisputable. A remarkable new generation of American fiction writers now seems poised to carry the sequence into the next millennium, adapting it to the jarring incongruities of postmodernism and the developing implications of chaos theory. The urgent need to make sense of contemporary culture and its violent preoccupations compels us to attend more closely as readers and critics to the fragmented images of twentieth-century life glimpsed in momentary clarity in the short story sequence.

NOTES

1. Writing in 1846 about the "Magazine Literature of America," Edgar Allan Poe remarked that "the *rush* of the age" called for "the curt, the condensed, the pointed, the readily diffused." The feverish pace of American life seemed more conducive to the reading and writing of short tales than of long novels. See his "Marginalia" in

Edgar Allan Poe: Essays and Reviews, ed. G. R. Thompson (New York: Library of America, 1984), 1,414–15.

2. Susan Garland Mann, *The Short Story Cycle: A Genre Companion and Reference Guide* (New York: Greenwood Press, 1989), 8–14.

3. I explore these modes and layers of signification more fully in "Toward a Poetics of the Short Story Cycle," *Journal of the Short Story in English,* 11 (Autumn 1988): 9–25. Because the term "cycle" carries implications of an overdetermined, even circular, arrangement that defines the genre rather narrowly, I now prefer the term "sequence," which (as Robert Luscher has persuaded me) places the formal emphasis on incremental meanings generated by a progression of texts.

4. Forrest Ingram, *Representative Short Story Cycles of the Twentieth Century* (The Hague: Mouton, 1971), 15–19.

5. Robert M. Luscher defines the sequence as "a volume of stories, collected and organized by their author, in which the reader successively realizes underlying patterns of coherence by continual modifications of his perceptions of pattern and theme." See "The Short Story Sequence: An Open Book," in *Short Story Theory at a Crossroads,* ed. Susan Lohafer and Jo Ellyn Clarey (Baton Rouge: Louisiana State University Press, 1989), 148. I have abridged Luscher's formulation to eliminate the test of reader response, which varies from person to person in relation to competence and purpose. I also concede the near impossibility of proving that certain sequences have been "organized by their author" and grant the decisive role, here and there, of certain strong editors. But I nevertheless assume that collections published within an author's lifetime tend to reflect that writer's preferences about organization and content.

6. See Susan V. Donaldson, "Dismantling the *Saturday Evening Post* Reader: *The Unvanquished* and Changing 'Horizons of Expectations,'" in *Faulkner and Popular Culture,* ed. Doreen Fowler and Ann J. Abadie (Jackson: University Press of Mississippi, 1990), 179–95.

7. For Mann's remark, see *The Short Story Cycle,* 12. At least six of the sixteen stories in *The Joy Luck Club* appeared first as separate short stories, as did five of the twelve sections of *My Father's Geisha.* This publishing scheme differs from the also pervasive tactic of placing in magazines short extracts from soon-to-be-released novels. Such excerpts lack the independence or formal cohesiveness that might be found in a story heralding a segmented novel.

8. Roger Shattuck, *The Banquet Years: The Origins of the Avant-Garde in France 1885 to World War I* (New York: Vintage, 1968), 331–52. Shattuck here describes the breaking apart of aesthetic unity as effected by the modernists — Jarry, Rousseau, Satie, and Apollinaire — he celebrates in this famous study.

9. Adams's ideas about the modern age inform the closing chapters of his famous autobiography. See *The Education of Henry Adams,* in *Henry Adams: Novels, Mont Saint-Michel, The Education,* ed. Ernest Samuels and Jayne N. Samuels (New York: Library of America, 1983), 1,068, 1,173–5.

Henry James's Incipient Poetics
of the Short Story Sequence:
The Finer Grain (*1910*)

RICHARD A. HOCKS

Many critics of Henry James are aware that after he completed the arduous task of selecting his novels and tales for Scribner's or The New York Edition (1907–9), revising all the chosen texts and composing his dense theoretical *Prefaces*, James went on to write something important other than his now much interpreted travel memoirs and autobiographical volumes. In fact, he composed and published five final tales between March 1909 and April 1910 – "The Velvet Glove," "Mora Montravers," "Crapy Cornelia," "The Bench of Desolation," and "A Round of Visits"; then he quickly republished them in book form with a new title, *The Finer Grain*, in October 1910, and changed the order as follows: "The Velvet Glove," "Mora Montravers," "A Round of Visits," "Crapy Cornelia," and "The Bench of Desolation." [1] Because the New York Edition's *Prefaces* are generally regarded as a veritable apotheosis of James's lifelong artistry – even by those who now contextualize or else deconstruct them – the status of five final tales said to have just "missed" making The New York Edition seems at first a bit like that of five cabooses standing stationary on a track parallel to that of the enormous luxury train to which they might have been joined. Edward Wagenknecht's observation in this regard is the norm: "Since the publication of The New York Edition was completed in 1909," he writes, "it was not possible to include any of them in that collection; they made their first appearance in book form in *The Finer Grain* (Scribner's, New York, and Methuen, London, 1910)." [2] Wagenknecht, that is, assumes that these tales appeared as *The Finer Grain* because they were too late to be absorbed into the architecture of The New York Edition. Certainly this is a plausible assumption, both because of the close proximity of these stories to James's famous edition and also because of the presence of his many earlier collections of tales from which James plucked innumerable stories, giving them an utterly new appearance and placement within The New York Edition.

At the same time, however, these last tales have intermittently provoked extraordinary comment. For example, R. P. Blackmur wrote in
1948: "[James's] fourth period began with a visit to America in 1904
and 1905 and might well have prepared him, had he lived longer or had
not the First World War intervened, for the still greater art of which we
can see the signs in the volume of stories called *The Finer Grain*, collected
in 1910."[3] Clearly such an assessment grants an accomplishment other
than the caboose separated because of mistaken scheduling; it suggests
instead that James was on the verge of a whole new "fourth manner."
There are, moreover, several major critics who have praised several of
these last tales, among them Ezra Pound, Dorothea Krook, J. A. Ward,
Peter Buitenhuis, Adeline Tintner, and Nicola Bradbury, although their
evaluations do not embrace the concept of the collection as something
greater than its individual parts. For that matter, it is hard to tell whether
Blackmur himself conceives of *The Finer Grain* as a unified artistic entity
or as a collection of tales that point individually toward a new direction
in James; presumably he means the latter. Pound praised all these pieces
as among James's best work; Nicola Bradbury speaks of "A Round of
Visits" as exhibiting at once "a strict sense of form" and eliciting the
quality James himself attributed to Shakespeare's *Tempest*, "'the joy of
sovereign *science*.'" For Dorothea Krook, "the relation between these stories [in *The Finer Grain*] and the novels appears to be that of the sketch
or study to the finished portrait," exhibiting the "prevailing mood and
atmosphere" of "harshness, grimness, pessimism – the Ecclesiastes
note" found in late novels such as *The Golden Bowl* and *The Ivory Tower*.
Adeline Tintner reads "The Velvet Glove" as a mock epic and "A
Round of Visits" as an analogue to *Paradise Lost*, and J. A. Ward, similar
to Krook, emphasizes James's sense of the experience of suffering and
pain, especially in "A Round of Visits" and "The Bench of Desolation."
Finally, Peter Buitenhuis responds to the title as an "accurate summa-
tion of James's effect in all this late short fiction," his manifesting the
"finest grain of consciousness and the richest compositional effect."[4]
These commentators and others have noted various important features
about *The Finer Grain* stories without, however, probing the collection's
status as a *sequence* – not simply as five tales of high merit, nor as an ap-
pendage to The New York Edition.

Very recently, however, this has all changed. Investigating *The Finer
Grain* as a short story sequence has become the endeavor of three quite
different James scholar-critics, and their hearty efforts, both individually
and together, suggest at once the great importance, yet also the lingering

problematic, of the whole enterprise. In their "Introduction" to a facsimile reproduction of *The Finer Grain*, W. R. Martin and Warren U. Ober propose that the volume presents James's very first "coherent vision" with "full scope" of the "grand concept of the intelligent imagination . . . which displays itself most conspicuously perhaps in art, but which – the stories show – must also be at work in all human relationships and affairs if the good life is to be achieved." Commenting on James's admiration of Turgenev's *A Sportsman's Sketches*, Martin and Ober further insist that "the carefully grouped, deeply related constellation of short stories, as opposed to collections with looser or more obvious connections, is, we believe, a distinctly modern phenomenon. It becomes a prominent feature of twentieth-century literature in English, and with *The Finer Grain* Henry James is a pioneer in this form."[5]

This is a wonderful initial thesis, and one could hardly ask for a more articulate and promising expression of it; yet the body of their argument quite unintentionally swerves away from its own claim. Martin and Ober write of the themes of "imagination," "art," and "life" implicit in the stories; they likewise affirm James's relation to both the "Romantic tradition" and to his distinctly post-Romantic Nietzschean imagination, his conception of the "artist-as-superman." This leads them to a peroration linking James's celebration of imagination and consciousness in the *Prefaces* and in "Is There a Life After Death?" (also written in 1910) to *The Finer Grain*. They thus conclude: "These [Prefaces] are *sui generis*, having a scope and an authority unmatched in the three-hundred-year history of the novel. *The Finer Grain* can be seen as a fruit of this great gestation, the culmination of a long striving for the highest coherence. What we find in the five carpets are variations of the same figure – the divine yet human faculty of imagination. Since Milton there has been no grander subject."[6]

Although I concur wholeheartedly with the elevated status Martin and Ober here accord James's imagination and sensibility, and have written to that effect for some twenty years, I continue to argue that James is less the Nietzschean artist (an idea first proposed by Stephen Donadio) and more the William Jamesian artist; but that really puts us together in the same general intellectual school. I also agree – and, again, have written on just this matter – that the *Prefaces*, a tale such as "A Round of Visits," and "Is There a Life After Death?" are extraordinarily comparable in poetic density and resonance.[7] And yet for all its legitimacy, Martin and Ober's argument for aesthetic and thematic parallelism seem a somewhat different matter from *The Finer Grain*'s status as a short story sequence, that is, as a distinct genre. In brief, they have proposed an important initial hypothesis, have even quoted from Forrest Ingram's classic definition of the short story cycle ("a set of stories so linked to one another that the reader's experience of each one is modified by his experience of the other"[8]) but have then somehow swerved away from that issue in proclaiming James's "divine theme" of the artistic "imagination."

A second recent attempt to deal with *The Finer Grain* as a short story cycle is Richard Gage's 1988 study, *Order and Design: Henry James' Titled Story Sequences*, the first to tackle this issue in James's vast corpus. Gage's is an ambitious attempt to argue "organic unity and connectedness," "thematic continuity," and "architectural form" in James's six short story volumes with "evocative titles," as well as in volume eighteen in The New York Edition. Gage's real interest is in thematic unity, a position that causes him sometimes to strain and overclaim Jamesian interlinkings, especially when dealing with *The Better Sort* (1903); or else his unhappily definitive proposal that *all* of James's titled story sequences interconnect precisely like the "dots" on Georges Seurat canvases, an analogy which, at the very least, reduces the intrinsic merit – as well as the process that Ingram calls "modification" – of each constituent James tale, a number of which, like "The Beast in the Jungle" in *The Better Sort*, are exceptional early modernist works in their own right.[9]

Gage has better luck with *The Finer Grain*, however, because there he wisely follows James's publisher's description and argues for a "grain"-women leitmotif as well as the necessary "graining" of male protagonists, "tested and proven in the furnace of human experience."[10] Even so, the lingering difficulty with Gage's long chapter on *The Finer Grain* is precisely the problem of the study as a whole, his excessive claims surrounding James's thematic "coherence, organic growth, development, and a sense of architectural balance" throughout *all* his titled short story volumes.[11] Once again, as with Martin and Ober, I agree that James is a great artist and craftsman, but I doubt that insisting so relentlessly on thematic unity and plot explication is the most convincing way of demonstrating the actual significance, architectural or poetic, of a collection like *The Finer Grain*.

The third and most recent attempt to come to grips with this group of stories is Richard Lyons's 1990 essay, "Ironies of Loss in *The Finer Grain*," an analysis that likewise sounds unabashedly thematic, yet in fact approaches the tales with a deftness and feel for their actual subtlety not present in Martin and Ober or in Gage; indeed, Lyons's conjunction of irony with loss already insinuates a quiet, subtle interlacing of mode with theme. This perceptive new analysis of the tales emphasizes their "complexities of tone and attitude" in treating "the various forms of loss" and "costs," including "the loss of illusions" and the "implicit threat to the imagination" – that is, *not* Martin and Ober's divine celebration of it. Lyons dissects not only the "social satire" and "element of self-parody" of these pieces but also their distinctive "mixture of comedy and pathos," and even their Chekhovian "intermingling of tragedy and comedy, an evocation of moods of loss, of transience, of ironies just fending off despair." He detects not so much a Jamesian fourth manner, as Blackmur had proposed earlier, but rather a "shift of emphasis," in which James accords "feelings of loss and defeat their full and richly shaded measure of irony and pity." Lyons's discussion of "The Bench of Desolation" is particularly fine.[12]

These three critics and their approaches are truly interesting to ponder together. Lyons, for instance, never discusses the genre of *The Finer Grain* as such, and, most significantly, refers to the individual tales *only* in the sequence of their *serial* publication, not in the different order of James's volume. Nevertheless, Lyons's thematic analysis conveys most successfully James's integrating preoccupation with deprivation, ambiguity, and irony, elements that mark the author's last collection as proto-modernist in conception and execution. Martin and Ober, one recalls, proposed James as precisely just such a modernist "pioneer in this form," and yet their analysis veered away from the claim. Lyons, in other words, seems to make good on Martin and Ober's "pioneer" thesis, while remaining uninterested in the sequence as a genre.[13] As for Gage, his vigorous insistence on "organic unity," "architecture," and "pointillism" sits most uneasily astride his actual methodology of plot summary and thematic explication, so unlike the fluid, nuanced thematics of Richard Lyons. In short, the difference between the *unity* Gage proclaims and the *integration* Lyons in effect conveys is the acute difference between a work that is premodern and one more distinctly modernist in mode. So if Martin and Ober are to be validated in their claim about James "the pioneer," it is Lyons who better confirms it.

Until 1895, Henry James's numerous collections of tales were simply and routinely miscellanies with titles taken from stories in them; thereafter all his volumes beginning with *Terminations* (1895) and *Embarrassments*

(1896) have titles newly devised. Although there are six such titled collections, as mentioned earlier, and also several untitled groupings of tales in The New York Edition, it is, I believe, *The Finer Grain* that in 1910 first presents us with a short story sequence proper. Its singularity and cohesion arise first from genetic evidence of two kinds. To begin with, we are told by James's amanuensis Theodora Bosanquet in her diary that:

> It is almost literally true to say of the sheaf of tales collected in *The Finer Grain* that they were all written in response to a single request for a short story for *Harper's Monthly Magazine*. The length was to be about 5,000 words and each promising idea was cultivated in the optimistic belief that it would produce a flower too frail and small to demand any exhaustive treatment. But even under pressure of being written by hand, with dictated interpolations rigidly restricted, each in turn pushed out to lengths that no chopping could reduce to the word limit.[14]

This tells us that the tales were composed more or less simultaneously and seems to confirm the closeness in composition already indicated by the contiguity of the magazine publications. In point of fact, one would be hard-pressed to say whether this and the evidence to follow confirms that James authored what Ingram would define a cycle of stories "*composed* as a continuous whole, or *arranged* into a series, or *completed* to form a set."[15] In any case, these compositional circumstances differ from any of James's other volumes, including those five others with newly devised titles (treated identically by Gage as exemplifications of organic unity).

The other singular feature about *The Finer Grain* is James's prefatory statement to his publishers, intended no doubt for the book jacket, purporting to explicate his book title and perhaps suggest an organizing principle. It reads as follows:

> *The Finer Grain* consists of a series of Tales representing in each case a central figure (by which Mr. Henry James is apt to mean a central and a lively *consciousness*) involved in one of those greater or less tangles of circumstance of which the measure and from which the issue is in the vivacity and the active play of the victim's or the victor's sensibility. Each situation is thereby more particularly a moral drama, an experience of the special soul and intelligence presented (the sentient, perceptive, reflective part of the protagonist, in short), but with high emphasis clearly intended on its wearing for the hero or the heroine the quality of the agitating, the challenging personal *adventure*. In point of fact, indeed, it happens in each case to be the hero who exhibits this finer grain of accessibility to suspense or curiosity, to mystification or attraction – in other

words, to moving experience: it is by his connection with its interest in the "grain" woman that his predicament, with its difficult solution, is incurred. And the series of illustrations of how such predicaments *may* spring up, and even be really characteristic, considerably ranges: from Paris to London and New York, and then back again, to ambiguous yet at the same time unmistakable English, and ultra-English, ground.[16]

This explanatory statement is unique to any of James's collection of tales, although it is hardly what most of us would call a dust jacket style. It is vintage late Henry James prose, thereby presumably telling us a great deal while at the same time making certain that the work it purports to describe remains what Robert Luscher would call "an open book."[17] Gage understandably seeks to use this document as his foundation from which to "unify" *The Finer Grain* around certain key points, particularly the "special" Jamesian "intelligence" or "consciousness" as well as the various "grain"-women who appear in the sequence. And one of Gage's best ideas is the possibility that "fine-grained timber is generally stronger than coarse-grained; that to be fine-grained means to be many-fibered," so that ultimately fine-grained characters in the volume "are not weak but strong."[18]

Nevertheless, the most salient feature of this supposedly descriptive passage is its rich elliptical abstractionism, the same quality found in late short fiction like "The Great Good Place" or "The Beast in the Jungle," as well as in the *Prefaces*. To be sure, one can easily identify the "sentient, perceptive, reflective" hero-gentlemen from each tale: John Berridge from "The Velvet Glove," Sidney Traffle from "Mora Montravers," Mark Monteith from "A Round of Visits," White-Mason from "Crapy Cornelia," and Herbert Dodd from "The Bench of Desolation." Correspondingly, the "grain"-women are quickly identifiable and perhaps even more plentiful: Amy Evans from "The Velvet Glove," Mora Montravers (and Jane Traffle, I believe) from "Mora Montravers," Mrs. Folliott (and perhaps Florence Ashe) from "A Round of Visits," Cornelia Rasch (and possibly Mrs. Worthingham) from "Crapy Cornelia," and Kate Cookham (but also Nan Drury, I suspect) in "The Bench of Desolation." Still, having said that, and having also given due acknowledgment to Jamesian interior reflectors of consciousness, one wonders where we are; interior reflectors of consciousness, after all, are the norm in the late James, hardly distinctive to *The Finer Grain*. This leaves us with the "grain"-women, all of whom come into conflict with their male counterparts (each with his "finer grain of accessibility . . . to moving experience"). Perhaps James's language citing "the active play of the victim's or the victor's sensibility" should engage us: "Victim" and "victor" suggest a pattern of forceful conflict, even war, between the male protagonists and their "grain"-women – in fact, the women might be thought of as going "against the grain" in their relationships with the "finer-grained" men. Other significant language includes the phrase "mystification or attraction," which carries multiple suggestions. The first is of James's "ghostly" realm, so dominant in this late period, one that gravitates toward the surrealistic sphere and joins the modernist landscapes of Eliot, Conrad, Woolf, and Pound. "Mystification" and "attraction" also convey the element of extravagance and the phantasmic found in these stories, while it also points toward the feature of a psychic parable or fairy tale so prominent in "The Bench of Desolation," "A Round of Visits," and "The Velvet Glove." An attractive "mystification" is also the quintessential element of the late Jamesian style, including the prefatory statement itself, and a crucial reason why its meaning remains fluid, implicitly making *The Finer Grain* an "open book" regardless of any discoverable "themes."

In a way, perhaps the least mystifying element in the entire statement is James's last sentence, in which he speaks of the geographical movement "from Paris to London and New York, and then back again, to ambiguous yet at the same time unmistakably English, and ultra-English, ground." That is, his statement makes sense *if* one recollects the difference between magazine and book publication: By placing "A Round of Visits" and "Crapy Cornelia" third and fourth in the volume (they are fifth and third, respectively, in order of magazine publication), James achieves in his settings the geographical trajectory he alludes to. Why he prefers that order probably stems from his perception that "The Bench of Desolation," the final tale (fourth in magazine appearance), has the sort of "Winter's Tale" resonance that makes it the ideal "anchor" among these five. Also, I suspect James realized that the same tale, however convoluted and extravagant its mode, by its dealing with lower-middle if not quite working-class people and set in "Land's End," where one gazes at the sea from the bleak marina, conveyed a sort of spiritual coastal finality, an end-of-the-land perspective that suits the end of the volume. Certainly the tale is "ultra-English" in its seaside setting on and beyond the edge of land, so to speak, but also in its comprehensive ethos in a way that the volume's other English tale, "Mora Montravers," set in more provincial Wimbledon, just outside London, is not. Furthermore, inasmuch as *The Finer Grain* is James's last published fiction, the fact that he chose the phrase "Land's End" to denominate his fictitious town of Properly is significant: For although "The Bench of Desolation" does not take place in the actual English locale of Land's End in Cornwall but is rather almost certainly Brighton on the southern coast near James's own seaside town of Rye, "Land's End" represents figuratively the westernmost point of land in mainland England closest to the United States, thus perhaps signifying James's own life and career as an American writer who lived in England and wrote international fiction. Such metaphorical overtones, however, cannot diminish the strong ironic and satirical elements inherent in James's fictitious name of Properly, given to a town long known for its sexual *im*propriety – namely Brighton.[19]

The geographical sequencing brings up another formal issue of no small importance. Once James decided his tales were to move "internationally" from Paris to London to New York and then back to England at "Land's End," he quite obviously had the choice with his two New York tales – "A Round of Visits" and "Crapy Cornelia" – of which to place third and which fourth. I do not believe he flipped a coin. "A Round of Visits" was his final tale published serially, and it is a very powerful work, a broad indictment of cultural values, a study of complicity, a violent narrative ending with a brutal suicide. "Crapy Cornelia," too, contains a critique of the present society by contrasting it nostalgically with the past, but the terms of the critique are less momentous and culturally resonant than in "A Round of Visits." Perhaps James felt that by putting "Crapy Cornelia" fourth in the volume the reader would get a slight "breather" between his two most powerful tales, "A Round of Visits" and the finale, "The Bench of Desolation," allowing a greater appreciation of each.

That is one possibility. However, I do not believe it was the principal reason for James's decision to place "A Round of Visits" third in *The Finer Grain*. He placed it third, I think, because "A Round of Visits" is the only story in which the protagonist's principal encounter is not with a woman but with another man: Mark Monteith's incredible maneuvering with Newton Winch in the final scenes leading up to Winch's suicide not only takes precedence over all the briefer previous "visits" with "grainy" women but even evokes that unmistakable aura of an encounter with one's own alter ego; it is almost as though James finally gives us the scene between the alter and the ego, so to speak, that did not quite transpire in "The Jolly Corner."[20] This story's formal element of asymmetry in this one respect within the collection probably dictated its placement in the final sequence: by putting it third, James created geometrical balance out of imbalance, for he flanked it on both sides with two tales in which the encounter conflicts transpire between the hero and a woman, not another man. Formal questions of this sort mattered deeply to James. For example, his "Preface" to *The Wings of the Dove* is largely preoccupied with his perception of, and worry over, its structural disproportion in the sequencing of the novel's ten books, so much so that he even discourses on a "misplaced pivot" occurring in Milly Theale's Book Fifth.[21] By contrast then, his positioning "A Round of Visits" third in *The Finer Grain* in effect creates or places his "pivot" symmetrically in the middle.

I would also suggest – though I would not press the point – that because James alluded to his geographical trajectory in the publisher's statement, perhaps the concept functions in an analogous way to T. S. Eliot's geographical sequencing in *Four Quartets,* as a way of using the "visiting mind" to engage the transnational issues besetting the modern world, while defining a "subtext" of one's own personal "pilgrim" odyssey as both an artist and a representative member of the same fractured community. If *The Finer Grain* is analogous to *Four Quartets'* international "pilgrimage" in this regard, it suggests that James's poetic mode, like Eliot's, is a modernist's reconception of Dante, a feature R. P. Blackmur believed James exhibited in the late novels as the "poetry of the soul in action."[22]

Far more certain in *The Finer Grain* is the formal, recurrent pattern of reversal. Like the St. John's River in New Brunswick, Canada, which flows toward the sea and then reverses itself in the wake of an overpowering high tide, each tale executes a phenomenal reversal in the interpersonal relationships between hero and "grain"-women. In "The Velvet Glove," after John Berridge becomes enamoured of the beautiful young woman he meets at sculptor Gloriani's garden (the same place where Lambert Strether had said "Live all you can" in *The Ambassadors*), he is later shocked to learn that she invites him "home" seductively only in order to persuade him to write a "puffing" preface for her trashy novel *The Velvet Glove,* written under her pen name Amy Evans. In "Mora Montravers," Sidney Traffle's fascination with the free lifestyle of his wife's niece Mora undergoes a cataclysm when, after Mora agrees to marry artist Walter Puddick with whom she is living in order to collect a bribe from Sidney's prim wife Jane, Mora immediately divorces Puddick and takes up with another "catch," so that Puddick can keep the benefit of her aunt's money. Sidney absorbs a second blow when he realizes that Jane likes Puddick well enough to let him keep the allowance, a twist that the resourceful Mora probably anticipated.

In "A Round of Visits," Mark Monteith, after being swindled out of his money by a broker-friend-turned-crook, calls on some mutual friends (female) to receive solace, only to find out that each one wishes him to "doctor" her instead. Determined finally that "Providence" is "breaking him to its will by constantly directing his attention to the claims of others" (162), Monteith casually visits an ill, old-time acquaintance, Newton Winch, only to discover with triple shock that Winch has mysteriously "improved" in sensibility, is guilty of larceny just like Mark's broker friend, and is at once awaiting the police and contemplating suicide, which he commits at the end of Mark's visit. In "Crapy Cornelia," forty-eight-year-old bachelor White-Mason, responding to the ambience of April in Central Park, decides to propose to nouveau riche Mrs. Worthingham, but at her residence he meets Cornelia Rasch, a friend from the old days. When Mrs. Worthingham speaks disparagingly of Cornelia, White-Mason reverses his decision and instead renews his acquaintance with "crapy" Cornelia, whose mellow old furnishings contrast with Mrs. Worthingham's gaudy appointments, and with whom he can reminisce indefinitely about the charms of old New York.

Finally in "The Bench of Desolation," Herbert Dodd, a second-hand bookseller, is threatened with a lawsuit by Kate Cookham for breach of promise. After fearfully paying her £270 of the £400 he "owes" her, Dodd loses his business, marries Nan Drury, has two daughters, sees all three die of poverty, becomes a clerk in the gas works, and sits on a desolate bench along the southern English seacoast. Suddenly after twelve years Kate reappears, now astonishingly "oh, yes – a real lady" (265) and wondrously solicitous of Dodd's welfare. Her "idea" all along has been to prove herself worthy of his regard as well as to bring him back his money fivefold from accrued interest. Though Dodd feels the "wail" of his lost family and senses that Kate's return is "at once a fairy-tale and a nightmare" (294), in which "the unforgettable and the unimaginable were confoundingly mixed" (287), his egotism has been so chastened, even brutalized, by suffering and poverty that he now feels both freedom and wounded pride alike to be the "thinnest of vain parades" and the "poorest of hollow heroics" (301). At the end, silent Kate's "arm pass[es] round him" and she is "beside him on the bench of desolation" (312).

I hope these brief summaries make clear that the patterning of reversals in *The Finer Grain* is every bit as insistent as the motif of irony through loss that Lyons explores so deftly and persuasively. Indeed, these reversals constitute the grammatical chain which makes Lyons's explicated

meaning possible, and thus constitute an avenue toward James's narrative deep structure, which might be conceived of as something like this:
the collision of extravagant expectation with the abyss of actuality.[23]

In any case, one could try improvising on Robert Luscher's theoretical point and propose that, although *The Finer Grain* has no "technically
uniting" figure like Sam Lawson in Harriet Beecher Stowe's *Oldtown
Fireside Stories,* on the one hand,[24] or else, say, an overt Joycean theme of
"paralysis," on the other, James's volume is deeply integrated through
its systematic reversals and *far* more resembles Joyce – whose *Dubliners*
(1914) was in preparation for several years before *The Finer Grain* appeared – than it does Stowe. And what this means is that James in 1910
wrote a quintessentially protomodernist short story sequence that, to
combine Forrest Ingram's terminology, seems at once both highly "arranged" and "completed."

Academic critical theory since about 1980 seems to have established (or
at least insisted a hundred times over) that Henry James is a modern,
indeed postmodern writer. Perhaps it is not so surprising, then, to conclude, as I have above, that *The Finer Grain* is a modernist work. Nevertheless, what makes this volume so distinctive is precisely its place both
very late in James's career yet also quite early in this century. James
seems to have "intuited" the modernist conception of a story sequence –
perhaps one reason Ezra Pound thought so highly of these particular
tales. The actual *narrative* relationship – as opposed to a thematic or formal one – between one tale and another in *The Finer Grain* might best
be called "tangential," in the same sense and for the same generic reasons that the narrative episodes in *The Waste Land* are tangential – made
all the more so, one recalls, by Pound in his radical editing of Eliot's
manuscript. What Eliot with Pound's help achieves is an ideological
"unity of disunity" (as all readers and editors who have worked hard to
put back together Eliot's "fragments" know so well), which seeks to express the core of modern life. Just as the typist and the clerk, let us say,
are not known to Marie, or either to Lil, Lou, Albert, and the other
figures in the pub, neither are James's men and women in the tales of
The Finer Grain.

Yet what James in his publisher's statement calls their "predicaments" resonate, as we have already seen, with recurrent concerns: loss
of illusion, irony barely distinguishable from despair, interpersonal exploitation by money or power, extravagant expectations foredoomed to

disappointment, retreat into the past, the high cost of investing emotional "interest" in another, and especially the lethal combination of hyperconsciousness with loneliness. The implicit community made up of James's characters in *The Finer Grain* definitely cuts across class, economic, and national boundaries, but the world in common is that of modernity, and the news is not very good. None of these characters will ever meet, and yet none of them who do meet ever deeply understand each other – with the striking exception of Mark Monteith and Newton Winch, and Winch's final response to that understanding is to kill himself; and Mark's is to tell the police, "I think I must practically have caused it" (185). The composite world of James's five tales is one of discontinuity and continuity: discontinuity from the standpoint of the characters with one another, both within and between tales; continuity from the standpoint of James's patterning through reversal, his integrated themes of loss, and his geometrical as well as geographical positioning of the tales. James's community is "invisible," in the language of J. Gerald Kennedy, both because its members are spiritually closed off from one another and also because the atmosphere in which they live and act, as James depicts it with his late prose of "mystification," is that of the phantasmagoric, the "ghostly," the surrealistic.

Related to the issue of isolationism and aloneness is the question of the sexes, obviously the preeminent one in *The Finer Grain*. The post-Freudian psychoanalyst Jacques Lacan has proposed that "there is no sexual relation," by which he appears to mean that men and women are fundamentally structured so differently that as human subjects they can never truly understand one another; they will have social and family relations, obviously, but at their core, he claims, there can be no true commonality of perspective. Lacan expresses this idea parabolically by telling of a young brother and sister on a train who, upon pulling into the station, look past each other out the window and see the signifying letters for the different rest rooms, "Gentlemen" and "Ladies." The sister concludes that the town is called "Gentlemen," and the brother that it is "Ladies." Brother and sister inhabit the same territory, but the name or language for it, by which each is structured, remains opposed; indeed, their condition with respect to each other is in a sense emblematized by the two separated tracks on which they "sit."[25]

This is quite obviously a very controversial thesis, but I cite it because I can scarcely think of a better way to describe the problematized "sexual relation" between the heroes, despite – or is it because of? – their "finer grain" of Jamesian consciousness, on the one hand, and the women "against-the-grain" with whom they would interact, on the other. In all five stories the social or family relation inevitably belies any fundamental sexual relation. John Berridge of "The Velvet Glove" totally misconstrues Amy Evans by imagining her a part of the "Olympian race" (11), and she greatly misconceives him. When she finally names her desire for his puffing, "log-rolling Preface" to her junk novel, Berridge feels

> this exquisite intimacy of her manner of setting him down on the other side of the abyss. It was as if she had lifted him first in her beautiful arms, had raised him up high, high, high, to do it, pressing him to her immortal young breast while he let himself go, and then, by some extraordinary effect of her native force and her alien quality, setting him down exactly where she wanted him to be – which was a thousand miles away from her. (38)

This passage – with its astonishing "Leda and the Swan"-like encounter – virtually serves as a key signature for the male–female relationships and reversals throughout the sequence. Sidney Traffle remains totally perplexed by "the sharer of his life" (94), his wife Jane; but with young Mora Montravers Sidney is "smashed into smithereens" (50) by "the treacherous fact of her beauty" (51). For despite her "extraordinary prettiness," she "opened out before him – a vertiginous view of a gulf," wherein "he knew the vague void for one he would never bridge" (69–70). Mark Monteith's encounter with Mrs. Folliott in "A Round of Visits" creates the same impasse, as the two lament their mutual victimization by larcenist Phil Bloodgood:

> She abused the author of their wrongs – recognising thus too Monteith's right to loathe him – for the desperado he assuredly had proved, but with a vulgarity of analysis and an incapacity for the higher criticism, as her listener felt it to be, which made him determine resentfully, almost grimly, that she shouldn't have the benefit of a grain of *his* vision or *his* version of what had befallen them, and of how, in particular, it had come; and should never dream thereby (though much would she suffer from that!) of how interesting he might have been. (150)

What makes this example particularly helpful is that it conveys what all the tales – but not all the examples – possess, the feature that, although James's viewpoint characters or "registers" are men, they are ultimately no more trustworthy than are the women with whom "there is no sexual relation." Critics like Gage or Martin and Ober, for instance, would do very well to attend to James's ironic use of the word "grain" in the passage above. In "Crapy Cornelia," White-Mason's reencounter with Cornelia Rasch serves only to separate him inexorably from Mrs. Worthingham; his renewed friendship with Cornelia has no intertwining love or sexuality, but is only a suture allowing each to acknowledge, Prufrock-like, "I'm old" (233). Finally, despite Herbert Dodd's "reduplications of consciousness" (271) and the fairy tale/nightmare return of Kate Cookham with his money to rejoin him on his bench of desolation, these juxtaposed figures remain the aggressive "grainy" woman (compared at one point to the witch Meg Merrillies) and the passive residual egoist. In fact, Kate Cookham and Herbert Dodd, as much as any two characters in *The Finer Grain,* exhibit the Lacanian hysteric and obsessive structure, respectively. In any case, their "togetherness" at the end is, once again, at best a suture, and their minimal mutual understanding is best articulated by Kate: "I've meant, for long years, I think, all I'm capable of meaning. I've meant so much that I can't mean more" (307). And when Dodd asks how, then, she persevered with such an incredible plan, she retorts, "But that's my story." "And mayn't I hear it?" he pursues. "No–because I mayn't hear yours" (311).

James himself is not, obviously, indebted to a psychoanalyst of the future like Lacan anymore than to a contemporary like Freud. Such elements of parallelism merely reinforce the modernity of *The Finer Grain.* The theme of "loss" explicated by Lyons happens also to be the fundamental principle that underlies Lacanian desire, and this profound drive is indeed common to *both* men and women, which is another reason why Lyons's overview of that motif is helpful and illuminating.

The metaphor of the finer grain includes the idea of the pearl of great price, but with the emphasis on the terrible price paid for the pearl. That is also why the collection remains open-ended and contingent, although integrated, rather than formally "unified." Its modernist tenor disallows the kind of closure suggested by a concept like organic unity. On the other hand, all five stories do, after a fashion, execute James's Maupassant-like twist, the reversal; but precisely in order to open things up rather than make the neat *point-devise.* Only with James's placement of the "pivot," "A Round of Visits," third in the sequence, do we have something extraordinarily "neat" in that sense, and at that level we are talking about the basic formal architecture of the sequence, not the world-view conveyed in the work: As Theodora Bosanquet's diary makes clear, James simply could not contain his vision neatly, and thus wrote loose and baggy monsters like his early-and-late master Balzac or even his formalist bête noire Tolstoy. There is, nevertheless, much formal configuration and even originality of genre in a collection that begins with a kind of romance parody and ends with a stark fable, although James, despite his systematic use of reversal, misses what Robert Luscher calls that "near-perfect equilibrium between the conflicting demands of the independent story and those of the continuous narrative."[26] James misses such an "equilibrium" in part because *The Finer Grain* was not quite "composed" as a sequence – although importantly "arranged" and "completed" – and in part because his vision was more fluid and contingent than, say, Joyce's orchestration in *Dubliners,* whose collection is only a bit more obviously groundbreaking. What is indisputable to any reader of James's 1910 sequence is that the mystifying idiom, the intricacy of tonal variation, and the phastasmagoric atmosphere are poetic and modernist in resonance. James's style in this regard can be described as "expressionistic" in tandem with the post-impressionist movement in art at the beginning of the new century. The difficulty attending these last tales arises not from their artistic integrity but from their anticipation of the tangential, fragmentary nature of modernity itself. Correspondingly, the more one reads James's publisher's description of *The Finer Grain* the less one can find a lasting expression of its unified wholeness, even though each successive reading does suggest its poetic density, analogous, say, to Keats's "vale of Soul-making" letter. Such poetic compression is the Dantesque feature Ezra Pound must have seen in these tales, and it is most likely one aspect of what R. P. Blackmur meant by James's inchoate "fourth manner." *The Finer Grain* is indeed an inchoate attempt at the modernist short story sequence in which James is burdened by a vision of twentieth-century life typified by Herbert and Kate's prolepsis of death on their bench of desolation and by Mark Monteith's awareness that "there was nothing like a crowd, this unfortunate knew, for making one feel lonely" (151).

NOTES

1. For a detailed publication history of these tales see Leon Edel, Dan H. Laurence, and James Rambeau, *A Bibliography of Henry James,* 3rd ed. (New York: Oxford University Press, 1982), 144–5.
2. Edward Wagenknecht, *The Tales of Henry James* (New York: Frederick Ungar, 1984), 161.

3. R. P. Blackmur, "Henry James," in *Literary History of the United States*, rev. ed.; ed. Robert E. Spiller, et al. (New York: The Macmillan Co., 1953), 1043.

4. See "Henry James," *Literary Essays of Ezra Pound*, ed. T. S. Eliot (London: Faber, 1954), 305; Nicola Bradbury, *Henry James: The Later Novels* (Oxford: Clarendon Press, 1979), 216, 220; Dorothea Krook, *The Ordeal of Consciousness in Henry James* (New York: Cambridge University Press, 1967), 326, 335; Adeline Tintner, "James's Mock Epic: 'The Velvet Glove,' Edith Wharton, and Other Late Tales," *MFS* 17 (1971–2): 483–99, and "An Interlude in Hell: Henry James's 'A Round of Visits' and *Paradise Lost*," *Notes on Modern American Literature*, 5, no. 2 (1981): Item 12 (cf. W. R. Martin and Warren U. Ober, "Dantesque Patterns in Henry James's 'A Round of Visits,'" *Ariel: A Review of International English Literature*, 12, no. 4 (1981): 45–54); J. A. Ward, *The Imagination of Disaster: Evil in the Fiction of Henry James* (Lincoln: University of Nebraska Press, 1961), 160–5; Peter Buitenhuis, *The Grasping Imagination: The American Writings of Henry James* (Toronto: University of Toronto Press, 1970), 210. Of the five tales, the two most frequently analyzed are "A Round of Visits" and "The Bench of Desolation," with "The Velvet Glove" next in the gaze of critics.

5. Henry James, *The Finer Grain: A Facsimile Reproduction*, ed. W. R. Martin and Warren U. Ober (Delmar, NY: Scholars' Facsimiles & Reprints, 1986), vi. All future citations from *The Finer Grain* will be from this edition and will appear parenthetically by page number in the text.

6. Ibid., xxii.

7. In *Henry James and Pragmatistic Thought* (Chapel Hill: University of North Carolina Press, 1974), 217–27, I have analyzed "Is There a Life After Death?" as the poetic document paralleling "The Jolly Corner," the *Prefaces,* and "A Round of Visits"; more recently, my *Henry James: A Study of the Short Fiction* (Boston: Twayne Publishers, 1990), 91–105, probably contains the most extended analysis in print of "A Round of Visits" as a self-standing tale independent of *The Finer Grain*.

8. Quoted by Warren and Ober, vi.

9. Richard P. Gage, *Order and Design: Henry James' Titled Story Sequences* (New York: Peter Lang, 1988), 292; for Gage's iteration of organic and thematic unity, see pp. 3–15, and passim.

10. Ibid., 289, 276.

11. Ibid., 290.

12. Richard S. Lyons, "Ironies of Loss in *The Finer Grain*," *Henry James Review*, 11, no. 3 (Fall 1990), 202–12.

13. It is surely significant that Lyons quotes only from volume 12 of *The Complete Tales*, never *The Finer Grain; The Complete Tales* prints the stories in sequence of their serial publication.

14. Theodora Bosanquet, *Henry James at Work* (London: Hogarth Press, 1924), 248–9. In her fine brief review of Gage, Adeline Tintner, *ALR*, 22, no. 2 (Winter 1990), 87, pertinently remarks that "in the case of *The Finer Grain*, the stories are clearly united in time and therefore united in James's mind."

15. Forrest L. Ingram, *Representative Short Story Cycles of the Twentieth Century* (The Hague: Mouton, 1971), 17.

16. Henry James, *The Complete Notebooks of Henry James*, ed. Leon Edel and Lyall H. Powers (New York: Oxford University Press, 1987), 577.

17. See Robert M. Luscher, "The Short Story Sequence: An Open Book," in *Short Story Theory at a Crossroads*, ed. Susan Lohafer and Jo Ellyn Clarey (Baton Rouge: Louisiana State University Press, 1989), 148–67.

18. Gage, 202, 276.

19. For his convincing identification of James's town Properly in "The Bench of Desolation" with Brighton, I wish to thank Mr. Lionel Kelly, Director of American Studies at the University of Reading in England, who along with Nicola Bradbury, a fine James scholar, kindly allowed me to try out this prepublished essay in seminar.

20. For more of this interpretation see my *Study of the Short Fiction*, 91–105.

21. See Henry James, "Preface," *The Wings of the Dove: A Norton Critical Edition*, ed. J. Donald Crowley and Richard A. Hocks (New York: W. W. Norton, 1978), 16.

22. R. P. Blackmur, *Studies in Henry James*, ed. Veronica A. Makowsky (New York: New Directions, 1983), 147; see also pp. 151–2.

23. For a fine theoretical statement of narrative deep structure in short story cycles, see J. Gerald Kennedy, "Toward a Poetics of the Short Story Cycle," *Journal of the Short Story in English*, 11 (Autumn 1988), 22–4.

24. Luscher, 163.

25. See Jacques Lacan, *Ecrits: A Selection* (New York: W. W. Norton, 1977), 152, and *Encore*, chapters 6 and 7 of Seminar XX (Lacan, 1972–3), 61–82; also Jonathan Scott Lee, *Jacques Lacan* (Boston: Twayne Publishers, 1990), 178.

26. Luscher, 165.

Toomer's Cane *as Narrative Sequence*

LINDA WAGNER-MARTIN

Jean Toomer's 1923 collage of fiction, poetry, and drama is a sequence of narrative forms riveted together by its title, *Cane.* The image of the sugar cane is Southern, nourishing, phallic, common, redolent – as Toomer says in his poems – of the Southern agrarian life. In "Georgia Dusk," his central image is of black men singing "the chorus of the cane . . . caroling a vesper to the stars."[1] Cane is also sweet, sensual, and a source of some of the (rare) pleasure in the lives of Toomer's black characters. The noun *cane* also is a homonym for the Biblical *Cain,* whose character suggests the bloody destruction of brotherhood and introduces the concept of immoral violence. The image of cane ties the reader to the earth, to the commonplace that was the touchstone of one current of American avant-garde literature in the early 1920s (represented by William Carlos Williams and Robert McAlmon's journal, *Contact*). Through that resonating image, Toomer creates place, time, and theme. The location is the South, both rural Georgia and urban Washington, D.C.; the time is the present; and one pervasive theme is the pitiful and yet self-defeating way black people live in contemporary America. *Cane* also explores the sexual lives of the blacks, and much of its narrative is expressed from a male perspective. It therefore fits neatly into mainstream American modernism, which was soon dominated by the writing of Ernest Hemingway, F. Scott Fitzgerald, John Dos Passos, and William Faulkner.

For all its similarity to other modernist texts, however, *Cane* is unique in American literature. In its wide-ranging eclecticism, it goes beyond the provincialism of much American writing. Toomer himself described his being saturated for the several years before writing *Cane** with the

---

* Between 1919 and 1922, Toomer wrote many poems, some of which he included in the 1923 *Cane.*

work of Walt Whitman, Afro-American writers and mystics, the Imagists, and the Symbolistes (here, Charles Baudelaire's *Les Petits Poemes en prose*). Toomer recalled as well, "Buddhist philosophy, the Eastern teachings, occultism, theosophy . . . challenged and stimulated me. Despite my literary purpose, I was compelled to know something more about them." [2] This complex of possible sources, coupled with *Cane*'s fragmentary structure and mixed genre base, makes the text as difficult to comprehend as Eliot's *The Waste Land*, yet *Cane* has never been accorded its due as a modernist tour de force.

From the almost radiant central image of the cane, Toomer's book extends through a number of themes and image patterns. The sexuality of black women and men; the poverty of black laborers; the warmth of the soil under the Georgia sun; the disdain of the dominant white culture; the search for soul and religious comfort; the importance of song, of smell, of the colors rife in nature; the self-imposed quandary of intellectualism; the mystery of eroticism – Toomer is, in some ways, reifying themes already pronounced in the writing of Sherwood Anderson, William Carlos Williams, and Theodore Dreiser; but because his focus is on black characters in the southern milieu, his writing seems quite different from theirs. The fragmentation of Anderson's *Winesburg, Ohio* is less problematic than Toomer's juxtaposition of diverse elements in *Cane* because Anderson uses only short stories, and those fictions are unified through the character of a continuing protagonist. As narrator and observer, George Willard does not vary from story to story. In contrast, Toomer writes fiction, sketch, poem, song, and drama; and whoever the narrator might be in *Cane* is faceless, nameless, and chameleonlike as he goes from being sympathetic and wise in stories like "Fern" and "Carma" to confused and weak as the title character of the play "Kabnis." Toomer's use of this shifting and unobtrusive narrator stems in part from his interest in nondirective Eastern beliefs: There are few judgment calls in *Cane*. Whereas the reader of the *Winesburg* stories knew that George was a sympathetic character, the reader of the *Cane* fragments is working doubly hard both to make the segments cohere and to decipher – or perhaps to create – one constant point of view.

The structure of *Cane* parallels its multiple, inclusive aims. The first part arranges poems and short fiction in a texture dominated by the fiction, most of it focused on women characters in erotic relationships. In the second part, which contains fewer poems, the stories are more diverse, almost postmodern in their minimalist impact, widely different in tone one from the other, more male-centered. The third part is given entirely to "Kabnis," a play about a northern black man trying to live in the racist and hostile South, shaped to show a spectrum of religious belief amid philosophical dialogue. Disparate as these parts are, the segments of *Cane* when read in order form a sequential narrative. The work begins in medias res, as the narrator observes the southern black women he finds so compelling and alluring. His first visit to the South has disoriented him, and he uses the lives of these women, objects for his male gaze, as entry points for understanding the unfamiliar culture. From the first story, "Karintha," through the next four, erotic force provides plot direction. Only with the concluding sixth story, "Blood-Burning Moon," does Toomer unleash his narrator's anger at the violent culture that pits white against black, broadening the focus of the narrator's view from the erotic to the political. Part II moves the reader to Washington, D.C., differentiated from the Georgia milieu by its urban setting and its more sophisticated people whose problems are intellectual rather than erotic. Part III, the open-ended psychological drama titled "Kabnis," returns the reader to the deep South, but here Toomer leaves the role of observer and appears to suggest answers for the cultural dilemma (it is interesting that most of those answers come from Eastern philosophies rather than American or European).

Even though "Kabnis" seems to circle back to the beginning, and the epigraph markings of each part shape the circle of the uroborus, Toomer has created a narrative with linear progression. What creates the movement is the journey or hegira format, reinforced by his apt placement of poems – each in a distinctive Imagist or lyric form – between the short stories of Parts I and II. The juxtaposition of story/poem/poem or story/poem/story also creates the sense of montage, so that "meanings" accrue for the reader rather than being didactically stated. Toomer described the process of composing *Cane* as creating a mandala, and its formal design as "the spiritual entity behind the work."[3] To see the collection as a symbol of integration, an arrangement of images from the unconscious that form a constellation, is to understand how pervasive Toomer's philosophical interests were.

Each part of *Cane* reflects an integrative order, and the fact that Toomer included poems he had written earlier – seeing their usefulness to the total structure of *Cane* – suggests that he saw the process of "writing" this book as an assemblage. He placed the poems from the previous three years in key places so that their themes either reinforced or contrasted with those of the stories surrounding them, although their tex-

tures often contrasted with the pervasive fictional tone. The sonority of
"Karintha" is undermined by the abrupt "sound of steel on stones" of
"Reapers," the first poem in the book. When the rat is killed by the
scythe's blood-stained blade, the reader transfers that terror to the objectively presented deaths in "Karintha," particularly that of her burned
baby. The second poem, "November Cotton Flower," foreshadows the
ominous narrative of Becky, "the white woman who had two Negro
sons. She's dead; they've gone away." The flat prose that recounts her
pitiful story continues the tone of the sonnet, which is filled with cold
winters, rusty cotton stalks, and dead birds. A more vivid illustration of
the way Toomer uses poems in juxtaposition is his pairing of "Face" and
"Cotton Song," one a startling Imagist picture of a tearful old woman
"nearly ripe for worms"; the other an evocative chant used as men lifted
cotton bales. Folksong set against modernist irony, the traditional qua-
train of "Come, brother, come. Lets lift it;/Come now, hewit! roll
away!" is itself broken with lines that mimic the sounds of the men's
hard labor:

> Nassur; nassur,
> Hump.
> Eoho, eoho, roll away!
> We aint agwine t wait until th Judgment Day!

Toomer reminds the reader that black speech or song, less evident in
his Imagist poems, is the background for this expression; and he regularly makes use of folk stanzas and patterns such as call-and-response.
The poems Toomer chooses to follow the strange story "Esther," the
only one of this section about a white woman rather than a black
woman, extend the theme of that story, which is the impact of one culture on another – here, the powerful sexual attraction the black man
holds for the white woman. "Conversion" ridicules the Christian imper-
ative that religion change black people's beliefs, whereas the parodic
"Portrait in Georgia" describes a beautiful woman whose physical
beauty means death to whoever attempts to possess it.

Toomer's choices of poems in Part II tend to be less bleak, less ironic,
and part of the progression of fiction in that section is reflective of options black men and women have in a more urbanized culture. "Storm
Ending" and "Her Lips Are Copper Wire" are more gently erotic, the
latter even comic, and the paired poems "Prayer" and "Harvest Song"
conjoin black lives with the Eastern beliefs in the primacy of the soul.
The opening lines of the former, in fact, could be placed in the "Harvest

Song": "My body is opaque to the soul./ Driven of the spirit, long have I sought to temper it unto the spirit's longing." "Harvest Song' is filled with images of being thirsty and hungry, searching for sustenance that is not evanescent or temporal. When these poems printed as separate works are considered along with the countless lines and stanzas that Toomer uses within his fictions as songs or refrains, the importance of the poems to *Cane* is irrefutable.

Toomer also wrote fiction as if it were poetry. This practice suggests that he saw genre distinctions as artificial, and that he understood that the methods of achieving organic form in poems – line length and stanza form chosen to reflect emotion, word choice to suggest pace and tone of speaking voice, assonance and consonance to create patterns of sound that underscored meaning – would work as well in fiction as in poetry. The great contrast between the form and language of the first story, "Karintha," and that of "Becky," "Carma," and "Fern," illustrates that these fictions are prose poems, evocative of a resonance that is unexpected in conventional narrative.

For all its diversity of form, *Cane* keeps the reader immersed in the present-day South. In 1923, most writing by black authors focused on inoffensive topics because publishers and many readers were white: Rather than offend those readers, black writers kept their fiction and poetry focused on politically "safe" subjects, many of them nostalgic. The battle among W. E. B. Du Bois, James Weldon Johnson, and Alain Locke about what appropriate subjects were and about the propriety of writers and artists being drawn from the elite (the educated blacks, termed the "Talented Tenth"), rather than from a larger spectrum of black artists, raged throughout the early twentieth century and well into the years of the Harlem Renaissance (of which *Cane* was the first prominent success).[4] For Toomer to hit the reader hard with the inequities of black life in the South, the racist and unameliorated violence permeating all life there, was a bold move that made him and his work highly visible. One supposes that his deflection of attention, his reluctance to being known as a black writer, stemmed in part from the flood of commentary that *Cane* evoked – and part of that commentary resulted from the difference between the writing of the black authors who were already known – James Weldon Johnson, Claude McKay, Countee Cullen – and what was seen as the radicalism of Toomer's work. As Cullen himself said of *Cane*, it was "a real race contribution, a classic portrayal of things as they are."[5]

There is no question that Toomer was writing out of what was to be seen later as the modernist aesthetic rather than from a primarily black artistic perspective. The collage organization, the juxtaposition of positive and negative, the seeming randomness of association, the reliance on the small and separable image – all these techniques were the basis of T. S. Eliot's *The Waste Land,* as well as, of course, James Joyce's *Ulysses,* both published in 1922. Toomer identified with the modernists, and called Eliot "an artist in the use of words."[6] As Cary D. Wintz comments, Toomer was also enthusiastic about Waldo Frank and his Greenwich Village associates, and Toomer's aesthetic position was based partly on that enthusiasm.

> He became involved in Frank's efforts to redefine American culture by focusing on the 'buried cultures' – the American Indians for Frank and southern blacks for Toomer – and adopted Frank's vision of art as a spiritual force which motivated people and defined the symbols that give life meaning. He evolved his literary style, which was reflected in the unorthodox structure of *Cane,* from the experimental literature of Crane, Frank, and . . . *Winesburg.*[7]

Toomer's *Cane* was itself so innovative that other writers knew about it and commented on its importance, as when Sherwood Anderson wrote to Gertrude Stein in March 1924: "There is a book by an American negro – Jean Toomer – called Cane [sic] I would like you to see. Real color and splash – no fake negro this time, I'm sure. Do look it up – Boni & Liveright."[8] Because Stein herself had written about black characters in her "Melanctha," published in 1909 as the longest segment of *Three Lives,* she often heard about minority writers and writing, and because during 1924 Hemingway was still a disciple of Stein's in Paris, it seems reasonable that he also knew about Toomer's book. Two years after *Cane's* publication in 1923, Hemingway was to write and publish the stories and vignettes of his *In Our Time.* (The first *in our time,* published in 1924, consisted of only the page-long vignettes, or prose poems, that Hemingway – himself a poet – understood as a blend form.) With Ezra Pound's "Make it new" sounding in his ears, Hemingway created a form for *In Our Time* that was less experimental than was Toomer's *Cane*: It used only prose forms, its title was thematically directive, and it moved alternatingly between the longer and more subjective stories and the seemingly objective vignettes that were based on either bullfighting or World War I experiences. Hemingway's structure was, in some ways, predictable, plotted, controlled (as was to be most of his writing throughout his career). Thematically, he alternated between the domestic and the exotic, searching for the formula that would attract commercial publishers. Unlike Toomer's work, in Hemingway's, the author's moral position was clear – and being able to identify that position was of inestimable help to the reader. Toomer's *Cane* was, in a sense, both exotic and domestic, simultaneously. What made *Cane* exotic was that its focus was black existence, a marginalized culture that had seldom been recreated in mainstream literature. What made it domestic was that Toomer was himself at least partially black, so he was trying to write about this experience as if he were privy to it. Much of the modernist tension of *Cane* accrues from Toomer's complicity in recognizing his own blackness yet feeling like an outsider to the black experience, being both intrigued and horrified by it. And part of his ability to avoid a consistent moral position was in some ways psychological: Whereas Hemingway was confident about his judgments of everything, Toomer in this period of his life was trying to maintain distance from all commitments, even from that of racial identity.

When Hemingway made the decision to use only prose within *In Our Time,* he in some ways closed his writing off from more radical experimentation: Gertrude Stein, E. E. Cummings, Dos Passos, Williams, Frank, Anderson, and others were all fusing separate forms to create new structures. Stein's prose-line "poems" in her 1914 *Tender Buttons* illustrated what was possible. Yet today, criticism still approaches texts by genre, even though critics of modernist and postmodernist writing know that defining a work arbitrarily on the basis of genre is to devalue work that should be considered. Cary Nelson points out that such exclusionary categorization will "consistently falsify the history of aesthetic innovation."[9] Nelson uses *Cane,* and its many similarities in form to William Carlos Williams's *Spring & All,* a montage of poetry and nonfiction prose, to illustrate how the division between a "poetic form" (*Spring & All*) and a fiction-based form (*Cane*) creates needless separations. To see both *Spring & All* and *Cane* as statements of their authors' respective aesthetics may be a more helpful means of comparing them. Both men, as writers, were intent on opening literature to people other than the elite, educated reader: Williams, like Toomer, had a multiethnic background and was more conscious than Toomer had been of the dangers of literary elitism (Williams's anger at Eliot's allusiveness and deference to Western culture within *The Waste Land* is illustrative). Both were friends of Waldo Frank, who persistently hammered away at elite modernist positions. For all three of these writers, considerations about established genre and form were hierarchical: Staying within proscribed literary forms was a means of reinforcing cultural prejudices that were already firmly in place. To make it new, in Pound's words, should mean making literature that would hold a new place in the world, making words accessible for readers who found themselves closed out of existing texts.

Toomer's "Blood-Burning Moon" provides insight into both the structural and thematic radicalism of his work. The sonorous prose rhythms are punctuated with the lamentlike refrain, and the ominous direction of the story is set both tonally and narratively. The reader hears the sorrow in this fiction. And in the story of Louisa, the black woman caught between the loves of the white Bob Stone (an ominous surname) and the black Tom Burwell ("whom the whole town called Big Boy," suggesting his importance within the black community), between the notions of white patriarchal power and racial equality, Toomer uses the erotic to approach the political. He makes it clear that Louisa enjoys her sexual relationship with the white man, even though she knows how dangerous it is for her to be so involved – in light of her black lover's feelings about the white culture. Rather than romanticize Louisa, Toomer draws her as an antiheroine, a woman passively waiting for two men to decide her fate. Despite their skin color, they seem almost interchangeable in her thoughts: "His black balanced, and pulled against, the white of Stone, when she thought of them" (28).

In this fiction, unlike his stories titled with the names of black women protagonists, Toomer's aim is to show passion itself, separate from personality; his title therefore reflects the role of the full moon, the emotion, rather than any single character. The first paragraph describes the moon providing an omen, "glowing like a fired pine-knot," visible through the door of the factory in which so many blacks work. The centrality of this emotional resonance appears in the poem that closes, and appears at intervals within, the story:

> Red nigger moon. Sinner!
> Blood-burning moon. Sinner!
> Come out that fact'ry door.

The conflation of passion and sin, the naming of the moon both "sinner" and "nigger," and the fusing of the color red with blood and fire – all accomplished in these three brief lines – explain Toomer's narrative line. When Tom and Bob argue over Louisa and when Bob whips out a knife only to find the faster Tom had already slashed his throat, the conflict is much less interesting than its context. For Toomer has spun a tale of community (the group speculating on which lover will win Louisa), of timeless eroticism imaged in the cane stalks, and of relentless passions. What is memorable about Toomer's writing is not the plotline, but rather the embedded scenes; for instance, these charting Bob Stone's journey to see Louisa in the full of the moon. In this passage, the speculation that she is also involved with Burwell makes him think of their respective roles in society:

> No sir. No nigger had ever been with his girl. He'd like to see one try. Some position for him to be in. Him, Bob Stone, of the old Stone family, in a scrap with a nigger over a nigger girl. In the good old days . . . Ha! Those were the days. His family had lost ground. Not so much, though. Enough for him to have to cut through old Lemon's canefield by way of the woods, that he might meet her. She was worth it. Beautiful nigger gal. Why nigger? Why not, just gal? No, it was because she was nigger that he went to her. Sweet . . . The scent of boiling cane came to him. (32)

Once he hears the men around the cane boil talking about him and Burwell, Stone becomes inflamed: "Sizzling heat welled up within him . . . Halfway along, a blindness within him veered him aside. He crashed into the bordering canebrake. Cane leaves cut his face and lips. He tasted blood. He threw himself down and dug his fingers in that ground. The earth was cool. Cane-roots took the fever from his hands." But the stasis is only temporary, and once the men see each other, Burwell severs Bob Stone's head from his body. The denouement is inevitable: The community kills Burwell by binding him to a stake and setting him on fire. As Toomer describes Burwell dying in the blazing pyre, he twice uses the description of the man as a stone ("only his head, erect, lean, like a blackened stone") as if to emphasize that the two men were alike, governed by the passion of eros and pride, and trapped in the influence of the full moon.

Because this narrative concludes the first part of *Cane*, it lingers as the mandala Toomer described as his ideal fictional construct. The tormented southern racial and sexual conflicts are given indelible expression, and the repeated refrain serves as a jeremiad for the human passions that create such situations. When Toomer opens Part II with the sketch of the materialistic and inhumane "Seventh Street," followed by that of the robotized "Rhobert," in mockery of people without emotions, the poignant lament of "Blood-Burning Moon" is reinforced.

Any reader who experiences Toomer's *Cane* is impressed with its versatility, its power as text, its emotional range and impact. Technically, formalistically, the work needs no defense. Toomer's mixing genres does not detract from the work's coherence as a unified text, and its organization manages to portray both a linear progression and a circular one. It is truly a cycle or sequence because of the various interrelationships within its parts,[10] and it achieves in addition the sense of a "surround," a contextualized presentation of the narrator's self-awareness after having been in the South, living in the South as a black, for the first time in his life. The effects of that experience stay with him even after he returns to Washington, and as a result of his new knowledge about racism and the complexity of the black life, he sees events in Washington with a new vision. Impossible to conceptualize in a simple linear fashion, Toomer's experiences – both objective and subjective – lent themselves to the kind of collage structure his linked tales, poems, songs, and drama form. Rather than the separable voices of the Canterbury pilgrims, *Cane* gives the reader a myriad of voices that are, in one mood or another, all germane to the various narrators' evolving understanding.

What sets Toomer's *Cane* apart from the modernist texts that are central to today's literary canon is its thematic complexity. Both female and male characters receive attention in Toomer's work; and in each case, the multiplicity and variety he succeeds in drawing show an artistic consciousness responsive to human problems. As a woman-centered text, *Cane* does more than describe the women protagonists in Part I as objects of the male gaze – although it also does that. *Cane* has, in fact, been criticized for its presentation of the five women's stories ("Karintha," "Becky," "Carma," "Esther," and "Fern") because Toomer seems more interested in the way the male observers react to the women's beauty and sexuality than to the characterization of the women themselves. But Onita Estes-Hicks points out in her discussion of *Natalie Mann*, Toomer's 1921–2 drama, that Toomer was early using strong women protagonists in a context reminiscent of Shaw's. Natalie Mann is a self-realizing heroine who insists on her own independence – as woman and as artist.[11] Alice Walker too has praised Toomer's portraits of women because the author clearly understands, and is capable of entering into, the women's consciousness.[12]

Besides being interesting in themselves, Toomer's portraits of women characters show his aim to integrate his philosophy with his technical and thematic concerns. From his Eastern beliefs, he viewed the elements of water, fire, wind, and sun as primary and necessary, for life and for sacrifice. Besides the literal name "Carma" (karma) appearing in the list of women characters, Toomer's descriptions of each woman stress one or another of these natural qualities. "Karintha" suggests the wind: "Karintha, at twelve, was a wild flash that told the other folks just what it was to live. At sunset, when there was no wind . . . her sudden darting past you was a bit of vivid color, like a black bird that flashes in light. . . . Karintha's running was a whir" (1). "Fern" suggests water: "Face flowed into her eyes. Flowed in soft cream foam and plaintive ripples . . . the curves of her profile, like mobile rivers. . . . Like her face, the whole countryside seemed to flow into her eyes" (14–15). In his densely poetic prose, Toomer includes a number of references to the East, to the state of people's souls, to the harmony that would lift people beyond either dissension or sexuality to a nirvana that might be attainable. For example, the initial description of Karintha – "Her skin is like dusk on the eastern horizon" – weaves her black beauty with a mention of the East, and the form of the poem combines imagist clarity with the call-and-response stanza (the refrain is answered in the second line, "O can't you see it, O can't you see it"). The beginning poem then, contrasts with the direct, almost explosive, prose opening, "Men had always wanted her . . . even as a child."

From this matter-of-fact statement, the reader is alerted to the social code: Karintha will be sacrificed to her male-dominant culture. The fiction reinforces her helplessness. Aside from her "carrying beauty" – as if it were some external quality – and having a shrill-pitched voice and a whirring walk, the reader is allowed to see Karintha only through the eyes of the men who seek her: old, young, lascivious. Similarly the "events" of her life (for the story has the chronology of her as a child, then at twelve, later as a mother, and finally at twenty) are all sexual events. Even the burning of her child in the pyramidal sawdust pile is described as inevitable, the product of her soul "ripened too soon," just as the male gaze ripened her beauty. Even in what appears to be a story about a young girl's sexuality, Toomer is probing toward explanations of the way people are destroyed by cultural responses (in this case, the way women are destroyed by the commodification of their sexuality). His story "Becky," with its cryptic, blunt prose and harsh assonance, narrates a story that is without mercy, just as the community has been toward the woman they were convinced was without redemptive possibility.

"Carma," with its synthesis of Eastern and Afro-American cultures, introduces one thematic center of *Cane*. As cane is the central symbol for Toomer's view of the complexity of black life, Carma/karma is one symbol for a stage in the development of essential black womanhood. Karintha is a passively sexual object; Carma is much more aggressive. "Carma, in overalls, and strong as any man, stands behind the old brown mule, driving the wagon home . . . She, riding it easy" (10), the narrative begins. Assuming power from her own self-knowledge, Carma does what she pleases, and that pleasing includes making love with the men she finds attractive. She accepts the results of her acts and does what she can to protect herself from social disapproval. Her trickery in the canebrake, making her angry husband think she had killed herself, leads to his killing an innocent man – and ending up imprisoned. But Carma is untouched by his outcome, and her narrative is appropriately open-ended. Although Carma is too interested in her own satisfaction to have reached nirvana, she is at a different stage than Fern, Esther, or Becky. Women such as Muriel in "Box Seat" and Bona in "Bona and Paul" share some of Carma's qualities – realistic and aggressive, they do not see themselves entirely as the male view portrays them. They exist on their own terms.

Toomer works with the image of woman as primitive force, as rooted center for life, in several of the middle-section stories. In "Box Seat," for example, in the midst of the tormented Dan Moore's aberrant behavior, Toomer embeds the surreal image of a black woman who knows herself and her place in the world:

> [Dan] shrivels close beside a portly Negress whose huge rolls of flesh meet about the bones of seat-arms. A soil-soaked fragrance comes from her. Through the cement floor her strong roots sink down. They spread under the asphalt streets. Dreaming, the streets roll over on their bellies, and suck their glossy health from them. Her strong roots sink down and spread under the river and disappear in blood-lines that waver south. Her roots shoot down. Dan's hands follow them. Roots throb. Dan's heart beats violently. He places his palms upon the earth to cool them. Earth throbs. Dan's heart beats violently. He sees all the people in the house rush to the walls to listen to the rumble. A new-world Christ is coming up. Dan comes up. He is startled. The eyes of the woman don't belong to her. They look at him unpleasantly. (62)

In the midst of images of sterility at the theater, the black woman's powerful, searching roots are a vivid contrast. To counter the sense of her life as bountiful, open to all who ask, Toomer creates the hostile second stage of Dan's recognition. After he has plundered her, following those roots in a kind of surreal rape image, the woman's eyes change; they look at him unpleasantly. She does not welcome his using her for his own purposes.

That has been the narrator's experience as well with the character Fern in the story of that name. Even though he assumes the power of narrator in her story, so that the reader sees her character and her life through his skeptical and yet sympathetic eyes, there are so many questions remaining at the end of the narrative that the reader must question the accuracy, the understanding, of the narrator. What he does tell firmly aligns his experience with Fern to the central image of the black woman in the theater. He feels "strange," and suspects he might be about to have a vision ("When one is on the soil of one's ancestors, most anything can come to one," 17); instead he embraces Fern, seeing that God flowed into her eyes, just as the countryside often did. Toomer's equation of woman with both the natural and the holy is here plainly imaged. Fern's reaction to the moment is inexplicable to her narrator; it brings her to both speech and song – talking in tongues, "calls to Christ Jesus," and then a broken singing: "a child's voice, uncertain, or an old man's." Unable to see Fern in the dusk, Toomer's narrator must rely on the uncertain, broken song, filled with anguish and pain.

These are the elements that close the mysterious narrative-drama "Kabnis." The old man – finally brought to speech beyond his mantra, the word "Sin" – is silhouetted in the glory of the rising sun while the child-woman Carrie Kate bows before him in obeisance. Kabnis himself has ascended to his work, called by his stolid wheelwright master Halsey, who would pour his life into his work. Taking off the robe of disguise (which makes of Kabnis an androgyne or a fool, "pompous in his robe, grotesquely so," 108), shamed by his bitterness and anger (the heat of his denial drawn from his hot forehead by Carrie's cool hands), Kabnis finally accepts his role as laborer, man, black man, southern black man. Though he fights his education at the hands of all his compatriots – resisting Halsey's practical injunctions, Lewis's larger definitions of purpose, and Carrie Kate's religious insistence, Kabnis at least survives his Walpurgisnacht, admitting that his lust (which Toomer describes as "weak approaches" to Cora, 108) has been only cold ash, a temporary solution to his many problems. Going into the cellar for his orgy, coupling with a Kore/Cora figure, and then returning to a higher stratum suggests the Demeter/Persephone myth, with the power of procreation and fertility resting finally with the matriarch.

Yet what does this ending have to do with Kabnis and his philosophical dilemmas? Of all the parts of *Cane*, readers have been most puzzled by this drama. Much of Toomer's work can be read meaningfully and accurately with reference either to modernism or to Afro-American issues and folklore, but "Kabnis" must be read as a treatise on Eastern theosophy. Toomer mentions that Mecca is important in understanding Father John, the meditative stonelike old man who lives in the basement; his fanciful description seems to be a clear allusion to the Kaaba, the black stone that is the most sacred Moslem object, housed in the center of the Great Mosque of Mecca. He also has Kabnis attempt to defame Father John by calling him "You old black fakir," a monk or ascetic, which he well may be. Carrie Kate has learned moral values by caring for the needs of Father John; because she has lived her apprenticeship, she knows a great deal more than do others in her culture. She has moved beyond the stage that Carma represented because she exists without attachment to pleasure, and she is also free from any need to make judgments about others.

The male characters of the play represent different stages of will, desire, and knowledge. Halsey may parallel Arjuna, the wheelwright of the *Bhagavad-Gita*, instructing Kabnis (a name suggestive of Krishna?) in life patterns he finds meaningful. There are some echoes of Krishna's profile in Kabnis's – their parentage is unknown, they are dark-skinned, they are sought after by women, they are mixtures of bravery and fearfulness, and they are preachers (or, as Kabnis claims, "I was born an bred in a family of orators, thats what I was. . . . Preachers hell. I didn't say wind-busters. . . . I said orators. O R A T O R S. Born one and I'll die one. . . . I've been shapin words after a design that branded here. Know whats here? M soul. Ever heard o that? Th hell y have. Been shapin words to fit m soul," 109). The seriousness of Kabnis's search for self is suggested in several key scenes, some of them stressing his feminine capacity to understand everyone, others like this, mentioning the word *soul* prominently.

Reading the play as a coded communication, with a scaffolding of Eastern belief, may provide alternatives to the kinds of interpretations that have dominated criticism of it, as for example Ann Massa's comment that Kabnis "is a tragic figure. He finds the black folk songs full of a 'weird chill.' They terrify him as much as the presence of the KKK." [13] Hardly in keeping with the rest of Toomer's intention in *Cane*, Massa's misreading results from the heavily modernist method of "Kabnis." It is Toomer's "Nine Characters in Search of an Author," yet because it occurs in an Afro-American work, Pirandello remains far from the reader's mind.

Experimental as the writing is, "Kabnis" yet continues the themes that are clearly expressed in the short fiction, poems, and prose poems of *Cane*: that people must find a source of personal and emotional sustenance and lead their lives as they plan them, choice after choice; that the optimum stage is that of a realistic nirvana, without dissension, conflict, or vain striving for material objects; yet that people must not live their lives away in sleep, passively accepting whatever force assaults them. The women in *Cane* awaken and come to their own sense of themselves and stop being sexual objects, and at the close of "Kabnis," the title character literally wakes from sleep and ascends the stairs to resume his work. A few years later, Toomer had become a serious follower of Gurdjieff, and in his teachings, the metaphor of awakening – of claiming one's own consciousness – was always positive: sleep suggests a trance state that results from negative self-awareness.[14] This theme appeared clearly throughout *Cane* in 1923. It may have been the author's first work, but it was in many ways to serve, as did Wallace Stevens's *Harmonium,* as a touchstone (or a mandala) to all the author's other writing. Toomer's aim in composing this unique and powerful work, regardless of its genre identification, was to provide his readers with a multifaceted approach to profound philosophical issues; and in considering those, questions of gender and race assumed important – but not crucial – places.

NOTES

1. Jean Toomer, "Georgia Dusk," *Cane.* Introduction by Darwin T. Turner (New York: Liveright, 1975 [1923]), 13; hereafter cited in text.
2. Jean Toomer, "Outline of an Autobiography," in *The Wayward and the Seeking, A Collection of Writings by Jean Toomer,* ed. Darwin Turner (Washington, D.C.: Howard University Press, 1980), 119; as quoted by Robert B. Jones in the Introduction to *The Collected Poems of Jean Toomer,* ed. Robert B. Jones and Margery Toomer Latimer (Chapel Hill: University of North Carolina Press, 1988), ix. For information about Toomer's life, see the Turner introduction to *Cane*; Cynthia Kerman and Richard Eldridge, *The Lives of Jean Toomer* (Baton Rouge: Louisiana State University Press, 1987); and Nellie McKay, *Jean Toomer, Artist* (Chapel Hill: University of North Carolina Press, 1984).
3. As quoted in Jones' Introduction, *Collected Poems,* xv. That introduction also gives much information about the order in which the poems were composed and what Toomer's rationale was for the different kinds of poetry written.
4. See Linda Wagner-Martin, *The Modern American Novel, 1914–1945* (Boston: Twayne,

1989); and *The Harlem Renaissance Re-Examined,* ed. Victor A. Kramer (New York: AMS Press, 1988).

5. Quoted in Cary D. Wintz, *Black Culture and the Harlem Renaissance* (Houston, TX: Rice University Press, 1988), 75.

6. Jean Toomer, "The Writer and the Literary Life," Lecture One in "The Psychology and Craft of Writing," 2–3, Jean Toomer Collection, The Beinecke Rare Book and Manuscript Library, Yale University, as quoted in Robert B. Jones, "Jean Toomer's *Lost and Dominant:* Landscape of the Modern Waste Land," *Studies in American Fiction,* 18, No. 1 (Spring 1990), 77–86.

7. Wintz, 79.

8. Sherwood Anderson to Gertrude Stein, March 1924 in *Sherwood Anderson/Gertrude Stein, Correspondence and Personal Essays,* ed. Ray Lewis White (Chapel Hill: University of North Carolina Press, 1972), 37.

9. Cary Nelson, *Repression and Recovery, Modern American Poetry and the Politics of Cultural Memory, 1910–1945* (Madison: University of Wisconsin Press, 1989), 180.

10. J. Gerald Kennedy, "Toward a Poetics of the Short Story Cycle," *Journal of the Short Story in English,* 11 (Autumn 1988), 9–25; *Short Story Theory at a Crossroads,* ed. Susan Lohafer (Baton Rouge: Louisiana State University Press, 1989).

11. Onita Estes-Hicks, *"Natalie Mann:* Jean Toomer's Feminist Drama of Ideas," *SAGE,* 5, No. 1 (Summer 1988), 21–4.

12. Alice Walker, *In Search of Our Mothers' Gardens: Womanist Prose* (Orlando, FL: Harcourt, Brace, Jovanovich, 1983), xi.

13. Ann Massa, *American Literature in Context, IV, 1900–1930* (London: Methuen, 1982), 122.

14. Kenneth Walker, *A Study of Gurdjieff's Teaching* (London: Jonathan Cape, 1957).

Hemingway's In Our Time:
The Biography of a Book

MICHAEL REYNOLDS

If you were not there at the time, Hemingway insisted, you could not possibly understand how things happened. He might have added that if you were there, you might be equally confused but in a different way. Of all the books in the Hemingway canon, none is more confusing than *In Our Time,* confusing now and then, confusing to reader and author, and particularly confusing to its bibliographers. It will remain that way forever, for its several parts – biographical, literary, editorial, and bibliographical – contain so many contradictions that any analysis will be flawed. Perhaps it is better that way, for so long as enigmas remain, the book lives; despite our proclaimed rage for order, there remains something about confusion that particularly delights us. Today the book and its attendant bibliography are a tangled ball of yarn. No matter which piece one selects to unravel first, the reader finds it snarled with another, and the unraveling becomes merely a rearrangement of the tangle.[1]

As an entry point, we might note that Hemingway published three volumes of short stories: *In Our Time* (1925), *Men Without Women* (1927), and *Winner Take Nothing* (1933).[2] Although all three titles imply a governing concept, only *In Our Time* has provoked numerous and divergent readings as a crafted sequence of stories with a sum larger than its parts. Neither the second nor the third volume evolved quite as complexly as did *In Our Time,* nor did Hemingway make any organizational claims for either of these volumes as he did for his first collection. From its earliest critical reading to the present day, *In Our Time* has provoked a wide range of response generated by the basic question: Is this book an interconnected sequence of stories to be read more like a novel, and if so, what is its governing principle? The easiest answer is, No, it is not. If the stories are read as discrete units, as they have been with great critical success, then *In Our Time* is no different structurally from several hundred other short story collections and, in fact, can be read as a predictable step in any young author's career. That response eliminates the need to ask more difficult questions, and as we shall see, the biography of the book in some ways supports such a view.

However, the collection's curious alternation of stories and vignettes, abetted by Hemingway's own remarks, has encouraged us to read, critique and teach the book as a conscious sequence of stories-as-novel in the tradition of Turgenev, Anderson, Stein, and Joyce. To do so forces one to ask: How could a barely educated, twenty-four-year-old writer produce a complex sequence of short fiction in his first book? If the reader replies, *impossible*, he or she is back to the first position: These are good stories, somewhat connected, but not a coherent sequence. Those determined for the sequence, but with no good answer to this question, might reply that Hemingway wrought better than he knew. This position allowed old New Critics and their children to treat the text as a discrete unit, uncomplicated by literary history or biography, while fostering the image of the dumb Hemingway who did not understand the depth of his own work.

There is, however, far too much evidence that Hemingway was intelligent, gifted, and well-read for the "Dumb Ox" epithet of Wyndham Lewis to apply any longer to Ernest. He may not have gone to an Ivy League college, as did most of his Paris literary friends, but by the time he was twenty-four, he had acquired a more useful literary education than most of today's college graduates and many of his early academic critics and literary friends. His Oak Park high-school curriculum, one of the most demanding in the country, included mostly the British classics but little American literature and almost nothing contemporary; but at sixteen he listed his favorite authors as O. Henry, Rudyard Kipling, and Stewart Edward White. When he returned to Chicago after the war, Hemingway fell in with a rather literary crowd, all of whom suggested new reading to him. Through his friends, Hemingway met and drank with Sherwood Anderson who loved to talk literary shop and give advice to young would-be writers. He directed Hemingway to the Russians: Dostoyevsky, Chekov, and Turgenev. He also told Ernest to read D. H. Lawrence and Gertrude Stein.

It was Anderson who sent Hemingway to Paris where one of his first stops was to join the lending library at Sylvia Beach's bookshop, Shakespeare and Company. In Paris, he quickly became a full-fledged member of one of the most literary crowds of the twentieth century. His friends and acquaintances included: Gertrude Stein, Ezra Pound, Ford Madox Ford, Robert McAlmon, Gerald Murphy, Louis Bromfield,

James Joyce, Archibald MacLeish, and John Dos Passos. Had Hemingway been as ill-educated as many once believed, he could never have held his own with that group. When he died in 1961, his Cuban library held over eight thousand volumes. He may not have gone to college, but few American authors were any better read than Ernest Hemingway.[3]

Included in his reading were the now classic short story sequences: *Winesburg, Ohio, Dubliners, Three Lives, A Sportsman's Sketches,* and one might add, Eliot's *The Waste Land.* Of all Joyce's work, Hemingway loved Molly Bloom, but it was *Dubliners* that he thought most likely to reach immortality.[4] To Turgenev's stories, Hemingway returned time and again, seeming never to tire of them. In 1927 he wrote himself a note: "Education consists in finding sources obscure enough to imitate so that they will be perfectly safe."[5] Certainly he learned that maxim at Pound's knee and reinforced it every time he picked up T. S. Eliot, all of whose books were in his library. My point, belabored as it may be, is now only too obvious: By the time Hemingway wrote the stories for *In Our Time,* he knew the genre of the short story sequence full well and was educated enough to challenge its masters. However it may rankle some ghosts of respected critics, we must finally admit that Hemingway knew what he was doing and that his craft does not depend upon the eye of its beholder. One might also note that over a period of sixteen years, Hemingway experimented more with the short story genre than almost any other American writer. From his "unwritten stories," which reduced the genre to a single paragraph, to his "The Snows of Kilimanjaro," which used a single story to hold a series of "unwritten stories," Hemingway continually stretched the limits of the genre.[6] If the stories of *In Our Time* form a sequence, then we must allow that Hemingway consciously crafted the collection that way.

However, the most cursory glance through the appended chronology of the book will raise interesting questions about Hemingway's authorial intentions, for the earliest parts of *In Our Time* were published in 1923, but the book did not reach its final form until 1955 when Scribner's reissued it with its 1930 "Introduction by the Author" retitled "On the Quai at Smyrna." With *Dubliners* or *Winesburg* there is ample evidence to support a governing plan for each of those books. *In Our Time* is different, with evidence to support both sides of the question. It may help to review the book's gestation before making any arguments for its coherence as a sequence of stories.

In February of 1923, Hemingway was in Rapallo, Italy, complaining about the meager surf and working on a series of sketches he called "unwritten stories." With most of his 1921–2 fiction lost when Hadley's valise was stolen in the Gare de Lyon the previous December, Hemingway was starting his career afresh. Having moved on from the "true" sentences of his "Paris 1922" sketches, he was now working on paragraphs done in different voices, for with his good ear, he could imitate almost anyone who caught his attention. One such voice was that of his war buddy, Chink Dorman Smith, with whom he had skied only two months earlier. He used Chink's voice to tell about the garden in Mons when

> Young Buckley came in with his patrol from across the river. The first German I saw climbed up over the garden wall. We waited till he got one leg over then potted him. He had so much equipment on and looked awfully surprised and fell down into the garden. Then three more came over further down the wall. We shot them. They all came just like that.[7]

That's how they all went – detached voices speaking, describing tightly focused events, small pieces of modern times.

By March he had six sketches finished, enough to send to Jane Heap for her "Exiles" issue of the *Little Review*. Three centered on Western Front experiences in the Great War; one came from the 1922 retreat of the Greek army across Thrace; another described a bull fight in Spain; the last one detailed the firing-squad execution of the Greek ministers at the end of the Greco-Turkish war. Only the retreat across Thrace came from Hemingway's direct experience; the other five, including that of the bullfight, came from secondary sources. Taken as a group, their thematic center was violence; however, they were not written as a sequence but as an experiment, and Hemingway needed a title before sending them on to Jane Heap. He jotted down a page of possibilities:

> Unwritten Stories Are Better
> Perhaps You Were There At The Time
> That Was Before I Knew You
> Romance is Dead
> The Good Guys See A Thing Or Two
> In Our Time
>   subtitle
> I Am Not Interested In Artists[8]

The April 1923 issue of the *Little Review* grouped the six vignettes as "In Our Time" without the subtitle.

By mid-August 1923 when the Hemingways returned to Toronto, Ernest had completed eighteen of his "unwritten stories," which he left with his friend and publisher, William Bird, to be the final installment in Ezra Pound's "*Inquest* into the state of contemporary English prose." Hemingway titled the book *in our time*. The first six vignettes were revised versions of the *Little Review* publication. The twelve new sketches ranged just as freely as the first ones, following no chronologic or geographic principle of organization and coming most often from secondary sources or out of his imagination. Nine were war-related, but from two different wars and three different fronts. Six came from the Spanish bullfights;[9] two involved American gangsters; and one was an anomaly about a young revolutionist. While Hemingway was working on his last vignette, the hanging of Sam Cardinella, he wrote Ezra Pound that the sketches held together quite nicely.

> The bulls start, then reappear and then finish off. The war starts clear and noble just like it did, Mons etc., gets close and blurred and finish with the feller who goes home and gets clap. The refugees leave Thrace, due to the Greek ministers, who are shot. The whole thing closes with the talk with the King of Greece and his Queen in their garden (just written). . . . America appears in the cops shooting the guys who robbed the cigar store. It has form all right. . . . I will commence the hanging.[10]

But the form had not dictated content; rather the sketches created the form. If there was a principle involved, it came from the title, *in our time*, which itself had not appeared until the first six vignettes were finished. Done in several distinct voices, Hemingway's "unwritten stories" were more like Eliot's *Waste Land* than any recognizable prose model.

Between August 1923 and January 1924 while the Hemingways were in Toronto, Ernest did no creative writing. However, in February when they returned to Paris, pent up stories began to explode from his head. During the following three months while assisting part-time on the *Transatlantic Review,* Hemingway wrote eight new stories, five of which centered on Nick Adams, who first appeared simply as "Nick" in one of the vignettes.[11] On May 2 Hemingway wrote Edward O'Brien for advice on his publishing career. He said he had ten stories finished and needed to get them moving. "What I would like to do would be bring out a good fat book in N.Y. with some good publisher who would tout it and have In Our Time [sic *in our time*] in it and the other stories, My Old Man and about 15 or 20 others. How many would it take?"[12] It was an ingenuous question, for Hemingway knew full well how many stories were in *Winesburg* and *Dubliners,* and his projected totals were roughly correct only if he included the vignettes.

Looking over the material at hand, he could find no obvious relationships like location in Anderson or Joyce, or gender as in Stein's *Three Lives.* These were not stories about a particular place, a single character, or a point in time. But then they were not written to be a book; there was no unifying concept at their inception. It was at this point in May 1924, when he thought he had almost completed enough stories for a book, that Hemingway began to write "Big Two-Hearted River," which was going to anchor the collection, hopefully in the same manner that "The Dead" anchored *Dubliners.* But before he could finish the story, his work on the *Transatlantic* interrupted the flow, and then came Pamplona and the feria of San Fermin. It was not until July 20, when he and Hadley were finally alone at Burguete, that he returned to Nick where he had left him on the river. During the intervening two months, his life had been very literary. While Ford Madox Ford was in America raising money for the *Transatlantic,* Hemingway edited a complete issue of the periodical, soliciting manuscripts and eliminating what he considered dead wood, including one of Ford's own columns. Then, during and after the Pamplona celebration, Ernest was in the company of Chink Dorman Smith, Bill Bird, Robert McAlmon, and John Dos Passos, all of whom were current in literary gossip and ideas.

It was after these events that Hemingway returned to Nick on the river and wrote his original ending to "Big Two-Hearted River," a pre-Borgesian tour de force that, had it worked, would have turned the collection of stories back on itself endlessly. Now he made Nick the author of all the stories in the collection, even those in which the character was Nick:

> Everything good he'd ever written he'd made up. None of it had ever happened. . . . That was the weakness of Joyce, the main one, except Jesuits. Daedalus in Ulysses was Joyce himself so he was terrible. Joyce was so damn romantic and intellectual about him. He'd made Bloom up. Bloom was wonderful. He'd made Mrs. Bloom up. She was the greatest in the world. . . . Nick in the stories was never himself. He made him up. Of course he'd never seen an Indian woman having a baby. That was what made it so good.[13]

Thinking aloud to himself, his mind jumping erratically from past to present, now Nick had as part of his memories Hemingway's past three weeks in Spain and all of Paris, including the Cézanne paintings Ernest so much admired. Nick wanted to write about country the way Cézanne painted it, breaking it down into its basic parts and then building it back up. "It was deadly serious. You could do it if you would fight it out. It was a thing you couldn't talk about. He was going to work on it until he got it. Maybe never, but he would know as he got near it. It was a job, maybe for all his life." [14]

He ended it with Nick hurrying back to his fishing camp, holding a story in his head to write. By mid-August he told Gertrude Stein that the story was finished. It was "100 pages long and nothing happens and the country is swell, I made it all up, so I see it all and part of it comes out the way it ought to, it is swell about the fish, but isn't writing a hard job though? It used to be easy before I met you." [15] "Nothing happens," he said quite proudly, trying to write a fiction so pure that it minimized character and conflict, leaving only setting and style, the painterly elements. He did not achieve anything close to that degree of purity, but it is interesting that he was trying and that he thought Gertrude, with her continuous present tense, would approve. But then it was Gertrude who sent him to Cézanne, claiming that she composed all of *Three Lives* while seated before a Cézanne portrait. It was also Gertrude who brought Flaubert's idea of pure fiction to Hemingway's attention.

He was so sure of the story that he had it professionally typed and placed at the end of the *In Our Time* manuscript. Two of the longer vignettes were revised into stories, "A Very Short Story" and "The Revolutionist," and "Big Two-Hearted River" was split into two parts, all of which made the volume seem longer than it actually was. Having arranged and rearranged the sequence of stories, Hemingway included all his new fiction, plus the stories from *Three Stories & Ten Poems* and used the "unwritten stories" from *in our time* as a counterpoint between stories. The book had, he thought, "a certain unity," which he tried to explain to Edward O'Brien. "The first 5 are [set] in Michigan starting with Up in Michigan . . . and in between each one comes bang! the In Our Time [*in our time*]." Without further explaining the "unity," he said that his long fishing story "finishes up the Michigan scene the book starts with." He was now calling the terse vignettes chapter headings, claiming that was what he first wrote them to be. "You get the close up very quietly but absolutely solid and the real thing but very close, and then through it all between every story comes the rhythm of the in our time chapters." [16] A month later Hemingway used a different metaphor to explain to Edmund Wilson that the interchapters separated the stories because

> that is the way they were meant to go – to give the picture of the whole between examining it in detail. Like looking with your eyes at something, say a passing coast line, and then looking at it with 15 X [power] binoculars. Or rather, maybe, looking at it and then going in and living in it – and then coming out and looking at it again.[17]

A week after Hemingway wrote Wilson, Gertrude Stein returned to Paris from her long summer at St. Remy; immediately he took her a copy of "Big Two-Hearted River," which he was certain she would appreciate. She returned it with the terse comment, "Remarks are not literature."[18] It was the ending she objected to, the ending that completely changed the collection, taking it to a different level of complexity. He read back over his "remarks," which were already circulating among the publishing houses of New York. Not yet confident enough to ignore Gertrude's criticism, Hemingway hacked off the last eleven pages of his typescript and added ten pages of new manuscript, ending the story where it began with Nick, the river, and the trout. Ahead of him, where the fishing would be "tragic," the river entered a swamp. As Nick moved back toward his camp, Hemingway ended the story: "There were plenty of days coming when he could fish the swamp."[19] In mid-November 1924, he told Robert McAlmon that he had "decided that all that mental conversation in the long fishing story is the shit and have cut it all out." It would be humorous, he thought, if some New York publisher took the book on the basis of that interior monologue.[20]

Thus did Hemingway's experiment with metafiction largely disappear beneath the surface of *In Our Time*. All that remained was the now enigmatic statement, "He had left everything behind, the need for thinking, the need to write, other needs" (179). Had Nick-as-writer remained in the ending, the reader would have been looped back to the beginning to reassess the stories in a different light; such an ending would also have borne similarities to Joyce's ending of *Portrait of the Artist as a Young Man*, where young Stephen Daedalus sets out to become the writer who may or may not be capable of writing *Portrait*.[21]

Hemingway's elimination of the obvious metafiction did not eliminate other unifying elements, nor did it completely erase the theme of the writer writing about a writer, which became a life-long obsession of Hemingway's. So many of his characters turn out to be writers, and their recurring concern is frequently the act of writing. In almost all of his novels, Hemingway keeps the reader continually aware of the writer in the rigging. *In Our Time*'s only remaining writer is the pathetic poet, Hubert Elliot, but the experimental nature of the interchapters and the stories, with their remarkably understated style in which little happened on the surface of the fiction, reminded Hemingway's contemporary reader that he was on new ground. Combining all he had learned from Anderson, Stein, Turgenev, and Joyce, Hemingway had forged an American style for his age.

In Our Time, even without its deleted section, remains Hemingway's most writerly book, in which he not only uses what his tutors taught him, but also pays homage to them in the process. Why else did he include "My Old Man," as good an Anderson story as Sherwood ever wrote, imitating his voice but leaving out the sentimentality? In "Three Day Blow," Hemingway gave us upper Michigan as Turgenev might have treated it. "Mr. and Mrs. Elliot" was written in the style and manner of Gertrude Stein's *Three Lives*. And Joyce was everywhere in the stories, helping with the down-beat endings and informing the selection of detail. He was particularly there in "Soldier's Home" when "Krebs looked at the bacon fat hardening on his plate." Including, as it did, all of Hemingway's previous fiction, *In Our Time* was a covert literary biography, showing forth all its author had learned since arriving in Paris three years earlier.

However, before the book reached print, other elements came into play, forcing Hemingway to make still more changes in the contents and their arrangement. Since his letter to O'Brien, he had once more rearranged the sequence so that it now opened with Nick Adams and his father the Doctor at "Indian Camp." On 5 March 1925, Hemingway received Boni & Liveright's acceptance of *In Our Time*, including a promise of a two-hundred-dollar advance against royalties. When the contract arrived, its cover letter asked Hemingway to eliminate what was now his second story, "Up in Michigan," which would create censorship problems in the America of 1925. Did he have a replacement? In fact, Hemingway had in hand "The Undefeated," a newly written story about an over-the-hill bullfighter that would have tied in very neatly with the six corrida interchapters, but he did not use it. Instead of taking that easy solution, he wrote a completely new story about the Michigan education of Nick Adams and called it "The Battler." Instead of inserting it in the second position left blank by excising "Up in Michigan," he moved the next three Nick Adams stories forward one position and slipped "The Battler" into the fifth position without changing the sequence of the interchapters. Whatever relationship he once saw between the vignettes and their accompanying stories was arbitrarily changed, but the book was finished. No more revisions, he told Liveright.[22]

The advance check arrived with Horace Liveright's apology for making his own revisions to "Mr. and Mrs. Elliot," which "would surely have made the book immediately suppressible. . . . galleys will be sent you very soon, and then you can change what I've done to suit yourself, bearing in mind, though, that it would be a pretty bad thing all around if your first book were brought into court for obscenity."[23] When Hemingway received his butchered story, he could not believe the changes. In New York it was apparently obscene for a husband and wife to "try" to have a baby. His story once opened: "Mr. and Mrs. Elliot tried very hard to have a baby. They tried as often as Mrs. Elliot could stand it. They tried in Boston after they were married and they tried coming over on the boat. They did not try very often on the boat because Mrs. Elliot was quite sick!" (109)

Taking his future in his own hands, Hemingway revised his paragraph to read: "Mr. and Mrs. Elliot tried very hard to have a baby. They were married in Boston and sailed for Europe on a boat. It was a very expensive boat and was supposed to get to Europe in six days. But on the boat Mrs. Elliot was quite sick."

Bereft of babies the opening sounded silly, its humor dead. It remained that way until 1930, when Scribner's negotiated with Liveright to bring out a new edition in which they restored Mr. and Mrs. Elliot's attempts to have a baby.

In early August 1930, Hemingway's editor, Max Perkins, asked Ernest to write an introduction for Scribner's new edition of *In Our Time*. On 12 August, Hemingway replied that he was "too busy, too disinterested, too proud or too stupid" to do as Perkins asked. He said he would return the text "with a few corrections, the original Mr. and Mrs. Elliot, and with or without a couple of short pieces of the same period."[24] What he sent Perkins was a laconic narrative done in a British voice describing the horrors at the 1922 Greek evacuation of Smyrna during their war with Turkey. Hemingway had not witnessed the event himself, but there had been graphic news coverage, and he had talked to men who were there. The style was "of the same period" as the interchapters, but the piece was probably written somewhat later, perhaps as late as 1926–7.

There is no evidence to suggest that the piece was originally written with the other vignettes in 1923, nor is there evidence that Hemingway wrote the piece specifically for the "Introduction by the Author," as it was called. Nevertheless, in what was to be his penultimate chance to focus the book, he chose to place the sketch as an introduction. When his first forty-nine stories were collected in 1938, the "Introduction" was changed, apparently by Hemingway, to "On the Quai at Smyrna." It was not until 1955 that another edition of *In Our Time* was printed in which "On the Quai at Smyrna" was the opening story.[25]

Understanding this complex and lengthy evolution of *In Our Time* may help us account for our difficulty in reading the collection as a unified sequence, but our perplexity remains. We have Hemingway's various statements about the collection's unity, statements leaving us not much the wiser for them. We can say with some certainty that the stories of *In Our Time* were not written to fit a preconceived plan, nor were the interchapters written to complement their attendant stories. The more we know, however, the greater our discomfort. We know that "Up in Michigan" should have been part of the book, but in 1955 when Hemingway apparently had the opportunity to reinsert it, he did not. And yet who would take out "The Battler" to restore "Up in Michigan"?

Despite all this, despite last-minute changes and flawed texts, *In Our Time* still has a coherence, but that coherence is not narrative. We are not merely following a particular character's life; we are not listening to a single voice. Attempts to force these kinds of unity find the reader either ignoring "My Old Man" and "Mr. and Mrs. Elliot" or apologizing for their intrusion. The fault does not lie with the author but with us, his beholders. For years we tried to read *The Waste Land* as a narrative because any poem longer than a page had to tell a story. Those same nineteenth-century glasses have distorted our reading of more than one modernist piece. About 1906, painters stopped telling stories, to the continuing unhappiness of some whose tastes remain in the previous century. Painters like Picasso, Braque, Miró, and Gris, painters whom Hemingway knew and in some cases collected, those painters abandoned plot, narrative, and most of character, flattened their canvases and continually called our attention to the artifice of their product. "This is not a pipe," says the clear label on Magritte's painting of a pipe. One might put a similar note – This is not a narrative – on the covers of *The Waste Land* and *In Our Time*.

Hemingway said once that he did not lead guided tours through his work, for the writing itself was difficult enough. He did, however, leave us a few clues to *In Our Time*. He eliminated Nick's interior monologue, but he left us the clue that Nick was a writer who had left the need for writing somewhere behind him. Hemingway also told us something by writing "The Battler" when he had another story in hand to complete his book. Both stories, "The Battler" and "The Undefeated," have a similar focus – an old, physically battered professional at the end of his career. The difference is the presence of Nick Adams in "The Battler" and his absence in the story of the bullfighter. Another clue was Hemingway's repositioning "Up in Michigan" from opening story to the second position, which moved "Indian Camp," a Nick Adams story, to the front so that the book opened and closed on Nick. All of these clues argue strongly that Nick is central to *In Our Time*, as we have always known, for he appears in half of the stories and in one vignette.[26] But those other seven stories prevent any narrative from forming, leaving us only certain that the "time" of *In Our Time* is that of Nick Adams, the period immediately before, during, and after the Great War.[27]

Our only other major clue is the "Introduction by the Author," for if Hemingway did not fully understand his book in 1924, he surely did by 1930. There, on the quai at Smyrna, the Greek refugees "screamed every night at midnight," and in the harbor there floated "plenty of nice things," such stuff as the narrator's dreams are made of. His detached, disembodied voice is British, his dark vision a sign of the times. It is not women giving birth in dark corners that disturbs him so much as the mothers refusing to give up their dead babies. In the end the Greeks break the legs of their baggage mules and dump them into the harbor to drown. "It was all a most pleasant business" (9–12). Similarly, in all but one vignette, we never see the war, only its aftermath, only the effects of violence on the mind of the beholder.

What we are left with is the New Historian's picnic, a book that assumes the reader is cognizant of the major events of 1910–24, which is no longer "our" time. We are never told which war or what front, but the clues are there. In 1925 the reader should have remembered the Greeks retreating across Thrace. It was in all the papers and on the newsreel screen. Hemingway assumes we understand the contemporary economics that allow his characters to live so idly in Europe, assumes we are familiar with the growing divorce rate. He assumes we remember the Russian revolution and have lived through the Palmer Acts that deported politically undesirable immigrants. He assumes we are living in Prohibition America. All of these assumptions are implicit in the title and embedded in most of the stories.

All of which takes us back to a qualification of our initial question: If the book is not a narrative then what holds it together as a coherent sequence? Let me suggest now obvious answers. *In Our Time* achieves its coherency in at least two ways, neither of them narrative. At its most subliminal level, the book is a literary biography of an American male learning to write in the postwar period. We see his homage to tutors – Turgenev, Joyce, Stein, and Anderson – and we see him moving beyond them in "Big Two-Hearted River," creating a style and attitude for his time. It is a young, brash writer showing us his "stuff," giving us an irreverent pastiche of styles and technique, a range of voices, blinding us at times with his brilliance. It is Hemingway at his most experimental, at a point in his career when he had nothing to lose and the world to gain.

At its more accessible level, the book is a series of long and short takes, close-ups and wide angles, creating a visual scrapbook of the age that spawned it. It is the repetition of thematic experiences that binds the collage together: war, violence, water, darkness, isolation, babies, and most centrally, failed relationships. Fathers fail their sons; lovers fail each other. In every story but one, the male–female relationship is either flawed, ruined, or missing. Nick ruins his relationship with Marge; the boxer is emotionally wrecked when his wife leaves him. The husband on the bed is not interested in his wife's identification with the poor kitty out in the rain. Unheroic, the enervated men accept disappointment as their inheritance and wounding as their inevitable due. In another part of the country, the jazz bands were playing hot music in the "speaks" where flappers strutted their stuff. It was the age of bathtub gin, bobbed hair, rolled stockings and sleek cars. But Hemingway's stories took a longer view of what was, in fact, an emotionally desperate period in our nation's history.

The opening story, "Indian Camp," set the tone and established the themes for all that followed: a father and son without a mother, a bloody Caesarian operation done without anesthetic, a wounded father cutting his own throat in the upper bunk; and Nick, watching it all, assuring himself later that he will never die. Played in different keys, almost every story is a variation on some thematic element of "Indian Camp" until we are alone with Nick isolated by his own choice on Big Two-Hearted River, trying to recover his poise. Behind him he has left, we're told, the needs to think and write, and he can stop his mind from working if he sufficiently tires his body. There the modernist and postmodernist come together: the writer writing about a writer who has temporarily killed the need to write. Beside the river, half afraid to face the swamp where fishing will be tragic, Nick Adams has nothing left to tell us about his era or its pitfalls. Unlike Gabriel Conroy at the end of Joyce's "The Dead," Nick is not in tears, but the two remain first cousins nonetheless. Both men, anchoring as they do the collections that house them, have come to realize the pathos of their situations. By 1930, when the music stopped and the jazz babies went on the dole, the rest of the country joined Nick to face the swamp, which had been waiting for them since the end of the war.[28]

APPENDIX: Chronology of *In Our Time*

August 1923	"My Old Man" and "Out of Season" are published by Robert McAlmon in Hemingway's *Three Stories & Ten Poems* (Paris: Contact Publishing Co.).
October 1923	The *Little Review* 10 (Spring 1923) publishes six sketches under the title "In Our Time."
January 1924	Edward O'Brien republishes "My Old Man" in his *Best Short Stories of 1923* (Boston: Small, Maynard & Co.).
March 1924	Bill Bird publishes eighteen sketches, including those in *Little Review*, in book form as *in our time* (Paris: Three Mountains Press).
April 1924	"Indian Camp," *transatlantic review*.
October 1924	"Mr. and Mrs. Elliot," *Little Review*.
December 1924	"The Doctor and the Doctor's Wife," *transatlantic review*.
January 1925	"Cross-Country Snow," *transatlantic review*.
May 1925	"Big Two-Hearted River," *This Quarter*.
June 1925	"Soldier's Home" is published by Robert McAlmon in *Contact Collection of Contemporary Writers* (Paris: Contact Publishing Co.).
October 1925	Boni & Liveright publish *In Our Time*, including sixteen *in our time* sketches as interchapters and another two converted to stories: "A Very Short Story" and "The Revolutionist." Of the fourteen stories, only

four were previously unpublished: "The End of Something," "The Three Day Blow," "The Battler," and "Cat in the Rain."

October 1938   Scribner's publishes *The Fifth Column* and the *First Forty-Nine Stories*, which includes all of the interchapters and stories from *In Our Time* but changes the "Introduction by the Author" to "On the Quai at Smyrna."

1955   Scribner's reissues *In Our Time*, opening with "On the Quai at Smyrna."[29]

Given the probability for printers' errors in each new edition and the authorial and/or editorial changes along the way, the comprehensive critic would do well to establish first that he is reading the correct text. Sad to say, we still do not have a standard edition of *In Our Time*.[30]

NOTES

1. Parts of this essay bring together fragments from my several previous publications. Without footnoting every point, I refer the reader to *Hemingway's Reading* (Princeton, NJ: Princeton University Press, 1981); and the indexes to *The Young Hemingway* (Oxford: Blackwell Publisher, 1986) and *Hemingway: The Paris Years* (Oxford: Blackwell Publisher, 1989).
2. Ernest Hemingway, *To Have and Have Not* (New York: Scribner's, 1937), which did begin as a series of stories, has been largely ignored as a failed novel worth small critical attention.
3. For substantiation and more information on this subject, see James Brasch and Joseph Sigmund, *Hemingway's Library* (Boston: G. K. Hall, 1981) and my *Hemingway's Reading* and *The Young Hemingway* (Oxford: Blackwell Publisher, 1986).
4. Ernest Hemingway, item 489, undated note on back of February 1927 letter, Hemingway Collection, Kennedy Library, Boston, MA.
5. Hemingway, item 489.
6. One might also note that Hemingway's *To Have and Have Not* and *A Moveable Feast* are, in fact, sequences of connected short stories, and his *For Whom the Bell Tolls* is thirty-percent short stories told by embedded characters to the central character who is a writer.
7. All quotes will be from Ernest Hemingway, *In Our Time* (New York: Scribner, 1958). This vignette is "Chapter III," 33.
8. Ernest Hemingway, item 92, Hemingway Collection, Kennedy Library, Boston, MA.
9. Having been twice to Spain since writing his first bullfight vignette, he now revised

the one written from hearsay and wrote five new ones based loosely on what he had seen.

10. Ernest Hemingway, letter to Ezra Pound, c. 5 August 1923, *Ernest Hemingway, Selected Letters,* ed. Carlos Baker (New York: Scribner, 1981), 91.

11. The last name, Adams, first appeared in an unpublished vignette that Hemingway wrote during the spring of 1923, entitled "Did You Ever Kill Anyone." In it a soldier named Adams is shot by an "old boche in a round cap and spectacles." Item 94a, Hemingway Collection, Kennedy Library.

12. Ernest Hemingway, letter to Edward O'Brien, 2 May 1924, *Selected Letters,* 116–17. The "ten stories" finished included "Up in Michigan," "Out of Season," and "My Old Man" from *Three Stories & Ten Poems* (Paris: Contact Publishing Co.: 1923).

13. Although this has been printed as "On Writing" in *The Nick Adams Stories,* I am quoting from the first, unrevised draft, item 274, Hemingway Collection, Kennedy Library, 91.

14. Item 274, p. 94.

15. Ernest Hemingway, letter to Gertrude Stein, 15 August 1924, *Selected Letters,* 122. Although we have no evidence that Hemingway had read the short stories of Henry James by 1924, Gertrude Stein, Ezra Pound, and Hadley Hemingway were all fans of James, who may have helped influence Hemingway's redefinition of what a short story was.

16. Ernest Hemingway, letter to Edward O'Brien, 12 September 1924, *Selected Letters,* 123.

17. Ernest Hemingway, letter to Edmund Wilson, 18 October 1924, *Selected Letters,* 128.

18. *Selected Writings of Gertrude Stein,* ed. Carl Van Vechten (New York: Random House, 1962), p. 207.

19. Hemingway, item 277, Hemingway Collection, Kennedy Library.

20. Ernest Hemingway, letter to Robert McAlmon, c. 15 November 1924, *Selected Letters,* 135.

21. My reading of *In Our Time* and its potential for metafiction is completely indebted to Debra Moddlemog's seminal and provocative essay, "The Unifying Consciousness of a Divided Conscience: Nick Adams as Author of *In Our Time,*" *American Literature* 60 (December 1988): 591–610.

22. Ernest Hemingway, letter to Horace Liveright, 31 March 1925, *Selected Letters,* 154–5.

23. Horace Liveright, letter to Ernest Hemingway, 1 May 1925, Hemingway Collection, Princeton University Library, NJ.

24. *Selected Letters,* 327.

25. Most of this paragraph is taken from Paul Smith, *A Reader's Guide to the Short Stories of Ernest Hemingway,* pp. 189–91.

26. In fact, the evidence seems so strong, that Philip Young rearranged the sequence of these and other episodes into *The Nick Adams Stories,* an almost coherent effort of the sort many wish Hemingway had written. But he did not.

27. One reason not to restore "Up in Michigan" was that it was set before the turn of the century. "He talked about . . . the Republican Party and about James G. Blaine." Blaine died in 1893.

28. There have been several thematic readings of the book, many of which are reprinted in my *Critical Essays on Hemingway's* In Our Time (Boston: G. K. Hall, 1983) and all of which have influenced my reading of the text, as have twenty-five years of teaching the book.

29. The most reliable sources of bibliographic information are Audre Hanneman, *Ernest Hemingway: A Comprehensive Bibliography* (Princeton, NJ: Princeton University Press, 1967) and Paul Smith, *A Reader's Guide to the Short Stories of Ernest Hemingway* (G. K. Hall, 1989). See also my *Hemingway: The Paris Years.*

30. See, for example, E. R. Hagemann's two studies: "A Collation, with Commentary, of the Five Texts of the Chapters in Hemingway's *In Our Time, 1923–38,*" *Papers of the Bibliographical Society of America* 75 (1979): 443–58; and "Only Let the Story End as Soon as Possible," *Modern Fiction Studies* 26 (Summer, 1980): 255–62.

Wright Writing Reading:
Narrative Strategies in Uncle Tom's Children

JOHN LOWE

Beginning with the Bible and proceeding all the way through the spirituals and blues, novel, poem, and the dance, Negro Americans have depended upon the element of narrative for both entertainment and group identification.

Ralph Ellison

Is the fiction of [the] world . . . capable of speaking itself and of displaying itself as a form of a story, necessary for the establishment of that moral authority without which the notion of a specifically social reality would be unthinkable?

Hayden White

Richard Wright, angry isolato, Communist Captain, and expatriate, first from the South and then from America, seems in many ways an unlikely writer to associate with Ellison's pronouncement. A more obvious candidate would be his old literary nemesis, Zora Neale Hurston, who built her narratives on leisurely pastoral, bright bolts of black music and folklore, dance, and a cornucopia of humor. Wright, in his rage, generally grim tone, and driven prose, seems diametrically opposed to the folk narrative in his moods and objectives. But many of our conceptions about Wright stem from an overconcentration on his angry, neo-gothic urban masterwork, *Native Son*. He could, and did, use folk materials to lend vitality to his realism, to ground his reinscriptions of memory and history, and to introduce his gospel of Communist brotherhood and struggle. Indeed, the book that preceded *Native Son, Uncle Tom's Children,* a sequence of short stories/novellas, commences in "Big Boy Leaves Home" with disembodied voices of the folk:

> Yo mama don wear no drawers
> Clearly, the voice rose out of the woods, and died away.
> Like an echo another voice caught it up:

Ah seena when she pulled em off . . .
Another, shrill, cracking, adolescent:
    N she washed 'em in alcohol . . .
Then a quartet of voices, blending in harmony, floated high
    above the tree tops:
    N she hung 'em out in the hall . . .
Laughing easily, four black boys came out of the woods into
cleared pasture. They walked lollingly in bare feet,
beating tangled vines and bushes with long sticks. "Ah
wished Ah knowed some mo lines t tha song." "Me too." [1]

The four boys are joined, as "speakers" playing out the quintessentially black verbal dueling of the dozens, by Wright as narrator; the "quartet" thereby becomes a "quintet" of blended folk voices, each rising with its individual inflection to form with the others a unified cry. This constitutes the pattern of the five stories of *Uncle Tom's Children* as well. Although each exists discretely and concerns a separate set of characters, all contain overlapping themes, symbols, motifs, and images, producing a powerful cumulative effect. Each tale leaves a trace subtly coiled inside those that follow. This seems particularly true of the first story, "Big Boy Leaves Home," which determines the narrative patterning for the sequence as a whole, one that mirrors the submerged history of black Americans through repetitive motifs and structures.

Although Wright employs several ingenious narrative strategies to further his aims, I shall concentrate here on three that interrelate: the rehistoricizing, through fiction, of the black experience; the use of biblical narrative patterns in the service of Communism; and finally, a narrative strategy that dramatizes and interrelates these two systems, Wright's compelling appropriation of the structure and language of torture rituals.

The five plot lines may be summarized briefly. In the first story, Big Boy and three friends, playing hooky, decide to swim in Old Man Hardy's "whites only" pond, and a stunned white woman discovers them. Big Boy asks her for their clothes; she screams, and when her soldier paramour shoots two of the boys, Big Boy shoots him. Galvanized by fear and rage, the black community arranges Big Boy's escape to Chicago, but for the night he must hide in a hillside kiln. His friend Bobo, caught trying to join him, is brutally tortured, tarred and feathered, and burned alive. After killing a bloodhound with his bare hands, Big Boy leaves for the North.

In the second story, "Down by the Riverside," Mann uses a stolen boat to get his wife, who is in labor, to a hospital during a flood. On the way he kills the white owner of the boat in self-defense. The wife dies at the hospital, and Mann finds himself conscripted for flood relief work, which leads him back to the dead white man's house. Unable to kill the white witnesses of his crime, he saves them, and they in return report him to the same authorities who earlier praised his heroism. After emergency militia sentence Mann to death, one of them shoots him as he tries to escape.

"Long Black Song" presents the yearning of a new mother, Sarah, for her lost lover Tom, as she awaits her aged husband Silas, who has been away selling his abundant crops. A white traveling salesman seduces her, leaving tell-tale evidence, and upon his return, an enraged Silas kills the man and then refuses to flee, preferring a shootout with the lynch mob. They burn him alive with the house as a horrified Sarah watches from a hillside.

"Fire and Cloud" paints the dilemma of an older minister, Dan Taylor, caught during a famine between the needs of a hungry congregation, the white power structure – which expects him to keep his parishioners from demonstrating – and Communist organizers, one white, the other black. Taylor's vacillation pleases no one; he receives a brutal beating by vigilantes, but finds the courage to lead poor whites and blacks in a successful march to City Hall for justice, declaring, "Freedom belongs t the strong!"

The final tale, "Bright and Morning Star," presents Aunt Sue, whose activist sons Sug and Johnny have converted her from Christianity to communism, along with much of the community, black and white. The sheriff and his thugs beat her senseless after she proudly taunts them when asked for Johnny's whereabouts and the names of party members. Weakened, she later reveals the names to a white Communist who turns out to be a Judas. She carries a concealed gun to the scene of Johnny's torture and manages to kill the traitor before he can reveal the names; as a result she and Johnny are murdered.

Even my bare-bones summary should indicate that it would be a mistake to read these stories *only* as discrete texts on a related theme. To do so would be to miss the carefully constructed space "in-between," that realm of surmise and dialogue where the individual narratives interweave and merge to form a kind of metanarrative. Indeed, the intertextual connections of *Uncle Tom's Children* present the rare case of a book that can be read over and over, as it offers, through its repetitive folk dialogics, a new book at each reading.

Paul Ricoeur has persuasively argued the linkage between the conceptualization of history and repetition. As in Martin Heidegger's *Being and Time,* each person's perspective develops from a personal history, one shaped and determined by the repetition of events. Everyone thus "transmits from him – or herself to him – or herself the resources that he or she may 'draw' from his or her past." Ricoeur notes that the German word for "drawing" is *holen,* the central unit of *wiederholen* (to "repeat" or to "re-collect"). In this sense, all of us can conceive of ourselves as having participated in the structure of our own fate through the patterns we choose to notice and honor. At the same time, of course, many of the events within this pattern are not chosen at all, but are rather imposed upon us by the world – a situation faced more often by oppressed peoples. Nevertheless, the idea of going through repetitive patterns of struggle gives each of us a history of response, which we can in turn "draw on." [2] This was expressed another way by Heidegger: "Only in communicating and in struggling does the power of destiny become free. Dasein's fateful destiny in and with its 'generation' goes to make up the full authentic historicizing of Dasein." [3] Simply put, "Dasein" (existence or being), which inevitably becomes shaped, and therefore "fated" by one's past, can be altered only by reaching to something outside the self – and in these tales, that usually means both the community and the cultural modes it has developed.

This idea can be fruitfully extended by linking it to the work of Houston Baker, who has applied Van Gennep's theories of the rites of passage to "Big Boy" and noted that the idea of passing into a state of "wholeness" involves an immersion in the "black (w)hole." Baker draws on the scientific phenomenon of the black hole, an area where "space and time disappear," where everything gets squeezed to its essential volume. Wright creates an equivalent mechanism in the kiln Big Boy and his friends helped create, which now offers shelter. But instead of a shaping fire, one finds the racial conflagration that forces Big Boy into a confrontation with both his own deepest essence and the cultural resources of his community that have in part generated it. Thus for Baker, the "black hole of science" and the kiln are both metaphors for the subsurface force of the black underground expressive will, "the subterranean *hole* where the trickster [like Brer Rabbit] has his ludic, deconstructive being," and where the hole becomes the domain of "wholeness." According to Baker, the onset of a life crisis instigates the rites of "the black (w)hole," which begin by withdrawal from the dominant white world, and then, in a second stage, desire awakens as the initiatee achieves an "ahistorical" sense of the black self's historicity; this liminal phase results in a negation of the white world's negation, and finally in a rewriting (and righting) of history and an awareness of his final separation from the white world, which in turns leads into the third, final phase, where he undergoes reintegration into the world, but not the old one. Instead, he becomes irretrievably transformed into the singularity of "black difference/black (w)holeness." Baker illustrates this thesis with "Big Boy Leaves Home," which does indeed fit this pattern, and clearly demonstrates Big Boy's affinity with the traditional trickster, Brer Rabbit, who asserts his "will," escapes from his hole, and defeats the "dogs"; in Wright's story Big Boy kills a very real dog to survive. As Baker notes, "The rabbit hole, black hole, train-whistle-heroic domain of Afro-American underground expressive *will* results in self-defense and escape"[4] and the driver of the truck who will take Big Boy to freedom is named Will.

We might note here how the first three stories of *Uncle Tom's Children*, in fact, all explore and limn the "black hole" of racism, and how the circular nature of the sequence as a whole is thus schematically appropriate to the overriding spatial and conceptual metaphor. Sarah, in "Song" feels that her ex-lover Tom's departure for the war "left an empty black hole in her heart, a black hole that Silas had come in and filled. But not quite." Clearly, the issue of (w)holeness looms large here, as Silas's acceptance of white finance capitalism has kept him from fulfilling his familial duties. Moreover, we know that cultural (w)holeness was on Wright's mind, for in 1937 he published his important essay "Blueprint for Negro Writing," insisting there that "A whole culture" could only proceed from folk culture that had been nourished by folklore and the black church; he decries the tendency of black writers to write of and for the "parasitic and mannered"[5] black bourgeoisie rather than the folk. Wright's position here accords with that of Mikhail Bakhtin, who repeatedly locates the "folkloric roots" of fiction in the people.[6]

FOCALIZATIONS OF F(L)IGHT

The narrative strategies we have examined thus far lead us to some basic considerations: How, after all, are the stories told? Originally, the sequence consisted of four stories: "Big Boy," "Down by the Riverside," "Long Black Song," and "Fire and Cloud." In the final version, Wright added "Bright and Morning Star" and prefaced the five stories with "The Ethics of Living Jim Crow," an autobiographical account of his early experiences of racism in Mississippi, particularly in the white-dominated workplace. Wright renders terrible events with reportorial diligence, employing a cool tone, which he would later modify when resetting this material in *Black Boy.* The encyclopedic narrative approach of this segment intentionally takes the reader through various worlds of work and differing types of outrages inflicted on the narrator by a variety of white racists. Wright thereby creates, respectively, a real-life verification, a "Tale of Truth," for the stories that will follow; a contrast in tone and narrative voice to the more passionately told tales; and a structural model for the fictions that take readers through the varieties of racism and the various personae in the black world. To state this another way using Gerard Genette's categories: Wright, as a figure involved in the story of "Jim Crow," performs the testimonial function, by indicating the source of his information, the precision of his memories, and the personal emotions these events have awakened in him, and thereby also contributes to the ultimate ideological effect of the sequence as a whole.[7] Adding "Jim Crow" and "Bright and Morning Star" to the original sequence forced the reader closer to a revolutionary awareness than the original four stories might have, and perhaps suggests that Wright had second thoughts about his readers' abilities to absorb the (W)right lessons; the original four tales allowed the audience the possibility of reading each discretely, as a narrowly focused melodrama, without experiencing a cumulative ideological effect. The final form of the sequence was designed to narrow that possibility, to write in a more determined form of reading.

The mode of narration for the short stories, with the exception of the first part of "Big Boy Leaves Home," told in third-person unrestricted narrative, is that of *personale Erzahlsituation,* a narrative rendered in the third person but largely confined to the consciousness of the central character. This replicates the method James uses in *The Ambassadors.*

Using Genette's categories, we may add that Wright "focalizes" his narrative internally through the consciousness of his most prominent figure. One sees this throughout *Uncle Tom's Children,* from the moment Big Boy and Bobo split up in the first story, setting forth the theme of "flight," through to the end of "Star," the concluding component of the dominant mode of "fight." This choice, of running or standing to face the enemy, characterizes each story.

The focalization of f(l)ight becomes *variable* in "Long Black Song," when Wright renders the first part of the story through Sarah, and the second through Silas, in the manner of Flaubert in *Madame Bovary,* which alternates between Charles and Emma as focal characters; on the other hand, the entire sequence, constituting, as we have seen, a primer on racial crimes, works rather in the manner of *multiple* focalization, as in Faulkner's *As I Lay Dying.*

Genette's internal focalization implies that characters can never be described "or even referred to from the outside, and that [their] thoughts or perceptions never be analyzed objectively by the narrator."[8] Accordingly, Wright's heroes move us through their mental struggles to find a way out of their agony, through the chain of discoveries they go through, and by the corrections in both perspective and action they attempt, rather than through authorial intrusion and commentary. The straightforward chronology seldom involves retrospective insets or flash-forwards. The stories roughly span twenty-four-hour periods and present the characters with impossible situations that must none-theless be faced immediately, thereby substantially increasing the dra-matic tension of the tales, and therefore, the reader's sense of involve-ment.

NARRATIVE AND THE (W)HOLE OF HISTORY

These focalization techniques prove useful in many ways, and they surely strengthen Wright's development of dramatic scene. In terms of the major figures and voices in *Uncle Tom's Children,* each comes to a mo-ment of epiphany where past, present, and future fuse in revelation. Each character, radically isolated by the narrative events, must attempt to "draw" resources from the past, an effort to create a repetition from personal history. Racism, however, has denied these figures access to such resources; the choices they are reduced to now – flight or fight – have no prior register; a history of direct, open opposition to white power would be unthinkable. Wright's manipulation of narrative has thus cruelly forced his characters, as the catastrophes of racist society do in life, onto a ground zero; the only choices open to them are those of submission, flight – an option none have exercised before – or radical, sometimes suicidal, revolt. And yet, the possibilities of repetition are still part of this ground; as Ricoeur states, repetition means the "'retrieval' of our most fundamental potentialities, as they are inherited from our own past, in terms of a personal fate and a common destiny. The ques-tion, therefore, is whether we may go so far as to say that the function of narrative – or at least of a selected group of narratives [such as *Uncle*

Tom's Children] – is to establish human action at the level of authentic historicality, that is, repetition."[9]

I would suggest that the ultimate "harmony" of the five "voices" raised in *Uncle Tom's Children* stems from a final assertion of self that comes from the annihilation of the flesh, a voice of pain that produces the need for the deepest kind of repetition, the most extreme sort of "*holen*/drawing" possible. In each case, because the character has no prior experience in enacting the various modes possible in these excruciating situations, acts of flight and "fight" constitute a virtual rebirth of the self, made possible by calling on the deepest resources of their being.

Wright enacts this drama through a ritual of pain, a pain so intense that the characters' responses constitute an almost sacral voice. Elaine Scarry has demonstrated that the Old Testament presents us with a God Almighty who finds evidence of his presence in man's world by inflicting pain, which in turn provokes a human cry. Similarly, dominant racists seek to create a sign of their power and dominance by inflicting pain on their subjects, thereby committing the worst type of blasphemy. For in the Bible but also in the racist's realm, belief in God or the white "master" finds substantiation through the text of the body.[10] Pain, or the threat of pain, forces the subservient figure to "testify" to the master's power, usually in words chosen by the master.

Each succeeding story in Wright's narrative plays off this traditional relation and subverts it. The "Christian" relation of the sinner and God, blasphemously mimicked by white Southerners, receives a Communist spin. Wright, too, features the mortification of the flesh; but he does more than document how this "ritual" is meant to function; he demonstrates that it can also be the generative ground for the new "word" of Communism, which indeed *is* "now in flesh appearing," in the sacrificial torture and deaths of Bobo, Buck and Lester; Mann, Lulu, and their child; Silas; Reverend Taylor; and finally, Johnny-Boy and Aunt Sue. As figures who have been denied, individually and communally, a history of active revolt, and as characters who have purposefully been denied by Wright, their creator, the possibility of covert or coded revolt – the more dominant type of "repetition" available to the focalized characters – each figure repeats, in their desperate and heretofore unthought-of defiance, their original act, precisely that of being born. Of course this also parallels the traditionally Christian trope of salvation, being "born again." In Wright's version, however, true salvation means rebirth in the Communist party.

The cost of submission and collaboration receives illustration here as well. Yeats says, "Too long a sacrifice / Can make a stone of the heart," and figures such as Deacon Smith in "Fire and Cloud" eventually become even worse, a Judas to their people. Throughout the sequence, opting for heroic rebellion prevents that fate, but often brings on a transfiguring death. Again to echo Yeats, each is "transformed utterly: A terrible beauty is born."

This replicates the pattern of classical tragedy, as Wright surely knew. Here, however, the flaw exists not in the characters, but in the social system that dooms them. And this pattern seems all the more painful because of the yearned-for solution of a return to order and domesticity, another pattern present in antiquity. Ricoeur reminds us that a return to origins can culminate in a return to home and hearth; this occurs in the epic of Ulysses, a model of the hero. Although their struggles are all related to these concepts, each one of Wright's figures – except, perhaps, Reverend Taylor – has that possibility annulled, in most cases physically, as in the burning of Big Boy's and Silas's houses and the death of family members.

This aspect of the narrative reveals Wright's intention of using this group of stories as a kind of semiotics of the history of the African-American family. His narratives mirror the actual history of the dominant culture's attacks on the integrity of black individuals and their families, but they also create, in their cumulative effect, their *own* history. Wright, like James Fenimore Cooper, Frederick Douglass, Abraham Cahan, and countless other American writers, understood the deep connection between history and narrative, and fiction's unique potential for revitalizing and even revising or correcting history itself. *Uncle Tom's Children* was written to memorialize the struggle of black Americans during the decades following the First World War, when white America was preoccupied with forcing the black man – and particularly the black soldier – back into his place. The economic vectors of the depression years actually facilitated this process, as response to the general need of all Americans became predicated on racial hierarchical models. Wright demonstrates this most powerfully in "Down by the Riverside"; the flood devastates all citizens, but whites have first claim on available boats, medical supplies, and so on, and blacks are conscripted into virtual slavery to help carry out that program.

Wright's stories were thus meant to *historicize* this kind of situation, this moment of conflict, which America's histories had omitted. Wright recreated it, fashioned a series of heroic responses, and projected them into the future as a rallying point for oppressed peoples, black and white, as in the united march of the poor of both races in "Fire and Cloud."

Wright's rock-ribbed narratives conceal an engine of rage and a fiery judgment and warning. The structural model evident here, the jeremiad, permits damning dramatization of social injustice, but also hints at possible solutions, thus highlighting Wright's prophetic nature. Biblical prophets condemned, yes, but they also offered the hope of restoration of the covenant if the people renounced their evil. Furthermore, as Whitman reminded us, prophecy has all too frequently been misunderstood as the predictions of a seer; a true prophet functions to reveal God. Wright felt he was doing that by directing us to the gods within us and by offering the solutions of the Communist party. Unfortunately, this secular "God" later failed him and other "believers" of the time.

It is fascinating to note that Wright was producing this kind of reading program at virtually the same moment that Lukács was formulating his masterful study, *The Historical Novel;* in the section "Prospects of Development for the New Humanism in the Historical Novel," he wrote:

> We see that all problems of form and content alike in the historical novel of our day centre upon questions of heritage. All aesthetic problems and valuations in this sphere are determined by the struggle to liquidate the political, ideological and artistic heritage of the period of declining capitalism, by the struggle to renew and fruitfully extend the traditions of the great progressive periods of mankind, the spirit of revolutionary democracy, the artistic grandeur and popular strength of the classical historical novel.[11]

Furthermore, Lukács makes it clear that what determines the success of a writer so motivated is his attitude toward popular life. In like manner, Wright, in *Uncle Tom's Children,* sought to fashion a new form of historical narrative, one deeply based in the realities of black culture and the spirit of "revolutionary democracy," precisely because he understood how impoverished American historical consciousness was at this particular moment, especially when it came to the scandalous history of lynchings and burnings in the South just after the war. This revised chronicle would provide Americans with an accurate and deeply disturbing depiction of a history their own complicity had created.

In light of this aim, it might seem curious that there are no temporal markers of any sort in the book, except in the references to the soldiers returned from World War I in "Big Boy Leaves Home." Wright seems to be intent on removing the boundaries of chronological time in order to liberate the resources of phenomenological time that historical narrative ignores; in so doing, he achieves what Ricoeur calls the "reinscription of historical time upon cosmological time," making the world of the narrative mythic and eternally relevant.[12]

We might further speculate that Wright also intends to memorialize, not just in his time, but for *all* time, the sufferings of a people for their descendents; as Bakhtin states, "One may . . . memorialize with artistic language only that which is worthy of being remembered, that which should be preserved in the memory of descendents. . . . Contemporaneity for its own sake (that is to say, a contemporaneity that makes no claim on future memory) is molded in clay; contemporaneity for the future (for descendants) is molded in marble or bronze."[13] And yet, increasingly moving in this direction after writing *Uncle Tom's Children,* Wright more and more cut himself off from the folklife that was his subject, retreating into the isolation of both the social rebel or outcast and the ironic separation of celebrity, eventually expatriating himself in France. As Lukács states, humanists of our time who write in protest often are tragically estranged from popular life and become increasingly dependent upon themselves. Richard Wright knew, when he was writing *Uncle Tom's Children,* that he had left the South forever, and the fictional personae he created in those pages are depicted through a form of historical elegy, an elegy not just for the dead. The bitter note that sounds again and again is that the search for (w)holeness on the individual level frequently leads to separation from the folk culture and death, or both. Only "Fire and Cloud" avoids this pattern; this story would seem a more logical conclusion to the collection than "Bright and Morning Star." Wright, however, abhorred any blurring of his message; witness his determination in *Native Son* to avoid Dreiser's mistake of creating ambiguity about the guilt of the central murderer. "Star" reveals his true stand regarding the church that "Fire and Cloud" possibly masks. Rather than a union of church and party, this story clearly draws powerful structures of faith and myth from black Christianity and reharnesses them to a new "morning star," the party. Aunt Sue, the embodiment of this process, represents the dimensions of what some readers would consider Wright's doubled blasphemy. Not only does he want the people to reject their religion in favor of his; he dares to use the forms, tropes, songs, and scripture of the black church to mount his argument.

In "Long Black Song," the salesman tells Sarah she needs the clock/
graphophone he is selling, but she replies, "We git erlong widout time
. . . we don't need no clock," referring to their base in natural time (108).
This simple utterance implies the divergence of black reality from recorded history as well. "Natural time," however, would also encompass
the concepts of *biblical* time, as embodied in the progression from Genesis, the creation of time, to Revelation, the end of time and human history. With this base established, we should return to the first story as the
genesis of the others, for the voices established by each story, repeated
and varied in those that follow, blend in a "song" of protest we may also
read as a howl of rage and sorrow, but one that encodes ethnicity and
history through the manipulation of biblical types.

"Big Boy" shifts from the Edenic to the hellish mode when the white
woman sees the nude boys; they instinctively cover their groins. Wright,
in glossing the Edenic scene, thereby sets up the first of a series of typo-
logical references in the sequence and actually inverts them, for the
white woman blasphemously takes on the role of God discovering the
sin of Adam and Eve. We find an element of fairy tale here too, in
the enchanted garden scene and in the woman's incantatory screams –
three times she calls for Jim, and issues a tripartite set of commands for
them to "go away"; similarly, there are three rifle shots, all set off on the
page in their own paragraphs: "CRACK!"

The ritualistic roles that all must play are clearly understood; as they
run through the woods, Bobo tells Big Boy "Theys gonna lynch us,"
and Big Boy's mother, asking questions in shorthand and getting them
back in kind, immediately understands that an old script has been set
in motion – "Lawd Gawd in Heaven, have mercy on us all! This is mo
trouble, mo trouble." But just how much is not clear until she hears
the dreaded words "white woman" intrude into the narrative. Saul, Big
Boy's father, an old man, seems clearly meant to represent an old de-
posed King, much like his biblical namesake. His heir, David/Big Boy,
will have to establish a new city/Temple in the North. These recurring
biblical allusions in the narrative should not surprise us. As Ralph Ellison has remarked, Richard Wright was "a possessor of that tradition"
established by the Negro church, "wherein you heard the lingering ac-
cents of nineteenth-century rhetoric with its emphasis upon freedom
and individual responsibility; a rhetorical style which gave us Lincoln,

Harriet Tubman . . . Frederick Douglass . . . and many other eloquent and heroic Negroes." [14] Part of that style and manner was of course reference to biblical figures as types.

To establish the unfolding pattern embedded in the structures of this first tale, we need to redefine the shift from the Edenic to the hellish. It modulates from the genetic to the apocalyptic, as it moves from images of creation/Spring to those of destruction/death in the lynching. To get at the final apocalyptic thrust of the cycle, also present at the beginning, we may return to the opening voices rising out of the woods, which refer us back to a seminal poem by Wright, "Between the World and Me." Trudier Harris has correctly earmarked this piece as the generative point of Wright's aesthetic, since metaphoric lynching, literal lynching, and the references to such events are everywhere in Wright's work. The poem, written just before "Big Boy," begins: "And one morning while in the woods I suddenly stumbled upon the thing, / Stumbled upon it in a grassy clearing." From the remains of this lynched body – "a design of white bones" – comes a voice of sorts, as the narrator imagines the mob, the roar, the gasoline: "My heart was circled with icy walls of fear." Then:

> The dry bones stirred, rattled, lifted, melting themselves into my bones. / The gray ashes formed flesh firm and black, entering into my flesh . . . a thousand faces swirled around me, clamoring that my life be burned . . . And then they had me. . . . Then my blood was cooled mercifully, cooled by a baptism of gasoline. / And in a blaze of red I leaped to the sky as pain rose like water, boiling my limbs. . . . Now I am dry bones and my face a stony skull staring in yellow surprise at the sun.

Thus after an initial survey of the scene, which Harris notes "approaches detachment," the speaker begins to identify with the body, to actually become the body en route to "a cathartic emotional 'death.'" [15] He can then be reborn into a new historical/human consciousness. Let us remember, however, that Wright specifically states, "The dry bones stirred, rattled, lifted, melting themselves into my bones." This refers to Ezekiel 37:1–14, where the Lord takes the prophet into the valley of the dry bones:

> And he said unto me, Son of man, can these bones live? And I answered, O Lord God, thou knowest. Again he said unto me, Prophesy upon these bones, and say unto them, O ye dry bones, hear the word of the Lord . . . So I prophesied as I was commanded . . . and the bones came together . . . and stood up upon their feet, an exceeding great army. Then

he said unto me, Son of man, these bones are the whole house of Israel; behold, they say, Our bones are dried, and our hope is lost: we are cut off for our parts. I will open up your graves . . . and bring you into the land of Israel. And shall put my spirit in you, and ye shall live, and I shall place you in our own land.

We know that Wright was familiar with this particular passage; he states in *Black Boy* that "the elders of the church expounded a gospel clogged with images of vast lakes of eternal fire, of seas vanishing, of valleys of dry bones, of the sun burning to ashes, of the moon turning to blood, of stars falling to the earth. . . . While listening to the vivid language of the sermons, I was pulled towards emotional belief." [16] The spiritual, "Them Bones," would of course have been familiar to him as well. The narrative strategy of *Uncle Tom's Children*, like "Between the World and Me," takes the "dry bones" of the reader's responses and fleshes them out via intense identification with the victims of the stories, to make the reader literally burn with the lynchers' gasoline, to feel the penetrating bullets, to hunger and thirst after bread, water, respect and justice. Wright thus begins a long strand of typology, primarily introducing Old Testament types here, but gradually doubling the typology with New Testament figures and building toward the images and prophecies of Revelation in the final story, as we shall see.

The first link to Old Testament mythology is to Genesis, as demonstrated earlier; Big Boy, living as he does in a pastoral world, must "fall" from his ignorance, as Adam did, hence the specifically Edenic aspects of "Big Boy Leaves Home," where he represents both Adam and Cain. Appropriately, this Genesis-grounded text opens Wright's larger narrative as well and leads next to "Down By the Riverside," an extension of the bondage/f(l)ight sequence, but also of the biblical referent, as Mann represents an ironic version of Noah, with echoes from the book of Job. The floodwaters create chaos but also ironically reinforce and underline hierarchy, in that who shall be saved first gets determined racially – "women and children first" has no meaning if those women and children are black. Mann's wife and child both perish, and when authorities send him to rescue the Heartfield woman and her children, the racist configuration of the scene inevitably leads Mann to the conclusion that he should kill them, an act thwarted by the literal shifting of the house itself, by an apparently hostile Nature.

Wright never makes specific reference to Noah and his ark, but then he doesn't have to; everyone must find a boat to escape the flood, and everything enters this narrative by twos. There are two shots to kill

Heartfield, two lighted windows, two visits to Heartfield's house, two soldiers, two nurses, and so on, thereby suggesting the biblical injunction to save in pairs, male and female. Mann's family, as completed by PeeWee, Lula, and Granny, contrasts symmetrically to Heartfield's (husband, wife, son, daughter) – that is, two males and two females, thus forming a black/white image of the family.

This biblical unifying device in the third story, "Long Black Song," finds expression in doubled typology, combining figures from both the Old and New Testament. Sarah, the central figure, *should* be the mother of a new chosen people; and Silas, the Abraham candidate, has devoted his life to capitalist acquisition to make this come about. Unfortunately, in so doing, his paterfamilias domestic self has atrophied, thereby leading to the collapse of his overall goal, a pattern Faulkner uses with Sutpen in *Absalom, Absalom!*

Wright draws his New Testament type from Silas, Paul's companion in Philippi (Acts 15). There, Paul cures a girl cursed with the spirit of divination, who is being hired out as a soothsayer by unscrupulous men; consequently, he and Silas are beaten and thrown into prison. As a result of their prayers, an earthquake throws all the doors open, thus permitting their escape, which the conversion of the warden assures. "But Paul said unto them, They have beaten us openly uncondemned, being Romans, and have cast us into prison; and now do they thrust us out privily? nay verily; but let them come themselves and fetch us out" (Acts 15:37). Like his biblical counterpart, Silas refuses flight and elects to stay "in prison," ironically, his home; he lets the enemy come to him. This story, like the "dry bones" passage in the Bible, serves as the subject of a beloved spiritual, "Who Shall Deliver Po' Me,"[17] that Wright undoubtedly knew.

Silas has been cited by several critics as the pivotal figure in the sequence, and the doubled typology of his stance indicates his function as a hinge between the old order and the new dispensation that the gospel of communism becomes in "Fire and Cloud." This story clearly builds upon the concept of Taylor as Moses; he shall lead his people out of bondage, out of the darkness of "Egypt" into the light of "freedom." Michel Fabre tells us that the story's final note came from Lenin, himself a Moses of sorts, specifically from his "Freedom Belongs to the Strong."[18] Taylor must grow into this stance however; initially, he vacillates between the demands of the elders, the white elite, and the communists, pleasing no one. Vigilantes subsequently torture him in the woods, filling Taylor with the fire of pain but also of hate, transforming him not into Moses, but into the biblical pillar of fire (Exodus 33:9) itself: "Like a pillar of fire he went through the white neighborhood. Some days thes gonna burn!" (167).

Once again, however, Wright employs doubled typology, transforming Taylor into Christ, and with good reason. One of the major problems Wright grapples with in these stories, paralleling his ongoing work with the Communist party, is how to use existing resources in the black community to further the cause of unity and freedom. Clearly, as Wright realized, a major source of strength, unity, and culture was the black church, yet that same institution had been co-opted by white interpretations of the Bible and a white God to shift black aspirations from earth to heaven. The problem for Wright, then, was to discover ways in which the church and Marx could meet, one that has recently been of paramount importance in liberation theology in Latin America. He no doubt found some clues in a book he bought in 1936, *The Bible Designed as Living Literature,* and as Michel Fabre notes, Wright quotes at random from the Bible in later works, especially *Black Boy, Savage Holiday, The Outsider,* and *Black Power.*[19] Moreover, one discovers a surfeit of biblical imagery interposed with communist motifs in the poems Wright wrote during the time that *Uncle Tom's Children* was taking shape. In these lyrics, as Fabre notes, "Wright constantly harks back to Christian formulas which seem the most appropriate for his political designs."[20]

The idea of Taylor as a black Christ could hardly be introduced *directly* by him, so Wright nudges the narrative that way by having Taylor depict his archrival in the church, Deacon Smith, as a "black snake in the grass! [folkloric signifier] A black Judas! [typological signifier]." And then more explicitly: "N when he ain doing that hes a-tryin his best t give me wrong advice, jus like the Devil a-tryin t tempt Jesus. But Ahm gonna march on wida hepa Gawd" (133).

God, however, gets replaced, at least as inspiration for the march, by the Communist party, which skillfully builds its networks and rhetoric around the structures and tropes of the black church, just as Wright does as an artist. Wright signals all this when Taylor arrives home and finds that the mayor and his men await him in the parlor and the deacons occupy the cellar, while Hadley and Green, the party organizers, sit in the Bible room. Their placement there, in the realm of the sacred "word," made possible by the displacement of the deacons to the cellar, underscores Wright's intent to reinscribe the gospels with a communist reading, beginning with the harnessing of the voice of Christ's chief rhetorician, Rev. Taylor.

The matter of authoritative voice plays a crucial role in democratic revolution. Wright originally intended this story to conclude the sequence, which begins by focusing on silence/immaturity in "Big Boy," expands into Mann's heroic but still silent action in "Down By," then explodes in suicidal, physical, and verbal defiance in "Song." In "Fire," the introductory passages, like those in "Big Boy," depict the central character moving reflectively through the landscape, internally engaged in a dialogue with God about the nature of the current crisis (famine) and reflecting about the history of his ministry and the voice that God has developed in him: "Yes, he had been like Moses, leading his people out of the wilderness into the Promised Land" (131).

Taylor attempts to deal with the crisis initially by leading the people in a call-and-response sermon, one that traces the entire history of the Bible, beginning with the Creation, going through Revelation and beyond to an appeal for a sign, and again we find doubled typology, first in the demand, "Speak t us like Yuh spoke t Jacob!" and then in the request, "Now show us the sign like Yuh showed Saul! [Who converted, became Paul] Show us the sign n well ack!" (138). Paradoxically, however, Taylor uses his voice here as a calmative to keep the people at bay, for he himself, like Saul before the "sign" appears, seems unwilling to act; he rushes from the room, "his ears filled with the sound of wailing voices" (139), a literal splitting of his voice from that of the folk. Eventually however, as noted, the fiery "sign" of his beating transforms him into Moses/Christ, with a voice and "gospel" to match; under the communist/Christian banner, he leads poor whites and blacks in the successful march for food and justice.

Wright pursued and extended this same theme in "Bright and Morning Star." Inexplicably, Lucien L. Agosta, in his otherwise perceptive examination of millennialism in "Fire and Cloud," fails to see how "Star" extends the march to Revelation, but then Agosta sees the story as being harmfully "tacked on." He accurately observes, however, that unlike the other stories, which present the two races "cursing and clawing . . . in an inextricable embrace," "Fire" ends with "an *exemplum:* whites and blacks cease clawing at each other and instead, draw from the strength of their union the energy to forge a new earth and a new heaven. As such, the millennial conclusion of the final novella (in the original design) is at least artistically validated by the development of this theme in each of the preceding novellas." [21]

Critics continue to argue about Wright's attachment of the final story to the original four. Whatever we might think about the opposing arguments, we must admire Wright's ingenuity in fitting "Star" into his original sequence. In terms of the unifying typology I have charted, the final tale completes the biblical parallel with a story tropologically modeled on the book of Revelation. The apocalyptic brutality of this tale surely eclipses everything that went before except the excruciating details of Bobo's immolation. Here Wright depicts the savage beating and later killing of an old woman, coupled with her witnessing of the crucifixion of her son. Clearly, Aunt Sue's resemblance to the Virgin mother would link her to the star of Bethlehem, but in fact the hymn Wright used for his title, "The Lily of the Valley," which critics usually classify as a "spiritual," draws its dominant imagery from the book of Revelation. The lyrics declare: "I have found a friend in Jesus . . . in Him alone I see All I need to cleanse and make me fully whole. . . . A wall of fire about me, I've nothing now to fear, With His manna He my hungry soul shall fill." The refrain refers to Christ as "The Lily of the Valley, the Bright and Morning Star, He's the fairest of ten thousand to my soul." Once again, we have reference to the (w)hole; moreover, when Christ speaks to John, he states, "I am Alpha and Omega, the first and the last: and what thou seest, write in a book, and send it unto the seven churches" (Rev. 1:11). Although the star as an emblem of Christ's gospel appears several times in the New Testament, the phrase "bright and morning star" occurs only once, in the last chapter of the last book of the Bible: "I Jesus have sent mine angel to testify unto you these things in the churches. I am the root and the offspring of David [we remember here the reference to David via Saul, Big Boy's father, in the first tale], and the bright and morning star" (Rev. 22:16).

These biblical models, so closely connected to the concept of voice, may thus be related to a narrative strategy, one centered on the testing of the hero's discourse, and connected to the concept of rebirth. Bakhtin has identified this as one of the most fundamental organizing ideas in narrative,[22] and in each of Wright's stories, voice or its absence precipitates a crisis and frequently its resolution as well, as we have noted in the above discussion of voice in the first three stories. In the fifth story, Aunt Sue's proud taunting of the sheriff and his goons causes both her catastrophe and her ultimate spiritual triumph. It could be said that the guns wielded by her, Big Boy, and Silas are "voices" of the folk as well.

At the same time, the testing motif, which relates thematically to motifs of rebirth, takes us back to Wright's central paradigm, his poem "Between the World and Me." There he creates an epiphany of horror in the woods before the lynch mob's victim, where "dry bones" live through the symbolic rebirth of both the "text" (the bones), the primary "reader" (the poet) and his audience, the secondary reader. Rebirth may come from the water or the fire; Big Boy sees Bobo's burning from the womblike hiding place of the kiln, a "female" structure he built himself, which had been penetrated by a black snake – a snake with white fangs that Big Boy has to kill before finding refuge. This "reading" of the fire as it renders the "bones" leads to the death of his old consciousness and the birth of another; he then leaves Eden, with his innocence gone forever.

The narrative strategies we have considered so far obviously create a great deal of repetition in the sequence, but black culture in general constantly utilizes repetition, as James Snead has recently demonstrated, as well as proletariat/propagandistic literatures. Moreover, we know from *Black Boy* that Wright's first rapturous experience in fiction was hearing the story of Bluebeard told to him by a young teacher. "My imagination blazed. The sensations the story aroused in me were never to leave me" (34). Since "Bluebeard" displays sets of ritualistic narrative repetitions, all culminating in murder, this early *oral* influence provides a personal ground for reading yet another set of repetitive narratives, the oral renditions of burning/lynching/beating rituals. Repetitions and variations on this paradigmatic scene throughout the sequence make the process of transubstantiation/baptism/rebirth ritualistic and, one hopes along with Wright, habitual. Wright clearly understood the role of what Heidegger calls "being-toward-death," and precisely these types of moments form the crux of each of the stories.

Moreover, repetition permits a "rereading" of what has been previously inscribed. When Wright presents Aunt Sue embracing the Party he reveals through her process of "rereading" both her past and the Bible what he went through in accepting the New Faith of Communism. As Michel Fabre has shown, in Wright's party-inspired poetry:

> the Marxist books become the Bible, and in 'A Red Love Note' the final notice of the proletarian to the capitalist echoes the Creator's curse on Cain; the deluge and the destruction of the Temple are the principal symbols of 'Everywhere Burning Waters Rise' [a title that obviously fuses the two modes of baptism]. Wright constantly harks back to Christian formulas that seem the most appropriate for his political designs.[23]

Our survey of doubled typology provides yet another justification for the placement of "Star" at the end of the cycle, as it caps the progression/repetition of political education scenes. In "Fire's" penulti-

mate message, the birth of an interracial brotherhood of consciousness
that truly signals a new millennium, Rev. Taylor figuratively receives a
baptism by fire through his beating and emerges reborn into the world
of collective revolt. A second baptism, however, "of clean joy" sweeps
over him when he stands up to the mayor, who finally capitulates to the
crowd's demands. "This is the way! he [Taylor] thought. Gawd ain no
lie! . . . *Freedom belongs to the strong!* (180). Thus we leave him with his two
"texts" – the Bible and communist procedure – curiously blended. Aunt
Sue, by contrast, has already gone through this process in "Star" and,
indeed, finds Christianity incompatible with Communism, in the former's interdiction of the violence that she finally accomplishes in the
service of the latter. The (red) star on the horizon, like the star of Bethlehem, represents a star of hope, and ultimately (it is said) peace, but a
star also signifies conflagration, a controlled and cleansing chaos of fire.
The story thus encodes both warning and hope, in the classic tradition
of the Jeremiad; Wright extends the brief interracial cooperation of
"Fire" into more permanent forms in "Star," and the interracial love
between Reva and Johnny-Boy provides a marker for this millennialist
goal. The story anticipates in many ways both the fiction (*Another Country*) and the nonfiction (*The Fire Next Time*) of James Baldwin, who would
nevertheless ridicule Wright's naivete as a protest writer.

THE NARRATIVE STRUCTURES OF TORTURE AND REBIRTH

All the foregoing illuminates Wright's motives and methods but somehow fails to account for the extraordinary power of the climactic scenes,
which have a narrative strategy of their own. Nowhere do these methods of focalization and repetitive narrative patterns become more
meaningful than in the scenes that involve torture, most prominently
Bobo's, Taylor's, and Sue's, but also that of Silas. Significantly, Wright
introduces all this in "The Ethics of Living Jim Crow," by depicting the
torture of the author himself. In most of the fictional renditions, torture
ironically produces a rebirth of the self, however brief. This flies in the
face of most cases of actual torture, however, which have been tellingly
examined by Elaine Scarry, whose theories prove most useful in our
final reading of the cycle, for a key element of Wright's program is instruction in the agency of pain and torture.

The opening story, "Big Boy Leaves Home" in some ways proves the
most shocking because of the multiple horrors of the lynching; but we
must remember that we *observe* the scene through Big Boy, rather than

feeling it through Bobo, or identifying with him via the author as in "Between the World and Me." We read the scene with mounting horror, but we do not feel it as direct sensation as we will in "Fire" and "Star," when we read the experience of physical pain directly through the bodies of Rev. Taylor and Aunt Sue, whose consciousness we share. The power of these scenes, we must recall, comes partly from the cumulative force of the inscribed memory of torture that begins with Bobo, memories created by Wright's narrative strategies.

Racists employ torture in the final two stories for the usual reason; the pain produced offers seemingly incontrovertible evidence of the power of the perpetrators, that is, the white establishment. In reality, however, those in power occupy unstable, unjustifiable positions; thus the need for the demonstration.

Wright had obviously given great thought to the script and semiotics of torture. As Scarry notes, torture scenarios are designed to convert real pain into a fiction of power; as part of the "script," victims everywhere are inevitably forced to stare at the weapon to be used against them. "[Rev. Taylor] saw a tall white man holding a plaited leather whip in his hand, hitting it gently against his trousers' leg. 'You know what this is, nigger? . . . This is a nigger whip!'" (161). Repeated questions accompany the beating; torturers inflict disorienting interrogation and intense pain in order to destroy the individual's world, in this case a black world that has suddenly become more threatening to the power structure because of the developing relationships among blacks, poor whites, and Communists. As this scene reveals, torturers view the content of answers to questions as secondary; the form and the fact of a reply matters much more. Here, after a perfunctory, "Well, nigger, what do you know?" the vigilantes use a whip to make Taylor pray; he eventually recites part of the Lord's prayer. As Scarry states, "The torturer and the regime have doubled their voice since the prisoner is now speaking their words." [24] Ironically, "their words" here mean an appropriation of God's words, thus constituting blasphemy; further, Taylor's plea to the white community throughout the story echoes the Lord's Prayer: "Give us this day our daily bread," a line he refuses to recite under torture.

The lines he does recite, however, have the effect of confession, which most people disdain; here, however, Taylor follows this surrender with a surge of resistance and anger, shouting, "Awright, kill me! . . . Yuh white trash cowards, kill me! . . . Well git yuh white trash some day! So hep me Gawd, we'll git yuh!" This leads to more whipping and a demand for him to "say that again, Goddam you!" (164).

This assertion of the self comes when Taylor realizes he will likely be killed; his voice becomes his last method of self-extension and enables him to transcend the prison-house his body has become. We also note this pattern in "Star," when Aunt Sue's fatal sin of hubris causes her to cry out after her brutal torture, "Yuh didnt git whut yuh wanted!" (197). In some ways, Wright's presentation of Aunt Sue's torture completes the "reading" of the subject he has forced on us, as unlike the torture of Bobo and Taylor, it takes place indoors, in her house. Twenty white men (setting up the proverbial twenty-to-one odds) invade her kitchen, looking for her son and for a list of Communist party members. Their seizure of her cornbread, greens, and coffee is accompanied by the muddy tracks of their boots across her floor; because those boots are soon employed kicking her, this invasion and profanation of the clean space that symbolizes her body presents both a premonition of her torture and a symbol of gang-rape. Wright skillfully transforms our traditional "reading" of the kitchen as a place of nurture, warmth, and familial unity into a torture chamber, and reminds us of Faulkner's similar achievement with the castration/death of Joe Christmas in Hightower's kitchen in *Light in August.* The room itself becomes a weapon as the men slap Aunt Sue into a wall. We remember too that the dog backs Big Boy up to the wall of the kiln; much of the drama inside the Heartfield house involves people being thrown against walls, and Mann constantly fights against walls of darkness; and the walls of Silas's burning house fall inward on his body. For Scarry, this form of torture represents all others, "the walls collapsing in on the human center to crush it alive." Wright thus makes us see how the subverting of the objects of everyday life – the conversion of the room and its artifacts into weapons – can unmake the person's concept of self and of world. As Scarry concludes, "the unmaking of civilization inevitably requires a return to and mutilation of the domestic, the ground of all making." [25]

This sequence thus asks "What are the forms/actions/functions of racism?" and attempts to answer by passing the question repeatedly through the prism of racial outrage; the resultant lines of illumination, passing through at different angles as the dramatic scene dictates, produce varying lines of narrative. The unbearable tension of the book comes from the question at the back of the reader's mind: What form will the horror take *this* time, and how will the victim(s) be different from those we have seen already?

Ultimately, Wright's narrative strategies reveal racism's most powerful qualities: Racial oppression terrifies because of its protean dynamic, its catholic taste in victims, and its ability to invade not only the public sphere but, more importantly, the intimacies of domestic, familial relationships, the mind, the body, and the larger family of man itself; bearing the power to falsify history, it masks and distorts a people's identity. As illustration, consider the line of racial crimes as balanced against the respective victims: "Big Boy" details torture, dismemberment, and the burning of a house and a human body. A teenage boy serves as the particular, focal victim, as witness, exile, and criminal. His family, members left homeless, become ancillary victims. "Down By the Riverside" presents forced servitude after the death of a spouse; the appropriation of property and the separation of family, and summary execution. Here, a mature man (Mann) serves as victim, whereas Granny and Pee-Wee, an old woman and a young child, play ancillary roles. Similarly, the entire black community's needs become subordinated to those of the whites in time of flood. "Long Black Song" presents a young wife physically seduced and economically conned by a white salesman; her middle-aged husband becomes a cuckold and is then burned alive by mob. Once again, white oppressors separate a black family, leaving a child fatherless. Vigilantes savagely beat a respected older minister in "Fire and Cloud," and again the black community gets slighted in time of general need (famine). Finally, in "Bright and Morning Star," an old woman suffers torture and death after both her sons endure torture, one before her eyes. We see Wright assembling an entire family of participants here, representing women in infancy (Ruth), youth (Sarah), maturity (Lulu), and old age (Sue); men find expression in childhood (Pee-Wee); teenage (Big Boy); young manhood (Jimmy, Johnnie Boy); maturity (Silas) and age (Taylor).

As in *Uncle Tom's Cabin*, *Uncle Tom's Children* presents a general pattern of disintegration, each story beginning with a whole family and then proceeding to chart its destruction and dispersal through racism. The "cabin", metaphor of familial unity and nurture, indeed is burned, both in "Big Boy" and "Song," and the "children" can survive only by banding together for communal strength; as Rev. Taylor shouts, "Freedom belongs t the strong!" The various stories of *Uncle Tom's Children*, read as a "family" of narratives, illustrate their own principles by the very structures of reading they impose; the members of the extended black family achieve individual wholeness through personal rebirth, repetition, communal strength, and meaning that reverberates across the voids of enforced separation.

NOTES

1. Richard Wright, *Uncle Tom's Children* (New York: Harper & Brothers, 1938), 17.
2. Paul Ricoeur, "Narrative Time," in *On Narrative*, ed. W. J. T. Mitchell (Chicago: University of Chicago Press, 1981), 171.
3. Martin Heidegger, *Being and Time* (New York: Harper, 1962), p. 436.
4. Houston Baker, *Blues, Ideology, and Afro-American Literature: A Vernacular Theory* (Chicago: University of Chicago Press, 1984), 152–7.
5. Richard Wright, "Blueprint for Negro Writing," in *Richard Wright Reader*, ed. Ellen Wright and Michel Fabre (New York: Harper & Row, 1978), 40.
6. Mikhail Bakhtin, *The Dialogic Imagination: Four Essays*, ed. Michael Holquist, trans. Caryl Emerson and Michael Holquist (Austin: University of Texas Press, 1981), 21.
7. Gerard Genette, *Narrative Discourse: An Essay in Method*, trans. Jane E. Lewin (Ithaca, NY: Cornell University Press, 1980), 256.
8. Genette, 192.
9. Genette, 179–80.
10. Elaine Scarry, *The Body in Pain: The Making and Unmaking of the World* (New York: Oxford University Press, 1985), 192.
11. Georg Lukács, *The Historical Novel*, trans. Hannah and Stanley Mitchell (Lincoln: University of Nebraska Press, 1962), 332.
12. Paul Ricoeur, *Time and Narrative* (3 vols.), trans. Kathleen Blarney and David Pellauer (Chicago: University of Chicago Press, 1984), 3: 128.
13. Bakhtin, 19.
14. Ellison, 208–9.
15. Trudier Harris, *Exorcising Blackness: Historical and Literary Burning and Lynching Rituals* (Bloomington: Indiana University Press, 1984), 100.
16. Richard Wright, *Black Boy: A Record of Childhood and Youth* (New York: Harper & Brothers, 1945), 89.
17. R. Emmet Kennedy, *More Mellows* (New York: Dodd, Mead, 1931), 116–23.
18. Michel Fabre, *The Unfinished Quest of Richard Wright*, 2nd ed., trans. Isabel Barzun (Urbana: University of Illinois Press, 1993), 160.
19. Michel Fabre, *The World of Richard Wright* (Jackson: University of Mississippi Press, 1985), 24.
20. Fabre, *World*, 40.
21. Lucien L. Agosta, "Millennial Embrace: The Artistry of Conclusion in Richard Wright's 'Fire and Cloud,'" *Studies in Short Fiction* 18 (1981): 126.
22. Bakhtin, 388.
23. Fabre, *World*, 40.
24. Scarry, *Body in Pain*, 36.
25. Scarry, *Body in Pain*, 45.

The African-American Voice
in Faulkner's Go Down, Moses

JOHN CARLOS ROWE

> On a riverbank in the cool of a summer evening two women strug-
> gled under a shower of silvery blue. They never expected to see
> each other again in this world and at the moment couldn't care
> less. But there on a summer night surrounded by bluefern they did
> something together appropriately and well.
>
> Toni Morrison, *Beloved* (1987)

Nearly thirty years ago, in *The Achievement of William Faulkner*, Michael
Millgate argued that the aesthetic unity of *Go Down, Moses* resulted from
Faulkner's successful representation of "the white-Negro theme." [1] Like
other literary formalists of his generation, Millgate focused on a
"theme" notable for its tension and conflict, in order to show how the
literary work effects "the conjunction, and in some measure the fusion,
of a number of disparate ideas" (201). For Millgate, this aesthetic synthesis depends crucially on the character of Ike McCaslin, "whose combination of sensitivity and long life would afford scope for the two complementary strategies of innocent childhood and retrospective old age"
(201). More than simply anchoring the thematic tensions of *Go Down,
Moses*, Ike *embodies* them in a complex character that serves as an ironic
patriarch for a new, redeemed South. Ike may never "father" the "new
family" that would transform the conflicts of Southern whites and African Americans into an openly miscegenated family, but this is surely
what Faulkner claims for himself as author in dramatizing the twinned
fates of the whites and African Americans of the McCaslin family as the
central action of *Go Down, Moses*. [2]

Ike is "father to no one" but "uncle to a county," and Faulkner creates what ought to be built in the moral space made possible by Ike's
renunciation of his family's legacy: the sins of slavery. Like Eliot's
Tiresias in *The Waste Land*, Faulkner's Ike can only bear witness to the
sinful world he inhabits. [3] As a consequence, Faulkner is Ike's supple-

ment, the patriarch who will cathartically purge the conflicts of the Old South in a new "genealogy" in which family secrets become the "news" of his literary narrative. Such a reading is, I think, extraordinarily close to Faulkner's own intentions, which explains how successful formalist interpretations of Faulkner have been long after their theoretical assumptions have been thoroughly deconstructed. As long as we continue to read *Go Down, Moses* as a "modern novel," we repeat the victimization of African Americans, in part by subordinating ourselves as readers to a literary authority often as paternalistic as that of the Southern patriarch.[4]

Even when the reader, the African American, the woman, and the child – all victims in Faulkner – are permitted by such a narrative to "speak," their voices are already echoes or necessary functions within the larger purposes of this modernist's story. It is for this reason, I think, that the interpretation of *Go Down, Moses* according to the "education" of Ike McCaslin has been so successful and yet remains so profoundly dissatisfying, not only for the cultural critic but also for Faulkner. Whatever Faulkner's modernist intentions in novels like *The Sound and the Fury* and *Absalom, Absalom!*, both of which certainly shape the "unity and coherence" of the stories in *Go Down, Moses,* he still understood at some level beyond the purely aesthetic that the political arguments of his major works demanded an African-American voice at once more rebellious and utopian than any of the voices he ever projected in his fictions.

The organization of *Go Down, Moses* in terms of the central action of Ike McCaslin's renunciation both empowers Faulkner as the author required to complete Ike's unfinished story and further marginalizes the African-American characters who paradoxically appear to have more substantial fictional realities than in any of Faulkner's previous works. Faulkner seems caught by the contradiction of his own aesthetic and political logics: On the one hand, he emulates the white Southern patriarch in the responsibility he assumes for his extended family; on the other hand, he knows that the sins of such families can be redeemed only by publicizing the scandal of slavery *and* by encouraging its victims to revolt against the social psychological habits that are as much the insidious "legacy" of slavery as the legal and economic bonds of postbellum racism.

As far as the formal definition of this famous short story sequence is concerned, my thesis regarding the complex interplay between Faulkner's expression – the genealogy from Ike to Author – and repression – the subordination of African Americans to the moral authority of Ike or Faulkner – would seem best served by considering the seven-part work as characterized by its "disunity, discontinuity, and never-ending strife."[5] This is Susan Donaldson's argument in "Contending Narratives: *Go Down, Moses* and the Short Story Cycle," which convincingly demonstrates that Faulkner's equivocal descriptions of the collection "as a novel and as a short story collection" might be interpreted in terms of what theorists have often claimed are the inherent "conflicts and tensions" of the literary form itself. Appealing as such an approach is, it tends to reaffirm Faulkner's modernist and even formalist intentions, insofar as it concludes by a certain inevitability that "Faulkner" (that is, the author-function of this name) encompasses this conflict and struggle. As Donaldson concludes her essay, the tensions and discontinuities in *Go Down, Moses* finally achieve a "small measure of victory" in the literary effort to resist the monologic discourse of the McCaslin ledgers with "the unending nature of" the literary struggle "to revise and transform" the ugly facts of those ledgers. Thus she may end her interpretation by recalling Faulkner's valorization of struggle, seeing the "contending narratives" as achieving a "modest victory" by resistance, asserting virtues we now identify closely with the ideology of modernism.[6]

While acknowledging the importance of Donaldson's approach in taking us beyond the obsession with the unity and coherence of *Go Down, Moses* in terms of Ike, "The Bear," and the related themes of the hunting stories, I want to propose a more radical "disunity" in this collection that focuses on Faulkner's ultimate inability to grant his African-American characters the independent voices he knows they must have in a truly "New" South. In this regard, Faulkner's text (and not just *Go Down, Moses*, but the Faulknerian text in general terms) must confront the fundamental limitation of the *family* as simulacrum for community, the public sphere, and the social relations of those who share the work of culture. It is the hypocrisy of the white Southern family that Faulkner criticizes so vigorously, exposing the violence and lies such families employ to maintain the illusion of racial "purity." Among the many consequences of the violence of slavery against African Americans, damage to the African-American family as a basis for community is one treated at length in Faulkner's fiction. Even in the face of his own literary critique of the violence done by slavery to Southern families, Faulkner insists upon reconstructing the family, offering another "ideal" that often finds its new genealogical basis in the relation of the literary author and reader.

In theoretical terms, the short story sequence may be an especially appropriate literary genre in which to explore problems with the family as social microcosm. Like other modern novelists, Faulkner understands how closely aligned the novel is with the form of the middle-class family. The novelist might revise drastically the meaning of the fictional family, as Faulkner does in *The Sound and the Fury* and Joyce does in *Ulysses,* but some such unit remains fundamental to the social-value system. In a similar manner, the polyvocal novels that Joyce and Faulkner made famous as the "signature" texts of high modernism generally depended on some orchestration of different narrative voices by way of an author-function as remote and yet definite as the Deists' conception of God. Bakhtin's "dialogic imagination" has had much appeal among scholars of the modern novel in part because it accounts for these polyvocal, polysemous, and often polyglottal dimensions in terms of the novel's "coherence," even its defining features.[7]

The short story sequence antedates the rise of the middle class and thus the dominance of the novel form, and it draws on prebourgeois forms like the historical chronicle and the fable that are not inherently tied to the family as the nucleus of community. To be sure, modern writers have often used the short story sequence as a means of representing the related destinies of several families. In this regard, *Go Down, Moses* appears merely another "novelized" collection like Joyce's *Dubliners,* in which the families represented share the cultural geography of a common Yoknapatawpha or Dublin. Yet when the definitions of families are as differently understood by the culture as the African-American and white families in Faulkner's South, families undeniably related both by the exploitation of African Americans and by the shared labor of social construction, then it may well be that the short story sequence permits the imaginative exploration of different social identities not exclusively tied to middle-class family structure.

I want to investigate the degree to which Faulkner's *Go Down, Moses* undermines the customary move of Faulkner's great novels to criticize the sins of the Old Southern, aristocratic, white family for the sake of constructing a New Southern, middle-class, white family that repudiates the sins of slavery and emulates the complex historical consciousness offered by the novelist. Insofar as Ike McCaslin's story in "The Old People," "The Bear" and "Delta Autumn" works out the logic of Faulkner's previous novels, our attention to his education is likely to reproduce the values of the modern, but still middle-class, novel. There is, however, another narrative in *Go Down, Moses,* and it is one that must be read in conflict with the sentimental "myth" of Ike McCaslin's *imitatio*

Christi. In the four other stories in *Go Down, Moses,* Faulkner attempts to give real voices, lives, and thus characters to African Americans, in ways that go far beyond his previous works.[8] Yet even as he tries to overcome the melodrama he recognizes in the nostalgia for "nobility" and "sacrifice" of an older Southern aristocracy represented by Ike in its passing, he also reaches what I consider a fatal limitation in his representations of these "other" voices – those African-American persons he knows must speak and write for themselves in order for any true redemption of the sins of slavery and racism to begin. In *Go Down, Moses,* Faulkner realizes the impasse of his own fictional project, even as he struggles impossibly to transcend imaginatively his own white Southern heritage.

Go Down, Moses is a sustained elegy for the disappearance of the Old South and the failure of the New South to overcome the moral ruin of a system built on slavery. But there is another kind of mourning organizing *Go Down, Moses* that works differently from the sentimentality shaped out of the tattered elegance of the de Spains, Beauchamps, and Edmondses. From the opening story, "Was," to the concluding, title story, "Go Down, Moses," Faulkner's collection is unified and coherent in its sustained mourning less for what has been lost than for what has been killed. From the murder of a man (Tomey's Turl), who could be traded in a card game in "Was," to the return from Chicago of Butch Beauchamp's corpse, all decked out in the good will of Gavin Stevens's collection from the shamed townsfolk of Jefferson in "Go Down, Moses," the legacy of racial violence is consistent from the antebellum to postbellum South, both as a fact of African-American experience and as what white Southern culture represses. "Is you gonter put hit in de paper? I wants hit all in de paper. All of hit," Molly demands of Mr. Wilmoth, the city editor, while they are waiting at the station for Butch Beauchamp's body to arrive from Chicago.[9]

It is just such publication of what Molly expects to be published in the paper, but never will be, that Faulkner insists redeems his own work from hopeless elegy, desperate nostalgia. What Molly really wants to be published in the Jefferson newspaper is hardly the headline: "Butch Beauchamp Executed for Murder of a Chicago Policeman," but that other headline that only literature could publish: "Roth Edmonds Sold My Benjamin. . . . Sold Him to Pharaoh," which is not just Molly's refrain but is intended to be that of the entire African-American community, as it tries to explain how "emancipation" has come to mean only another insidious sort of economic and psychological bondage for its children (362–3).

"Go Down, Moses" ends in a curiously ambivalent way that underscores the conflict between the two narratives I find wrestling for dominance in *Go Down, Moses:* Ike McCaslin's myth and the stories of the African Americans struggling to set themselves free. Molly's desire to publish "in de paper" what has happened to Butch Beauchamp is communicated to the reader in a final conversation between the two white men, Gavin Stevens and the newspaper editor, Wilmoth. Leaning out of his motor car, Wilmoth asks Stevens, "Do you know what she asked me this morning?" and Stevens knows enough to say, "Probably not" (364). But even as both of them sense they cannot know the inner experience of the African-American's oppression, each concludes Faulkner's narrative (the story and the collection) by trying to do so. Although both of them have "protected" her from the truth that Butch was executed for murdering a policeman, Wilmoth suspects that "if she had known what we know even, I believe she would have" still wanted it "all in de paper" (365). Gavin Stevens reads the grandmother's intentions more predictably, with all the benign paternalism of the white liberal: "She just wanted him home, but she wanted him to come home right. She wanted that casket and those flowers and the hearse and she wanted to ride through town behind it in a car" (365). As Millgate concludes, "nowhere in the whole of Faulkner's work is there a more persuasive dramatization of the gulf dividing the white man's mind from the Negro's than the scene in which Stevens, confronted by Molly's grief, flees from the house in a kind of terror" (212).

There is yet another reading that Faulkner leaves unwritten in the gap between Molly chanting her own version of the African-American spiritual – "Roth Edmonds . . . sold my Benjamin" – and Mr. Wilmoth quoting her strange question to Gavin Stevens: "Is you gonter put hit in de paper?" In this implicit reading, what Molly wants published in the paper is just the "news" that Roth Edmonds, surviving representative of the sins of slavery, is responsible for the fates of African Americans who are as doomed by their migrations north, like Butch's flight to Chicago, as their ancestors were by their captivity in the slave-holding South. Gavin Stevens vainly imagines that "Aunt Mollie" wants only the imitation of propriety and respectability that she identifies with white culture – casket, flowers, hearse, car, published obituary. Faulkner knows better, even as he cannot quite bring Molly to say what the two white men "quote" without understanding: She wants the heritage of slavery to be "published" in "de paper."

So much for good intentions. Faulkner does publish that headline, again and again, in that curious literary repetition-compulsion that characterizes his genius and his special regionalism, but it is not enough, or perhaps it is simply too much. For like the town newspaper of this better, moral sort, Faulkner's *Go Down, Moses* offers to publicize the South's original sin for the sake of reform: a new and better community, full of knowledge of its sinful past. All the celebrated mythopoeia of "The Old People" and "The Bear" works not simply to mourn a vanished America but to lend a myth to this new, reformed community. Much as we would like to think that *Go Down, Moses* deals with the ugly facts of the Southern past, it deals as much, if not more, with the utopian future beyond slavery, that remote future Ike McCaslin can imagine only at its remotest: "Maybe in a thousand or two thousand years in America" (344).[10]

There is little need for Faulkner to repeat in *Go Down, Moses* the historical analyses of the tangled human motives that permitted chattel slavery, the systematic rape of African-American women by whites for power and profit, the entanglement of Southern agrarianism with post-bellum capitalism, and the wrecks of families for the sake of the fiction of the taboo against miscegenation. These and many more historical issues are the essence of Faulkner's earlier works, such as *The Sound and the Fury* and *Absalom, Absalom!*. What is missing from those two great novels is just what *Go Down, Moses* attempts to add: a future for the South beyond the cynical and racist judgment of that foreigner, Shreve, in *Absalom* that "the Jim Bonds will inherit the earth" or the shooting (again and again) of Charles Bon as he crosses the shadow of the gate at Sutpen's Hundred or the endlessly repeated suicide of Quentin Compson in *The Sound and the Fury*.

This is elegy with a vengeance, like the revenge Molly Beauchamp would take on all the Edmondses and McCaslins and Compsons and de Spains for selling her Benjamin to Pharaoh. Yet such vengeance, insofar as it suggests an apocalyptic revelation of what the slave-owning South has destroyed in itself, is also intended to establish a new visionary community. It is in this that Faulkner stumbles, perhaps inevitably, on the very elements in his own background that cannot be reformed, the white southernness that can never be read entirely out of his fictional histories. It is clear enough that what is wrong with the New South (even before it was called such) is simply an elaboration of the sins of the Old South. The card game that Hubert Beauchamp plays first with Uncle Buck, then with Uncle Buddy, for the twinned wagers of Sophonsiba and Tomey's Turl, for ownership of a woman and a slave, is played again and again in these stories without regard for history. It is the same game that Lucas plays with the St. Louis drummer for the "divining machine" that will find the buried treasure in the Indian Mound in "The Fire and the Hearth," and the same game that informs Lucas's crazy quest for buried treasure. Just as the churn in which he discovers the $1,000 gold piece that perversely doubles Hugh Beauchamp's "bequest" of the tin pot stuffed with IOUs in "The Bear," so does the "cheat" of this game find itself revealed in the game of dice, which the bereaved Rider exposes as he forces the white nightwatchman to open his hand to reveal the "miss-outs" with which he has cheated his workers for years in "Pantaloon in Black." Butch's game in Chicago was the numbers "that people like him make money in," Gavin Stevens tells Miss Worsham, but the ghetto game was already learned at home from the white slaveowner or the white nightwatchman at the Lumber Mill, as Ike McCaslin learns surely enough from the numbers game of the ledgers in the Commissary (357).

The numbers game was run in everyday Southern life before and after the Civil War. It is the numbers game that Nat Beauchamp runs on her father, Lucas, when she bargains for a new backporch, a stove, and that husband, George Wilkins; just as marriage becomes the equivalent of the same game to save Lucas and George from Patcham Penitentiary for their illegal stills. But the reader is supposed to know all this; the original numbers game began as white traders counted the slaves in the holds of their ships, and white masters totted their profits in the children of rape and even paid those children, as Buddy and Buck did, with the paternal "legacy" that would "take care of them for life." That frivolous, most dangerous game structures the elegy of *Go Down, Moses,* but it takes us no further than the previous novels, gives no warrant for a collection of stories other than the customary repetition-compulsion that most often bespeaks repression. It is just such repression that encourages us to read the collection according to the three stories that shape the myth of the vanishing wilderness and its moral equivalent, Ike McCaslin, last individualist on the much diminished frontier.

But that narrative of Ike's unsuccessful sacrifice only distracts us from the other unwritten story of "What Is To Be Done?" for which Faulkner has often been reproached for his answers. Renunciation is, of course, disallowed from the outset, either for the sons and daughters of slaves or for the nominally "legal" heirs of white slavers. Ike's renunciation is no more Christological than Quentin's suicide, no more redemptive than Shreve's racist surrender to the Jim Bonds inheriting the earth in his outburst at the end of *Absalom, Absalom!*. *Endurance,* as in "they endured," is no redemption either, although Faulkner tries that here and there, but with a tired hand, knowing already in *Go Down, Moses* that the lifelong endurance of the African American has permitted only the same oppression and exploitation with a vengeance. The real sacrifice is the one recorded in Faulkner's somewhat stilted dedication of the volume:

> To Mammy
> CAROLINE BARR
> Mississippi
> [1840–1940]
> Who was born in slavery and who gave to
> my family a fidelity without stint or
> calculation of recompense and to my
> childhood an immeasurable devotion and love
> [Dedication, *Go Down, Moses*]

It is Caroline Barr's century that frames the narrative, even if Faulkner can only "name" her with the slave name, "Mammy," and the white paternalism inscribed in his testament to her "nobility" for "fidelity without . . . calculation of recompense."

It is recompense that the African Americans refuse when offered by Ike, again and again in the stories telling his side of the myth; but it is recompense that African Americans deserve and begin to demand in the other stories of the collection, recompense not just for the lost wages, the lost land, the abused bodies, the broken families, but also for the voices and words stolen from them: the power to *represent themselves.* Lucas Beauchamp is as barred from the white law in "The Fire and the Hearth" as chained slaves were, despite his $3,000 in the Jefferson Bank, his magical farming, his profitable still in the woods, his wariness of the drummer's swindle even in the midst of his own treasure madness. He may defy the law, as he does when he marches before the chancellor to retrieve the paper of divorce filed by Molly, sick of his whiteman's craziness for treasure, or when he creeps into Edmonds's bedroom with his open razor to avenge his manhood (yes, it is his manhood, not Molly's honor, that he is saving as he wrestles Edmonds for the pistol, saved again by the pistol's misfire). He may defy the law, but Lucas never beats the law, because the true law sits on his head in that carefully tended beaver hat (or the worn vest or the watch-chain) given him by McCaslin fifty years before.

It is that *beaver hat* that Rider doesn't wear when he flashes his razor against the throat of the cheating nightwatchman in "Pantaloon in Black." Rider imitates Lucas when he "rented the cabin from Carothers McCaslin and built a fire on the hearth on their wedding night as the tale told how Uncle Lucas Beauchamp, Edmonds's oldest tenant, had done on his forty-five years ago and which had burned ever since," as if connecting his story with Lucas's, "Fire and the Hearth" with its successor, "Pantaloon in Black" (134). But Rider more consistently than Lucas tries to break the family bonds of obligation that continue to subordinate African Americans to their old slave masters. Rider insists upon paying for everything he uses with money that clearly represents his labor. He is a new kind of self-reliant man, who knows better than Ike (or his transcendentalist ancestors) *why* independence is so important. Lucas accepts the propriety of the law, respects its rituals and symbols; Rider refuses such legal conventions, speaking forthrightly when Maydew comes to arrest him. "'Awright, white folks. Ah done it. Jest dont lock me up' . . . advising, instructing the sheriff," Faulkner adds, as if to remind us that Rider has his own voice, even though he is being quoted here (152). It is not the "law" of Jefferson that gets Rider – he tears the prison bed from its anchors, the bars of his cell from the wall. It is a wonderful scene, tragicomic in the way it renders trivial for just a moment the power of the white folks' law, now that Rider

had done tore that iron cot clean out of the floor it was bolted to . . . and throws the cot against the wall and comes and grabs holt of that steel barred door and rips it out of the wall, bricks hinges and all, and walks out of the cell toting the door over his head like it was a gauze window-screen, hollering, "It's awright. It's awright. Ah aint trying to git away." (153)

In the end, however, if the "law" can't hold him, the Birdsongs will, as the deputy reminds us: "Of course Ketcham could have shot him right there, but like he said, if it wasn't going to be the law, then them Bird-song boys ought to have the first lick at him" (153). We are reminded here that the "white folks" still have the community of their families to crush even the most willful and furiously honorable self-reliance, like Rider's. The law won't even properly recognize Rider's family: "So we loaded him into the car, when here come the old woman – his ma or aunt or something," and it is true that the old woman cannot do anything to save him from the Birdsongs (152). What saves Rider in the moment he reveals the law to be powerless to contain him is in fact "them chain gang" African Americans who have come back to the jail, who obey Sheriff Ketcham's order, "Grab him! Throw him down!" Rider throws them off and out of the room "like they was rag dolls," reminding us, "'Ah aint trying to git out,' until at last they pulled him down – a big mass of . . . heads and arms and legs boiling around on the floor" (154). The Birdsongs are a *family*, but the group on the floor of Ketcham's jailhouse is a big mass, a metonymy for that "old woman – his ma or aunt or something." And if they save Rider for the moment, it is only for Sheriff Ketcham's bullet or the Birdsongs' lynching.

In moments such as these, Faulkner wants us to understand how crucial it is for African Americans to have a sense of community built from shared labor, just as the heritage of slavery was their shared violation, the theft of that labor. Yet in just such moments, it is the family that returns as Faulkner's model, as if he cannot quite see clearly what African Americans struggling against slavery generally understood so well: that the "family" and the "community" are synonyms in the common work of abolition.[11] Nearly half a century later, Toni Morrison in *Beloved* would rewrite this ugly scene, in which the African American is condemned to dig his own grave, build his own prison, abandon her own child, witness her brother's whipping, crush his own spirit. In the prison in Alfred, Georgia, Paul D will join the other men in the "chain up" in their collective escape from the rain and mud rising in their cells, diving down beneath the mud and walls:

> For one lost, all lost. The chain that held them would save all or none, and Hi Man was the Delivery. They talked through that chain like Sam Morse and, Great God, they all came up. Like the unshriven dead, zombies on the loose, holding the chains in their hands, they trusted the rain and the dark, yes, but mostly Hi Man and each other.[12]

Lucas Beauchamp is too dependent on white symbols in his bid for economic independence. He is still caught in the social psychology of the old and tangled genealogies. Rider is too insistent upon a complete and utter independence, not only from white culture but also from his own community, driven there no doubt by his experience of other workers' acceptance of the racial and economic hierarchies. In Morrison's rewriting, the chaingang's escape is a consequence of the coordinated labor that is as much the physical effort as the communication, in that beautiful figuration in which the "chain" becomes the telegraph cable, and "they talked through that chain like Sam Morse." This is the new speech that Morrison roots in the African-American community forged

in the resistance to slavery and consolidated by its history from Reconstruction to the civil rights movement.

"Blood relations," we know from "The Old People" and "The Bear,"
have nothing to do with family descent, inheritance, genealogical tables.
That way madness lies, again and again, not as a consequence of some
perverse biological theory of secret incest, but simply as a result of the
unnaturalness psychically and sociologically bred into the South by its
power-hungry patriarchs. "Blood relations," family bonds, are born
even more perversely of Thomas Sutpen's recognition and refrain, "Because I own this rifle," from which all else issues in the violent procreation that follows his childhood scene of instruction when he is sent to
the servants' entrance of that plantation in Tidewater, Virginia. The
"blood relations" for Faulkner ought to be symbolized in the sweat and
blood of shared labor, which ought to be the meaning of the blood that
Sam Fathers daubs on the cheeks of the young Ike McCaslin following
his first kill of deer in "The Old People." This is the "'blood hot and
strong for living, pleasuring, that has soaked back into'" the earth of
which Cass McCaslin tells Ike at the end of "The Old People" (179). To
be sure, this is part of the customary white rationalization of the sins
brought on by slavery: "'And even suffering and grieving is better than
nothing,'" although Faulkner is careful to remind the reader: "'There
is only one thing worse than not being alive, and that's shame'" (179).
Above all, Cass naturalizes this economy of community, in which "'the
earth dont want to just keep things, hoard them; it wants to use them
again'" (179). "Using" the grief and suffering of the African American
"again" may be what Faulkner at times appears to be doing with the
"sin" of the South and all the melodrama of the General Compsons and
Major de Spains. But there is also a sense in which Faulkner wants to
think *beyond* the "natural family," damaged by the violence of slavery, to
some community beyond the biological family.

The distinctions among the "blood" shared by way of common violence (the blood that stains the hands of the children of white slaveowners), the "blood" earned in the common cause of the hunt, and the
coordinated labor of building a community are finally very hard to
make, since each version participates in the basic economy of the South,
old and new, and desperate as he is to do so, Faulkner cannot quite
identify the moral boundaries. Given the evasiveness of the law on just
these issues – its tendency to slip from the defense of property to the
justification of violence, both displacing the human concerns at stake –
how could Faulkner do much more than merely worry about the new

circulation of "blood" through the political, legal, economic, and familial "bodies"?

Presumably, Faulkner's utopian alternative is the "treasure" that Lucas hunts with the damnfool "divining machine," which falls on him in the form of a gold coin when the Indian Burial Mound collapses on him, and which Rider furiously uncovers as he buries Mannie in the opening paragraph of "Pantaloon in Black," building anew the Indian Burial Mound disturbed first by Lucas, then by the sheriffs hunting for his still in "The Fire and the Hearth." Once again, it is Rider who "speaks" in ways that Lucas cannot, with an eloquence of action independent of the "white folks":

> Flinging the dirt with that effortless fury so that the mound seemed to be rising of its own volition, not built up from above but thrusting visibly upward out of the earth itself, until at last the grave, save for its rawness, resembled any other marked off without order about the barren plot by shards of pottery and broken bottles and old brick and other objects insignificant to sight but actually of a profound meaning and fatal to touch, which no white man could have read. (131–2)

Except for Faulkner and the reader, who are meant to "read" the "profound meaning" of these shards of history as equivalents to the Southern history Faulkner is uncovering for a similar purpose of ritual mourning, only to build up again the Indian Mound for those willing to read unlike the "white man." It is little wonder that Rider concludes this little act of grave-digging art with his characteristic dignity and self-reliance: "Then he straightened up and with one hand flung the shovel quivering in the mound like a javelin and turned and began to walk away." This is just the moment in which the old woman the white folks don't recognize is identified for us by the narrative, by Rider's actions and by her own: "An old woman came out of the meagre clump of his kin and friends and a few people who had known him and his dead wife both since they were born, and grasped his forearm. She was his aunt. She had raised him. He could not remember his parents at all" (132).

All this and more is quite splendid, both stylistically and intellectually: the measure of Faulkner's genius. The sanctity of human labor is invoked at every turn as the redemption of mourning, hard work and discipline being the values that might transform a society based so foully on the theft of another person's treasure: his or her own productivity. The racist clerks, the red-neck sheriffs, the submissive Southern tenant farmers (white and African-American) are simply dismissed to the mar-

gins of the landscape in *Go Down, Moses;* only those who recognize implicitly their responsibilities to the community are given any space, the
fictional equivalent of a body. Faulkner vivifies them, whether they are
proud and sure, like Lucas and Sam Fathers, or determinedly confused,
like Boon Hogganbeck and George Wilkins, or transcendentally above
any law other than the community established by such labor, like Molly
and Rider.

Their labor is not some throwback to a fantastic georgic, not some
celebration of agrarian delights "before" slavery, the lumber mill, the
city, the automobile. It is always a labor of symbolic relations, not to be
confused with symbolic labor, but the real labor of establishing relations
among men and women according to their shared needs. Those needs
encompass the customary wants of hunger, thirst, shelter, and reproduction, but are embraced more widely by the primal need of human exchange, of that intercourse through which the members of a community
take responsibility for what they have made. Thus the horrid comedy of
the entangled hunt for Tomey's Turl and for Miss Sibby's mate in "Was"
is redeemed in part by Lucas and George and Carothers hunting for
the runaway wife, Molly, fleeing her treasure-mad husband. The per-
versity of that opening comedy is rendered apparently charming by
Lucas's ritual renunciation of the "divining machine" that he sets, all
polished and clean, on Roth Edmonds's dining-room table, amid the
landlord's lonely meal.

All of this is intended, I think, to redeem the mythic vision of Ike in
"The Bear," not so much in the form of the primeval, which Faulkner
reminds us has its dangers for man, else there would be no need for
community in the first place, but more enduringly as the symbolic
speech that is meant to communicate the tangled family fortunes of the
McCaslins and the tenant Beauchamps in "The Fire and the Hearth."
In many ways, this story would be the centerpiece of the collection, the
hinge of the door that Faulkner hopes to open to a future, "in a thousand or two thousand years in America" (344), rather than simply the
lid he lifts repeatedly to expose the dead, as in "The Bear" and its satel-
lites – "The Old People" and "Delta Autumn" – which so generalize the
Southern mythos in the American Quest as to render the genius loci a
mere forest mist. It is much harder to read "The Fire and the Hearth"
than "The Bear" outside its Mississippi context, harder yet to wrench it
into a general narrative of American initiation. The regionalism of
"The Fire and the Hearth" encompasses problems of race, gender, and
class that have wider significance for modern America, but it is nonethe-

less a narrative that begins with the very specific socioeconomic problems facing African Americans in the New South.

And yet "The Fire and the Hearth" is still part of Faulkner's problem, because it achieves that fragile redemption of the racist and sexist comedy of "Was" only by reinstating subtly a class system as insidious for our own age as the slave system of the Old South. After all, the labors of this utopian community are delegated according to the responsibilities virtually determined by the history uncovered. Carothers "Roth" Edmonds is no "innocent" Ike, no preternaturally old child refusing his patrimony. In "The Fire and the Hearth," Roth accepts the necessary rule of the landlord, and he wields it generally with the compassion that comes from his knowledge of the heritage he shares with Lucas and Molly, with Nat and George Wilkins. Threatening his sharecroppers with the law, he always saves them for his more temperate and humane laws. Leveling ultimatums, threatening them with exile, Roth always surrenders before their weaknesses, in the most decidedly paternal manner. There is no need to detail this paternalism; others have related how benignly Roth tolerates the foibles of his tenants, only to expose his secret motivation: the purification of his own history through his hard-won right to rule. Alternatively, he appears at times intent on proving his authority by virtue of his hard work, even when that work involves little more than occasional attention to the accounts, tolerance of his tenants' whims, and selective knowledge of the larger historical scheme.

Of course, he is Molly's child, but only as a consequence of being orphaned at birth by his mother and rejected by his father, Zack. Of course, he knows the history of miscegenation in the ledgers, which is why he is so often interrupted writing at his own accounts. His right to rule is never clearer than in those moments of compassionate and pained recognition of his own ancestry in the nobility of his African-American tenants, as when Lucas crosses the Square to buy Molly that nickel's worth of candy, the same candy Roth ritually brings her each month to remind himself and her of his debt:

> He stood beside the car and watched Lucas cross the Square, toward the stores, erect beneath the old, fine, well-cared-for hat, walking with that unswerving and dignified deliberation which every now and then, and with something sharp at the heart, Edmonds recognised as having come from his own ancestry too as the hat had come. (125)

That damned, absurd beaver hat, with its presidential pretense, that reminder of every man's need for authority, leaves Lucas still comic, and allows Roth Edmonds and perhaps the reader to forget just what both are forced to recognize fleetingly: that the ancestry Roth shares with Lucas derives its real nobility from the African Americans' refusal to submit to the brutalizations of the white slaveowner and then the white landowner (or just the plain white owner). The vision that Roth Edmonds has so fleetingly just a few paragraphs before the end of "The Fire and the Hearth" occurs in a sustained way at the beginning of this last chapter (chapter 3). It interrupts yet another "solitary supper" that he "couldn't eat." It is a perfectly imaginary moment, close to the Faulknerian sublime, in which Roth:

> could see Lucas standing there in the room before him . . . the face which was not at all a replica even in caricature of his grandfather McCaslin's but which had heired and now reproduced with absolute and shocking fidelity the old ancestor's entire generation and thought . . . and he thought with amazement and something very like horror: He's more like old Carothers than all the rest of us put together, including old Carothers. He is both heir and prototype simultaneously of all the geography and climate and biology which sired old Carothers and all the rest of us and our kind, myriad, countless, faceless, even nameless now except himself who fathered himself, intact and complete, contemptuous, as old Carothers must have been, of all blood black white yellow or red, including his own. (114–15)

Roth's vision is the closest, I think, that any character comes in *Go Down, Moses* to imaginative identification with Faulkner, who is also amazed and very nearly horrified by the visible thought of that face, which declares that the African American is the proper ruler, has the only right to authority, is the proper redeemer of community. The antecedence is only nominally ambiguous, strategically confusing the "he" and "his" in the twinned destinies of white masters and of African Americans, but there is no radical undecidability here. It is Lucas alone who is meant to gloss those pronouns, so that we see only *him* at the end of the long historical and syntactic labyrinth that is Faulkner's encounter with his invented Minotaur. Lucas is now Theseus, and Faulkner and Edmonds are too noticeably versions of King Midas. Both Roth and Faulkner must repress the heroism of Lucas Beauchamp, encouraging us (or, at least, Faulkner) to drift from "The Fire and the Hearth" in the direction of "The Bear" and its more conventional wisdom. For the generative power of Lucas Beauchamp is transformed hastily into that of the patriarch, quite a different figure indeed, "impervious to time" as well as to different races, intent only upon the maintenance of his undeniable selfhood, his insistent self-reliance and self-generation.

In a way, Lucas's "manhood" helps Faulkner and Roth Edmonds "defend" themselves from the more terrifying vision of an African-American authority different from that of the Southern patriarch. It is easier to imagine the African-American community centered on the familiar ideal of the "white folks": the self-made man. Lucas is that alright, but only as we recognize the jaunty angle of that beaver hat. The beaver hat is not only presidential; it links Southern history with manifest destiny, with the "capital" trapped originally by those Astors, and all that links Northern capitalism with the violence of the South. Unlike Rider, whose last words are prophetic – "Hit look lack Ah just cant quit thinking. Look lack Ah just cant quit" – Lucas knows when to stop thinking, knows when to repress the powers Faulkner is finally afraid to grant him (154). Refusing Roth's offer to lend him the divining machine from time to time, Lucas commands him:

> "Get rid of it. I dont want to never see it again. Man has got three score and ten years on this earth, the Book says. He can want a heap in that time and a heap of what he can want is due to come to him, if he just starts in soon enough. I done waited too late to start." (126–7)

Wiser than Boon Hogganbeck, Lucas renounces modern machinery, but thereby joins company again with the dependent Boon, in effect commanding Roth Edmonds to take care of him and his.

Rider, too, is finally caught by a system in which the "work" of community reproduces the authority of the "white folks" or their surrogates. He never would be caught dead in any beaver hat nor fool with any divining machine, but he works in the mill, where he gambles with a foreman who cheats him with both "white-out" dice and the contract for Rider's labor. Nevertheless, Faulkner needs "Pantaloon in Black" between "The Fire and the Hearth" and the hunting stories, because he knows Lucas is too conventional, too much the "white folks'" African American, even when, perhaps especially when, Roth Edmonds acknowledges Lucas's superiority. Recalling the story of when Lucas entered Zack Edmonds's bedroom and put the pistol to his head, just the misfire saving them both, Roth grants: "And by God Lucas beat him . . . Edmonds." He goes further, thinking that even as an African American, McCaslin can be:

a better man, better than all of us. . . . Yes, Lucas beat him, else Lucas wouldn't be here. If father had beat Lucas, he couldn't have let Lucas stay here even to forgive him. It will only be Lucas who could have stayed because Lucas is impervious to anybody, even to forgiving them, even to have to harm them. (112)

For all that Faulkner grants Lucas in this moment, he nonetheless makes him available for the "white folks" imaginary, where he himself can begin to be "mythified," not entirely unlike that bear. What is needed is what Faulkner cannot give: African-American identity that can govern its own historical representation and thereby earn some "recompense" for its "devotion and love" and work.[13]

In his interview with Gwynn and Blotner, Faulkner said of progress: "But if in the end [change] makes more education for more people, and more food for more people, more of the good things of life – I mean by that to give man leisure to use what's up here instead of just leisure to ride around in automobiles, then . . . it was worth destroying the wilderness."[14] The divining machine and Boon's shotgun are in themselves just versions of those "automobiles" – just for people "to ride around in," but they are also metaphors for the machinery of writing and publishing, for the "divining machine" that Faulkner uses to find the often terrible treasure in the Indian Mound. Roth offers to lend that machine to Lucas from time to time, but Faulkner makes sure that we know how much Lucas fears such writing (although he is careful to let us know that Lucas can read and write) and would rather leave it to Roth and Faulkner. Perhaps Molly knows better, for she wants the editor to put "it" in the paper. Not the bare facts of Butch's pathetic end in a Joliet prison, but the African-American mourning that is also her right to rule: "Done sold my Benjamin. . . . Sold him in Egypt." Gavin Stevens may think that "It doesn't matter to her now," but Faulkner knows better and does publish her dirge. If it captures the sufferings of African Americans before and after slavery, then it does so only at the discretion of the Carotherses and Faulkners. The real divining machine remains stored in their attic.

Of course, I am arguing that Faulkner created a fictional conflict in *Go Down, Moses* that demonized his own literary authority, indicting it as part of the history of white masters from cruel slaveowners to paternalistic landowners. If Faulkner forgets himself in "The Old People," "The Bear," and "Delta Autumn," purposively creating an alter ego in Ike McCaslin, then he criticizes himself in "Was," "The Fire and the

Hearth," "Pantaloon in Black," and "Go Down, Moses" as a double of
Roth Edmonds or Gavin Stevens or even Mr. Wilmoth. Beyond this it
would be unreasonable to expect any writer to go, even one as brilliantly
divided between a corrupt past and a utopian future as Faulkner.

Still, captives of the white imaginary as constructed by Faulkner and
enacted by Roth Edmonds or Ike McCaslin, African Americans in *Go
Down, Moses* nevertheless begin to speak and act in ways that exceed the
customary melodrama of Faulkner's grand narrative in the novels. To
be sure, they "speak" primarily in quotations, even their Southern dia-
lects imitated (and thus mimicked) by paternalistic landowners or racist
sheriffs. Lucas is still not *really* the "father" of us all, and Rider never
really escapes the law. But these symbolic actions remind us with our
own horror of recognition how rarely African Americans speak or act
in Faulkner's other narratives; how silent and impervious and enduring
they are.

So it is not the "racial theme" that is explored in *Go Down, Moses* as
much as it is the African-American voice that begins to challenge the
sentimental romance of the Old White South. Faulkner does not control
or command these conflicts; they begin to crack his own voice. This
would be the case whether the parts were distinguished as stories with
separate titles or arranged as numbered chapters, as Random House
proposed for a reissue of *Go Down, Moses*.[15] We can always read a "story
sequence" as if it were a novel, as I have argued so many professional
readers of Faulkner have done by emphasizing the hunting stories and
the myth of Ike's *Bildung*. But one motivation for choosing a short story
sequence may well be the author's sense that its inevitable formal disparities – the seams and sutures of the different parts – may challenge
assumed unities and tacit coherences. In the age of the novel's dominance, the short story sequence may well help question the presumed
naturalness of the self-reliant hero, *his* narrative of "education," and the
representative function of that process in the work of socialization.

It may well be that none of these qualities actually inheres in the short
story sequence as an entity because, since Kant, aesthetic "qualities" do
not belong to the "art work" in an unproblematic way but rather belong
decisively to our modes of perceiving the art work. Understood in this
way, what I have interpreted in Faulkner's *Go Down, Moses* might be considered a way of reading literary narratives differently from "novels."
Although in the popular imagination, Toni Morrison will continue to
be hailed as a "novelist," she strikes me as a storyteller who understands
the need for communal and collective tellings that will transcend the

limitations and bourgeois ideology of the novel. Like *Go Down, Moses,* *Beloved* is not a "novel," but a collection of stories, less separated than those in Faulkner's sequence, to be sure, but nonetheless stories that cannot be read apart from their disparities. The difference between *Beloved* and *Go Down, Moses,* however, is that the stories of *Beloved* belong to Sethe, Paul D, Sixo, Denver, Stamp Paid, the Cherokee, and that runaway servant, Miss Amy Denver of Boston, and other victims who are redeemed in part and in passing by their abilities to tell the stories of their oppression and thereby imagine alternatives to it:

> Sethe was looking at one mile of dark water, which would have to be split with one oar in a useless boat against a current dedicated to the Mississippi hundreds of miles away. It looked like home to her, and the baby (not dead in the least) must have thought so too. As soon as Sethe got close to the river her own water broke loose to join it. The break, followed by the redundant announcement of labor, arched her back. (*Beloved*, 83)

Craig Werner has argued that the African-American literary tradition substituted "call and response" for the "repetition and revenge" that characterizes Faulkner's narratives.[16] Between my epigraph and this closing quotation from Morrison, I am trying to invoke my own version of "call and response" to transfigure Faulkner, as I think Morrison herself has done so eloquently and consciously throughout her writings.[17] I also want to suggest that "call and response" as both a rhetorical mode fundamental to African-American culture and integral to the polyvocal short story sequence may help us understand why this form has played such an important part in African-American literary history, not only as it has offered an alternative to the novel but also as it has expressed what DuBois termed "twoness," "this double-consciousness, this sense of always looking at one's self through the eyes of others."[18]

To say it another way, Morrison put it in the paper, all of it, just as Molly wanted it, maybe even better.

NOTES

1. Michael Millgate, *The Achievement of William Faulkner* (New York: Random House, 1966), 201.
2. See Millgate, 201–2: "His answers to these needs were Isaac (Ike) McCaslin and the numerous other members, black and white, of the McCaslin family; and the fact that there exists a McCaslin family tree, drawn by Faulkner himself, is perhaps suggestive

of the degree to which the family was created for a specific purpose, not evolved slowly from Faulkner's original conception of the world of Yoknapatawpha County."

3. Most critics agree that Ike's Christological associations are ironized by Faulkner in ways that question both Ike's and Christianity's redemptive powers. As Lewis Simpson puts it in "Isaac McCaslin and Temple Drake: The Fall of New World Man," in *Nine Essays in Modern Literature*, ed. Donald E. Stanford (Baton Rouge: Louisiana State University Press, 1965): "I would agree with Robert D. Jacobs" that Ike "in his total aspect" is "'a pathetic figure, slightly comic, certainly ineffectual.' He represents only the nostalgic possibility of modern man rising in the guise of New World man to a new and better moral condition."

4. Millgate goes to some trouble to account for what he considers the apparently "disturbing" "shifts in period, setting, theme, and personnel which occur" in *Go Down, Moses* (Millgate, 203). These disparities are almost always explained by Millgate's appeal to the "novelistic" features of the collection. These qualities are, in turn, established by the nearly exclusive consideration in Millgate's interpretation with Ike's education in the hunting stories.

5. Susan Donaldson, "Contending Narratives: *Go Down, Moses* and the Short Story Cycle," in *Faulkner and the Short Story: Faulkner and Yoknapatawpha 1990*, ed. Evans Harrington and Ann J. Abadie (Jackson: University Press of Mississippi, 1992), 129.

6. Donaldson, 147.

7. See M. M. Bakhtin, *The Dialogic Imagination: Four Essays*, ed. Michael Holquist, trans. Caryl Emerson and Michael Holquist (Austin: University of Texas Press, 1981), 327, for example: "If the novelist . . . is deaf to organic double-voicedness and to the internal dialogization of living and evolving discourse, then he will never comprehend, or even realize, the actual possibilities and tasks of the novel." Although she does not cite Bakhtin, Donaldson's approach to *Go Down, Moses* is clearly influenced by Bakhtin's conception of the dialogic and heteroglossic features of the novel.

8. The four stories I wish to treat as critical readings of the three hunting stories are: "Was," "The Fire and the Hearth," "Pantaloon in Black," and "Go Down, Moses."

9. Faulkner, *Go Down, Moses* (New York: Random House, 1970), 364.

10. Ike is thinking specifically of miscegenation, although he must be thinking of the social *acceptance* of miscegenation, since the African-American woman who prompts this reflection is the mother of a son fathered by Roth Edmonds. She is the granddaughter of James Beauchamp ("Tennie's Jim").

11. See my "Between Politics and Poetics: Frederick Douglass and Postmodernity," in *Reconstructing American Literary and Historical Studies*, ed. Günter Lenz, Hartmut Keil, and Sabine Bröck-Sallah (New York: St. Martin's Press, 1990), 206–7.

12. Toni Morrison, *Beloved* (New York: A. A. Knopf, 1987), 110.

13. See Craig Hansen Werner, "'Tell Old Pharaoh': The African-American Response to Faulkner," *The Southern Review* 19 (October 1983), 711–36; and Eric Sundquist, "Faulkner, Race, and the Forms of American Fiction," in *Faulkner and Race: Faulkner and Yoknapatawpha*, ed. Doreen Fowler and Ann J. Abadie (Jackson: University Press of Mississippi, 1987), 1–34.

14. Joseph L. Blotner and Frederick L. Gwynn, eds., *Faulkner in the University: Class Confer-*

ences at the University of Virginia, 1957–1958 (Charlottesville: University of Virginia Press, 1959), 117–18.

15. See Millgate, 203: "Dated January 10, 1949 [an unsigned letter from Random House] mentions plans for re-issuing *Go Down, Moses,* recalls that Faulkner had emphasized in conversation the fact that he considered it a novel rather than a group of stories, and asks whether, when the book was re-issued, he would like to insert chapter numbers in addition to the titles of the individual sections. That Faulkner did not accept this suggestion may have been due in part to his familiar reluctance to return to work which was behind him . . . ; but he may also have recognised the force of the observation, also made in the letter, that it might be a mistake to eliminate the section titles altogether because of the way in which they had become accepted as part of the text."

16. Werner, 725.

17. In *Playing in the Dark: Whiteness and the Literary Imagination* (New York: Random House, 1992), Toni Morrison privileges Faulkner as a white male writer who does not succumb to the prevailing demonization of "blackness" in canonical American literature. Morrison sets Faulkner's partial recognition of how the African heritage of America enriches our language, culture, and being against the image of the "white curtain" into which Poe's Pym disappears.: "Does Faulkner's *Absalom! Absalom!,* after its protracted search for the telling African blood, leave us with . . . an image of snow and the eradication of race? Not quite. Shreve sees himself as the inheritor of the blood of African kings; the snow apparently is the wasteland of unmeaning, unfathomable whiteness" (58).

18. W. E. B. DuBois, *The Souls of Black Folk* (New York: Viking Penguin, 1989), 5. In the quest for literary forms appropriate to African-American culture and experiences, African-American writers have often written short story sequences and other works that should be considered to broaden and enrich any generic definition. Works like DuBois's *The Souls of Black Folk,* Zora Neale Hurston's *Of Mules and Men,* Langston Hughes's *Simple Speaks His Mind* and *The Ways of White Folks* are just some examples of African-American writings that resist consciously the canonical literary forms (especially the novel) and embrace more collective and folkloric modes of narration in the interests of building community.

Meditations on Nonpresence:
Re-visioning the Short Story
in Eudora Welty's The Wide Net

SUSAN V. DONALDSON

A good many critics have noted that Eudora Welty's elusive short stories strain toward moments of revelation and discovery, what Welty herself calls the "still moment" in the short story of that title in *The Wide Net*.[1] It is fiction, Michael Kreyling argues, marked by the desire "for some resolution in but also beyond the plot," a resolution that illuminates the underlying unity of the dreamlike fragments characterizing so many of her stories.[2] Nowhere, in fact, would this affinity for the "still moment" seem to be more pronounced than in *The Wide Net*, Welty's second collection of stories, which might more accurately be called a sequence of stories, nearly all of which resonate with brief flashes of illumination and awakening.[3]

In this respect, Welty, who quite often eludes the attempts of her critics to categorize and classify her, appears to ally herself with modernist writers who revere the Word for its capacity to transform and re-create a disorderly and fragmentary world.[4] Historians of the short story, in fact, have argued that such a "still moment," or epiphany, if you will, serves as the central distinguishing mark of the modernist short story in particular. Yet it is in *The Wide Net*, published in 1943, that Welty submits the notion of illumination to the sort of radical questioning that contemporary feminist critics and deconstructionists would readily recognize and appreciate, and does so in a form – the short story sequence – that both offers and withdraws the possibility of unity. Like so many contemporary critics, she is wary of the reverence accorded to what Jacques Derrida would call "this privilege of the present-now" – its insistence on mastering and appropriating anything exterior, strange, or foreign to establish unity.[5] Accordingly, in story after story in *The Wide Net* she exposes the drive for power underlying the desire for illumination and the illusory nature of immediacy and revelation created by those brief moments of epiphany. Arranged in a loose sequence, the stories together ponder the tensions between the desire for illumination, mastery, and unity and the muted acknowledgment that such moments of revelation may be as elusive and as tantalizing as the ordering principle linking the tales themselves.

The result is that Welty in this short story sequence, lying somewhere in the frontier between novel and short story collection, rewrites a "master fiction" – the modernist short story rendered whole and complete by the moment of illumination. If she, like so many writers of her generation, is attracted by that moment, she is nonetheless as ready to undermine its authority and integrity as Derrida is to probe and resist "the metaphysics of presence." Like Derrida, then, she uses the tools she has inherited from modernist fiction "to destroy the old machinery to which they belong and of which they themselves are pieces."[6] In doing so, she suggests in *The Wide Net*'s sequence of stories the possibility of a new aesthetic of short fiction, one for which questioning, openness, and transformation constitute both subject and technique.

Welty's subversive strategies, explored in a short story sequence published fifty years ago, seem all the more remarkable if one considers the general acceptance of the term and notion of epiphany by scholars and short-fiction practitioners alike. Literary histories of American and English short fiction turn readily to James Joyce's famous definition in *Stephen Hero*, where epiphany is described as "a sudden spiritual manifestation, whether in the vulgarity of speech or of gesture or in a memorable phase of the mind itself." It was the duty of the literatus, Joyce's narrator goes on to say, "to record these epiphanies with extreme care, seeing that they themselves are the most delicate and evanescent of moments."[7] Also regularly cited is Sherwood Anderson's declaration "that the true history of life is but a history of moments." Only in these "rare moments," Anderson adds, do "we live."[8]

Such moments, historians of the short story argue, helped dislodge plot from its place of importance in short fiction and in turn provided a central organizing and unifying principle for short stories produced after World War I.[9] Rather consistently, critics ranging from Austin Wright to Philip Stevick and William Peden observe that the moment of illumination or revelation came "to seem especially characteristic," in Stevick's words, "of fiction in the twenties and consistently after." It was a notion that appeared "particularly modern," Stevick suggests, because even though pre-World War I stories included "epiphanies" serving as the climax of action, ". . . American stories after the war, often presenting themselves as 'plotless,' sketches in the style of Chekhov or Joyce, offer an epiphany as the only justification for the story, its single, low-keyed climax." [10] Yet that "low-keyed climax" still retained the power to illuminate, to unify, and ultimately to transform the materials of the story; and the result, Austin Wright suggests, is "an attempt to sharpen and concentrate the focus of the short story – to find the unifying principle most appropriate to the absolute magnitude of the short story, most capable of yielding that sort of concentrated richness that we are accustomed to find in great art." [11]

As John Gerlach points out in his fine book, *Toward the End: Closure and Structure in the American Short Story*, this emphasis on unity, on a single effect, may have a good deal to do with our anticipating the ending of each story. [12] In this respect, of course, the modernist story has much in common with the short story as defined by Edgar Allan Poe, who stressed the importance of the single effect in his famous 1842 review of Nathaniel Hawthorne's *Twice-Told Tales*. Indeed, literary historians like Walter Allen tend to see singleness of effect as the one central trait that nineteenth-century tales share with twentieth-century stories. As he notes at the beginning of his study of the short story in English, "We feel that we are reading something that is the fruit of a single moment of time, of a single incident, a single perception." [13]

This is a characterization of the short story that Eudora Welty in her own musings about the genre would seem on the surface of things to confirm. "I'm quite certain that by nature I'm a short story writer rather than a novelist," she once remarked in an interview. "I think in terms of a single impulse, and I think of a short story as being a lyric impulse, something that begins and carries through and ends all in the same curve." Yet she warns – and we would do well to heed her cautionary note – "it may not be that in the working out." [14] For Welty is a writer who is acutely aware that fiction, as she notes in *The Eye of the Story*, is "empowered by a sharp and prophetic awareness of what is ephemeral." [15] Its difficult task, she once observed, is "to hold transient life in *words*," much as the photograph seeks "to capture transience," an apt analogy for a writer who once worked as a Works Progress Administration photographer. [16] For like a photograph, the short story by Welty's lights observes an uneasy and ever-shifting truce between the "single impulse" toward which the short story strains and the evanescence of the materials to be "captured," and the drama that often engages Welty's attention is the frequent breakdown of that truce.

If Welty herself, then, yearns for the "single effect," the moment of transformation and unity, she nonetheless dismantles that moment as soon as she evokes it to suggest just how elusive such singleness can be.

Reading *The Wide Net* from a feminist perspective, one discovers, in fact, a certain resistance to the modernist notion that the world can indeed be re-created and reunified by the transformative powers of the Word. For as Susan Stanford Friedman has observed, it was more often than not the aim of male modernist writers in the early twentieth century to "create what the culture could no longer produce: symbol and meaning in the dimension of art, brought into being through the agency of language, the Word or Logos of the twentieth century."[17] If reality itself seemed disorderly and fragmented, it could be re-created, modernist texts suggested, through "mastery of the Word," uniting words and their meaning, parts and their whole, the story and its epiphany.[18] Order could be imposed through the moment of illumination provided by the Word, binding within its boundaries meaning and purpose.

Such acts of mastery, of course, involve strategies of interpretation bound up with the imposition of power. For that moment of unity and control is achieved only, as Derrida would remind us, by refusing to acknowledge contradictions, anomalies, and opposing possibilities. A center is made possible, after all, by the definition of its margin, an inside by the designation of the outside, a contained self by expulsion of its other. And if that center is to be maintained, everything on the margin must be subject to conquest and mastery, to "appropriation," Margaret Homans writes, that "works to make the world one."[19] Strangeness and disorder must be transformed into familiarity and unity, otherness swallowed up by the self.

This yearning to appropriate and to master – so earnest and yet so dangerous – is the motivating force of narrative in *The Wide Net*, a sequence of stories largely set along the legendary Natchez Trace from its earliest fabled days to the twentieth century. Story after story shimmers with wonder and mystery, attracting and eluding the effort to control and unify. As Robert Penn Warren pointed out in his seminal essay on Welty more than forty years ago, her men and women wander in "a season of dreams," a phrase he borrows from "First Love," the opening story.[20] They inhabit a world, like early nineteenth-century Natchez in "First Love," seemingly on the verge of "transfiguration," where everything shines with portentous significance.[21] Like Josie, the little girl in "The Winds," they are all dazzled by the strangeness they yearn to reach out and grasp: "There, outside, was all that was wild and beloved and estranged, and all that would beckon and leave her, and all that was beautiful. She wanted to follow, and by some metamorphosis she would take them in – all – every one" (221). It is mystery, ultimately, that Welty's figures seek to make their own, and like Josie again, they all reach their hands "out after something that flew ahead" (214). And because they do "put out their hands," their worlds suddenly glitter with possibilities ripe for resolution. As one character observes in "The Wide Net," the second story of the sequence, "Everything just before it changes looks to be made of gold" (176).

Hence William Wallace Jamieson's world in "The Wide Net" – significantly, the title story of the collection – resonates with undefined omens and signs when William Wallace goes looking for his missing wife Hazel with a host of friends. In the anticipation of the search, everything suggests a resolution just out of reach – the suddenly mysterious Pearl River, where Hazel has supposedly drowned herself; the net for dragging the river that unexpectedly looks "golden, strung and tied with golden threads" (176); the huge dark snake, called the King of the Snakes, undulating through the water; and the tiny town, "somehow" looking "like new," through which the search party marches (184). Everything suggests the possibility of a moment when all is revealed, understood, and made whole, a moment that William Wallace and his fellow seekers can claim as their own.

A similar sense of anticipation propels Josie in "The Winds" and the fat man who tells the story of "The Purple Hat." They both live in a world in which the possibility of revelation charges their surroundings. Josie, for instance, is drawn to her mysterious neighbor Cornella, who always seems to Josie a little older, richer, and wiser than she can ever be; and although Josie is convinced that she can never "catch up" (214), she nonetheless lives in greedy anticipation of "the season of gifts," when all secrets will be revealed (219). She, like the time of the story itself, set in the equinox, is poised on the edge of change, and the flashes of lightning illuminating the house and the faces of her family during the night storm at summer's end suggest something of the bright instant of revelation she seeks. "When would the day come," she wonders, "when the wind would fall and they would sit in silence on the fountain rim, their play done, and the boys would crack the nuts under the heels?" (219).

This sort of yearning characterizes the storyteller in "The Purple Hat" as well, for he is just as determined to await that final moment of revelation as is Josie. To patrons of a sleepy bar he recites a story that elicits and frustrates his best efforts to find that moment of illumination. The story he tells is one of a woman in a purple hat and her young male companion who meet night after night in a New Orleans gambling house, but somehow the narrator – to his irritation and fascination – can never quite find the ending of his tale. From his position on the catwalk above the gambling tables, he has twice seen the woman murdered by her young man, but somehow she always manages to reappear – and with the inevitable purple hat. She must be a ghost, he concludes, but this resolution, of course, is impossible to confirm. When a listener finally asks if she *is* a ghost, the storyteller says simply, "I'll let you know tomorrow" (227). In a sense, then, "The Purple Hat" becomes a story about stories and the anticipation they create.

But if this particular storyteller is frustrated in his best efforts to "find" an ending and a moment when all is revealed, other storytellers in *The Wide Net* discover that such moments of closure and revelation may be illusory. This is the lesson learned by Solomon, the dignified old black farmer married to "Livvie" in the story of that title, for the beginning of the tale is colored by Solomon's unspoken assumption that Livvie's story has come to a resolution in her marriage. It is, after all, the culminating moment in Solomon's own story "that all his life he had built, little scrap by little scrap" (237). Indeed, to ensure that his wife's ending is the same as his, the old man forbids Livvie to venture out to consort with anyone else, and for years the young woman lives uneventfully in a world "where the days would go by and surprise anyone that they were over" (229–30). But Livvie's own story abruptly emerges with the arrival of the glamorous Cash McCord, to whom Livvie is instantly drawn, and on his deathbed Solomon is forced to acknowledge that Livvie's tale begins where his ends. As he tells both Livvie and Cash,

> "When Livvie married, her husband were already somebody. He had paid great cost for his land. He spread sycamore leaves over the ground from wagon to door, day he brought her home, so her foot would not have to touch ground. He carried her through his door. Then he growed old and could not lift her, and she were still young." (239)

Recognizing that the symmetry of his own tale cannot enclose Livvie's emerging story, Solomon hands to his young wife his silver watch, a gesture reminding us that endings can also be beginnings and that "revelations" can signify defeat as well as mastery, doubleness as well as unity.

Just as unsettling in its resistance to imposed unity is "Asphodel," set as so many of the stories in *The Wide Net* are along the dark and mysterious Natchez Trace.[22] For nothing could initially appear more orderly or settled than the story told by three rather self-complacent women about

two aristocrats, Miss Sabina and Mr. Don McInnis, caught in an un-
happy marriage. To the three narrators, "Miss Sabina's was an old story,
closed and complete. In some intoxication of the time and the place,
they recited it and came to the end" (206). Like the domineering Miss
Sabina, who vengefully breaks into the post office and destroys all those
secretive letters that seem "beyond her domain" (205), the narrators
leave no room for loose ends or contradictions in their smug little commentary. It dispatches both Miss Sabina and her rakish husband to
quick and orderly deaths and Asphodel, McInnis's lordly manor, to deserted ruins.

As soon as they finish their narrative, though, Mr. Don McInnis himself abruptly emerges from the ruins of Asphodel like an unbottled
genie, and he is quickly followed by hordes of dancing goats. The magical suddenness of this appearance suggests nothing so much as the configuration of revelation or epiphany, but strangely enough, it is an "illumination" that appears outside the narrative sequence established by
those three orderly narrators. Mr. Don McInnis and his goats explode
on the scene after the actual telling of the story, and as such, his presence
serves to disrupt rather than to unify or order the act of storytelling.
From the perspective of those three orderly narrators, he is a disturbing
reminder of all the otherness and strangeness repressed or discarded
to make a tidy narrative; but he also represents all that is beckoning,
mysterious, and forbidden, "a great, profane man" (202) whose wildness
the storytellers "all worshipped" (203).

Like so many mysterious and beckoning figures in *The Wide Net*,
though, Mr. Don McInnis remains just out of reach, an elusive bearer
of illumination lying outside the boundaries of the story and the task of
storytelling. He and those other emblems of mystery and wonder inhabiting the dark country of the Natchez Trace suggest that such a moment
of illumination may be a fata morgana, an illusion both extending and
withdrawing the possibility of resolution and unity. From beginning to
end, in fact, the stories of *The Wide Net* question the possibility of achieving any sort of resolution. If they shimmer with anticipation and
yearning, it is because that anticipation ultimately remains unfulfilled.

Nowhere, in fact, is unfulfilled longing made more painfully plain
than in the sequence's opening story, "First Love," which traces the infatuation of a twelve-year-old deaf boy named Joel Mayes with the legendary Aaron Burr, on trial for treason in 1807 Natchez. For it is in his
obsession with Burr that the mute and solitary boy discovers a world

beckoning with the possibility of some undisclosed meaning. Having lost his parents in an Indian raid on the Natchez Trace, Joel lives an untouched and uneventful existence until Aaron Burr happens on the scene and ushers in "a season of dreams" (153). Simply the sight of Burr opening his cloak in a dark room discloses for the boy "a panorama in his own head, about which he knew first of all that he would never be able to speak – it was nothing but brightness, as full as the brightness on which he had opened his eyes" (157). Touched by that brightness, the boy finds every waking moment heightened with portent and anticipation. Even though he is locked in his silent world, he feels "driven to know everything" (163). At times he takes his thoughts down to the river and tries to "read" the currents as he searches everywhere for some final meaning, waiting for the moment "when there might have been a revelation" (165).

It is a moment, though, that never comes. Joel's longing to grasp the mysteries suggested by Burr's distant and glamorous presence is defeated by the boy's deafness and muteness, by his inability to harness language:

> What Joel saw before him he had a terrible wish to speak out loud, but he would have had to find names for the places of the heart and the times for its shadowy and tragic events, and they seemed of great magnitude, heroic and terrible and splendid, like the legends of the mind. But for lack of a way to tell how much was known, the boundaries would lie between him and others, all the others, until he died. (165)

Estranged by silence, Joel is ultimately forced to confront his own limitations and losses – his inability to speak, Burr's eventual departure, and the deaths of the boy's parents in that terrible scene on the Natchez Trace. The final moment of revelation for which he yearns will always elude him.

Joel shares this plight with all the earnest seekers in *The Wide Net*'s Natchez Trace country, for that elusive final moment by Welty's lights always invites and always evades the eager grasp of the creative imagination. Indeed, "First Love," like the rest of the stories in *The Wide Net*, focuses as much on the pressing needs of the imagination and the making of fiction to meet those needs as it does on a strange and magical time along the myth-laded Natchez Trace. As a good many commentators have observed, Welty's fiction is to a great extent about fiction itself – its constant making and remaking – and *The Wide Net* is no exception.[23] Like William Faulkner before her, she constantly shifts the reader's attention, in the words of Danièle Pitavy-Souques, to "the *telling* of the story as opposed to the story proper."[24]

Above all, what absorbs Welty's energies in *The Wide Net* in particular is the ever-shifting and never-consummated courtship of the imagination. The writer is especially drawn to the yearning to "capture" and to master all those mysteries – that otherness – tantalizingly out of reach. In one of the essays collected in *The Eye of the Story*, Welty herself observes:

> For some outside signal has startled or moved the story-writing mind to complicity: some certain irresistible, alarming (pleasurable or disturbing), magnetic person, place or thing. The outside world and the writer's response to it, the story's quotients, are always different, always differing in the combining; they are always – or so it seems to me – most intimately connected with each other.[25]

Hence the short story sequence is particularly suited to Welty's elusive and quicksilver fiction. As J. Gerald Kennedy has recently observed, the short story sequence, largely a product of the twentieth century, is essentially "a hybrid occupying an odd, indeterminate place within the field of narrative, resembling the novel in its panoramic view of life (often focused upon a particular time and place yet composed of autonomous stories evoking different characters and problems)."[26] Such a hybrid in turn, as Forrest Ingram has ably argued, creates a peculiar tension between the individual stories themselves and the overarching framework of the sequence itself. Indeed, Ingram adds, the short story sequence requires reading strategies that can be described only as revisionary because the movement from one story to the next requires constant modification and adjustment. For Ingram, in fact, the short story sequence is defined largely by the reading strategies it elicits. "A story cycle," he suggests, "is a set of stories so linked to one another that the reader's experience of each one is modified by his experience of the others."[27]

More to the point, perhaps, Robert M. Luscher has commented on "the form's kinship with disunity" and has suggested that the writer of the short story sequence "courts disunity in order to achieve 'victory' over it by setting up a new set of narrative ground rules that rely heavily on active pattern-making faculties." It is that final "victory," strikingly enough, that so many students of the short story sequence emphasize in their descriptions and definitions of the form. As Luscher observes, "Our desire for unity and coherence is so great that we often use our literary competencies to integrate apparently unrelated material, so long as we are sustained by the faith that the work possesses formal wholeness."[28]

But what if that wholeness itself turns out to be chimerical, the creation of a mere yearning for unity? It might well be, as Kennedy has suggested, that discontinuity and fragmentation are as crucially important for understanding the short story sequence as are underlying patterns of "formal wholeness."[29] Certainly Welty's own short story sequence suggests that the stories in *The Wide Net* are bound as much by the different faces of failure confronting her seekers after unity as by the bonds of anticipation and yearning. Each tale, after all, traces the delicate maneuvers of the imagination's courtship in a particular time and place, but both the maneuvers and the courtship itself change as we move from story to story. From the opening pages of "First Love" to the haunting conclusion of "At The Landing," the quest for mastery and illumination steadily shifts, alters, and reforms. No dance between the "story-writing mind" and "the outside world" is the same. If any constant remains in this sequence of stories, it is the mysterious and ever-winding Natchez Trace itself, the dark road that never seems to end or begin.

Significantly, it is on the Natchez Trace of old that "A Still Moment," the most important piece in the sequence, is set. For the dark depths of the wilderness road prompt the question that haunts *The Wide Net* as a whole: "Is the radiance I see closed into an interval between two darks, or can it not illuminate them both and discover at last, though it cannot be spoken, what was thought hidden and lost?" (195). Here far more than anywhere else in *The Wide Net*, Welty directly addresses the longing of the imagination – the story-writing mind – to master everything exterior, mysterious, and elusive in a single moment, and here above all she exposes that "still moment" as an illusion born in the midst of loss and yearning. Not for nothing, then, has Welty herself observed in an interview that "A Still Moment" might be "the story that did what I wanted to more than any other story."[30] As the third tale in the sequence, placed in what F. Garvin Davenport has called a "pivotal" position, "A Still Moment" articulates most clearly and painfully the imagination's obsession with unity and the illusory nature of illumination and unity.[31]

That passion for unity links the three central characters of "A Still Moment," which, like "First Love," is set in the early days of the Natchez Trace; and it is on the wild Trace that those characters, drawn from historical figures, momentarily converge – a traveling evangelist named Lorenzo Dow, an infamous bandit named James Murrell, and the mysterious artist John James Audubon. Unlike Joel Mayes in the opening story, though, these figures possess formidable imaginative resources and their confrontation with the "outside signal" is considerably less one-sided.

Fired by religious passion, Lorenzo reads everything about him as "signs sent from God" (189), and his dearest wish is to resolve everything earthly and multiple into the unity of divinity. "To transmute a man into an angel," the narrator tells us, "was the hope that drove him all over the world and never let him flinch from a meeting or withhold goodbyes for long" (194). In contrast, the bandit James Murrell, who meets up with Lorenzo on the Trace, is driven by the need to slay everything exterior in order to exert his own existence. He is, in a sense, Lorenzo's exact opposite – a man yearning to destroy anything strange and wondrous, to slay each man he encounters in order to "solve his mystery of being" (192). Both abruptly stumble upon Audubon, also a driven man, an artist-naturalist who feels compelled to seek out "secret life" and to translate it into his journals and his paintings (195).

As different as these men are, though, they are momentarily drawn together in that fleeting moment when they see a white heron alight on the Trace, a bird that seems to embody for each man his own peculiar longings:

> What each of them had wanted was simply *all*. To save all souls, to destroy all men, to see and to record all life that filled this world – all, all – but now a single frail yearning seemed to go out of the three of them for a moment to stretch toward this one snowy, shy bird in the marshes. It was as if three whirlwinds had drawn together at some center, to find feeding in peace a snowy heron. (196)

Characteristically, both Lorenzo and Murrell see the heron in terms of their own obsessions, one sacred and the other profane. Lorenzo looks upon the bird "such as a man may bestow upon his own vision," and Murrell sees "only whiteness ensconced in darkness" and the brand "H.T." on the thumb intruding "into his own vision" (195). Each man claims the heron for his own and, in so doing, violates its beauty and mystery. Only Audubon, the artist who truly "appreciated" the fleeting sight, acknowledges both his desire to appropriate and master and the impossibility of fulfilling that desire (198). He abruptly shoots the lovely heron so that he can paint it, but he knows that any picture, any representation he produces, will never be as lovely or as whole as that still moment: "He knew that even the sight of the heron . . . had not been all his belonging, and that never could any vision, even any simple sight, belong to him or to any man" (198).

That still moment is precious and hauntingly beautiful, in short, precisely because it is born in an instant of death and loss, and nothing that Audubon paints can ever re-create that flash of illumination. It becomes for him – and in *The Wide Net* he is nearly alone in coming to this recognition – an emblem of the goal toward which his art and the act of representation strain and can never achieve: "As he had seen the bird most purely at its moment of death, in some fatal way, in his care looking outward, he saw his long labor most revealingly at the point where it met its limit" (198). And just as Audubon acknowledges that the act of representation can never fully capture the sight of the heron, so too does Welty herself offer us in this story what Danièle Pitavy-Souques aptly calls a "reflection on representation," one that acknowledges the miragelike nature of epiphanies and illuminations sought by the "story-writing mind." [32] In the midst of Welty's stories of eager seekers and fevered anticipation, "A Still Moment" unveils the sought-after moment of revelation as a fata morgana created by an acute awareness of loss and absence. [33] The fulfillment that such moments seem to offer originates in yearning, in the sense that something is always missing. As the narrator of the preceding story, "The Wide Net," observes, "When you go looking for what is lost, everything is a sign" (179).

In this respect, Welty's reflections on representation in *The Wide Net* bear a startling resemblance to Derrida's examination of the play of absence and presence in *Of Grammatology* and *Speech and Phenomena*. Much like Derrida, Welty probes the "privilege of the present-now," the luminous moment and truth that *appear* to make everything else secondary and less than whole, and her probing gives rise to something very like what Derrida in *Speech and Phenomena* calls a conflict "between philosophy, which is always a philosophy of presence, and a meditation on nonpresence." [34] If the stories in *The Wide Net* sympathetically portray worlds and lives trembling with the possibility of "transfiguration" straining toward moments of revelation, they remind us at the same time that such moments are illusory, creations of the signs we see when we go looking for what is lost.

Derrida, as well, in his own meditations on nonpresence, probes and questions the independence of signified from signifier, absolute truth apart from the representational systems that seek to describe it. "The sign, the image, the representation, which come to supplement the ab-

sent present," he observes in *Of Grammatology,* "are the illusions that side-
track us." They all seem to point to a missing truth or signified for which
the sign of representation serves as substitute. But the very absence of
that missing truth and the signs that appear to serve as substitutes are
the "conditions of the desired presence."[35]

Audubon, of course, acknowledges something very like this sad
"truth" in his shooting of the heron, and his realization colors our reading of other quests for illumination in *The Wide Net.* We discover, as
Pitavy-Souques once pointed out, that Welty "questions her art in the
very moment she is creating it."[36] But if so many of the tales in this
sequence expose the illusory nature of illumination and the yearning for
mastery implicit in seeking a final unity, the concluding story, "At The
Landing," hints at an alternative to the still moment.

Like "First Love," the opening tale in the sequence, this last story
explores the growing obsession of a sheltered youngster, in this case, the
infatuation of a young girl named Jenny with a wild and rakish fisherman called Billy Floyd. And like "First Love," again, this attraction to
a strange and mysterious figure touches Jenny's world with wonder.
Suddenly The Landing – the tiny, lost town where she lives, deserted
even by the river that once bordered it – no longer seems quite so con-
fining. Where the stories part company, though, is in Jenny's growing
"moral knowledge of a mystery that is in the other heart" (245). Accepting Floyd as "living and inviolate" (245), the young girl resists the
drive to master and to unify characterizing so many of those who precede her in *The Wide Net.*

Instead, Jenny increasingly renders herself open and vulnerable to
those around her – to Mag, the albino girl who romps with Floyd, to
Floyd himself, and even to the nameless, knife-wielding men she meets
along the riverbank. The price she pays for this vulnerability is fearful
indeed since she is raped first by Floyd and then by those nameless men.
But because she eschews mastery for openness, she is awarded brief moments of insight into the inner lives of those around her. Watching Mag
play with Floyd, she suddenly realizes that she "had felt whatever Mag
had felt. If this was a vision, it was the first. And it did not frighten her;
she knew it only came because she had felt what was in another heart
besides her own" (246).

These are moments, moreover, that have little to do with the unity
or final resolution toward which so many of *The Wide Net*'s seekers strain.
Through those flashes of insight she senses the world around her as
"multitudinous." For her, "nothing was single any more" (256). Even
her own sense of self expands and multiplies: "She herself was more

people than there were people in The Landing, and her love was enough to pass through the whole night, never lifting the same face" (256). Looking ahead, she sees something like the multiplicity marking the rainbow of light refracted through the prisms she touches in the beginning of the tale. Behind her is the narrowness of The Landing. Before her lie not the certainty of resolution but the possibilities of end-less change and "only a sense of journey, of something that might hap-pen" (254).

It is a story, ultimately, that ponders transformation rather than the stasis of a single moment, multiplicity rather than unity, vulnerability rather than mastery. And if "At The Landing," like so much of Welty's fiction, suggests a certain opacity or elusiveness, it is because this story – along with the rest of *The Wide Net*, for that matter – resists the "singleness of effect" achieved in still moments. As Welty has repeatedly noted, short fiction in general should be subject to constant change, constant transformation. "A short story is not the same thing when it ends as it was when it began," she observes in her own history and ex-amination of short stories. "Something happens – the writing of it. It *be-comes*." [37]

In this sense, Welty's concerns in *The Wide Net* appear to have a good deal in common with the kind of feminist aesthetic defined by critics like Jane Marcus. Such an aesthetic, Marcus declares, is grounded in transformation, not stasis or unity. Accordingly, it is an aesthetic aptly figured by Penelope, weaving her tapestry each day and destroying it each night.[38] Welty herself does much the same in *The Wide Net*; she offers us the tempting fata morgana of illumination only to expose its illusory nature. Finally, her interests lie not so much with the re-creation of the world through the Word as with the process of re-creation itself, and it is the endless variety of this process, of transformation in general, that emerges as both subject and technique in *The Wide Net*, indeed, as the tie that paradoxically binds story to story to "create" a sequence. As Welty herself gently notes in *Short Stories*, "Variety is, has been, and no doubt will remain endless in possibilities, because the power and stirring of the mind never rest. It is what this power will try that will most perti-nently define the short story." [39]

NOTES

1. Ruth Vande Kieft, for one, notes in her study of Welty: "The flashes of insight which come to the heroine of Dorothy Richardson's novels, Virginia Woolf's preoccupation with 'the moment of importance,' Joyce's 'sudden spiritual manifestations' or 'epiph-

anies' — are all closely related to the various moments of revelation which appear in Miss Welty's fiction" (Ruth M. Vande Kieft, *Eudora Welty*, TUSAS 15 [New York: Twayne, 1962], 179). Similarly, Michael Kreyling says of Welty's work: "The moment of vision is built upon the particular world each fiction summons into existence. The climactic experience of each of Welty's fictions is not only the resolution of a plot but a denouement of the form, in which the world appears in its integrity before the reader, allowing him to realize how and when the parts become whole" (Michael Kreyling, *The Achievement of Eudora Welty* [Baton Rouge: Louisiana State University Press, 1980], 175).

2. Kreyling, xvi.

3. See, for example, F. Garvin Davenport, Jr., "Renewal and Historical Consciousness in *The Wide Net*," in *Eudora Welty: Thirteen Essays*, ed. Peggy Whitman Prenshaw (New York: Pocket Books, 1984), 189–200.

4. See Chester E. Eisinger, "Traditionalism and Modernism in Eudora Welty," in Prenshaw, *Eudora Welty*, 3–25; and Danièle Pitavy-Souques, "A Blazing Butterfly: The Modernity of Eudora Welty," *Mississippi Quarterly* 39 (1986): 537–60.

5. Jacques Derrida, *Speech and Phenomena and Other Essays on Husserl's Theory of Signs*, trans. and introd. David B. Allison (Evanston, IL: Northwestern University Press, 1973), 62.

6. Quoted in Gayatri Chakravorty Spivak, Translator's Preface, in Jacques Derrida, *Of Grammatology*, trans. Spivak (Baltimore: Johns Hopkins University Press, 1976), xix.

7. James Joyce, [Epiphanies — from *Stephen Hero*], *A Portrait of the Artist as a Young Man*, ed. Chester G. Anderson, Viking Critical Ed. (New York: Viking, 1968), 288.

8. Quoted in Ellen Kimbel, "The American Short Story, 1900–1920," *The American Short Story, 1900–1945*, ed. Philip Stevick (Boston: Twayne, 1984), 63.

9. See Philip Stevick, Introduction, *The American Short Story, 1900–1945*, 15, 5; and William Peden, *The American Short Story: Continuity and Change, 1940–1975*, 2nd rev. ed. (Boston: Houghton Mifflin, 1975), 8.

10. Stevick, Introduction, 4, 5.

11. Austin McGiffert Wright, *The American Short Story in the Twenties* (Chicago: University of Chicago Press, 1961), 266–7.

12. John Gerlach, *Toward the End: Closure and Structure in the American Short Story* (University: University of Alabama Press, 1985), 160.

13. Walter Allen, *The Short Story in English* (Oxford: Oxford University Press [Clarendon Press], 1981), 7.

14. Scott Haller, "Creators on Creating: Eudora Welty," *Conversations with Eudora Welty*, ed. Peggy Whitman Prenshaw (New York: Pocket Books, 1984), 345.

15. Eudora Welty, *The Eye of the Story: Selected Essays and Reviews* (New York: Random-Vintage, 1977), 168.

16. Eudora Welty, *One Writer's Beginnings* (Cambridge: Harvard University Press, 1984), 85, 84. Stevick notes that documentary photography in the late 1800s and early 1900s had a strong impact on the development of short fiction. Both photography and modern short fiction, he argues, shared "that peculiar optical acuity that comes not so much from observing as from knowing what the camera can do" (Stevick, Introduction, 18).

17. Susan Stanford Friedman, *Psyche Reborn: The Emergence of H.D.* (Bloomington: Indiana University Press, 1981), 97–8.

18. Shari Benstock, "Beyond the Reaches of Feminist Criticism: A Letter from Paris," in *Feminist Issues in Literary Scholarship*, ed. Shari Benstock (Bloomington: Indiana University Press, 1987), 25.

19. Margaret Homans, *Women Writers and Poetic Identity: Dorothy Wordsworth, Emily Brontë, and Emily Dickinson* (Princeton, NJ: Princeton University Press, 1980), 38.

20. Robert Penn Warren, *Selected Essays* (New York: Random House, 1958), 157.

21. Eudora Welty, *The Wide Net*, in *The Collected Stories of Eudora Welty* (New York, 1943; New York: Harcourt, Brace, Jovanovich, 1980), 153. Subsequent references to this edition will be cited parenthetically within the text.

22. Peter Schmidt offers quite a persuasive reading of this story as a "slapstick" parody of Faulkner's *Absalom, Absalom!*. See his *The Heart of the Story: Eudora Welty's Short Fiction* (Jackson: University Press of Mississippi, 1991), 132–5.

23. See, for example, Schmidt, *passim;* J. A. Bryant, *Eudora Welty*, University of Minnesota Pamphlets on American Writers No. 66 (Minneapolis: University of Minnesota Press, 1968), 68–82; Kreyling, 174, 176, 177; Carol Manning, *With Ears Opening Like Morning Glories: Eudora Welty and the Love of Storytelling*, Contributions to Women's Studies No. 58 (Westport, CT: Greenwood Press, 1985), *passim;* and Pitavy-Souques, "Blazing," 554.

24. Pitavy-Souques, "Blazing," 554.

25. Eudora Welty, *The Eye of the Story*, 108–9.

26. J. Gerald Kennedy, "Toward a Poetics of the Short Story Cycle," *Journal of the Short Story in English* 11 (1988): 12.

27. Forrest L. Ingram, *Representative Short Story Cycles of the Twentieth Century: Studies in a Literary Genre* (The Hague: Mouton, 1971), 19.

28. Robert M. Luscher, "The Short Story Sequence: An Open Book," *Short Story Theory at a Crossroads*, ed. Susan Lohafer and Jo Ellyn Clarey (Baton Rouge: Louisiana State University Press, 1989), 158, 155.

29. Kennedy, 14.

30. Joanna Maclay, "A Conversation with Eudora Welty," in Prenshaw, *Conversations with Eudora Welty*, 315.

31. Davenport, 195.

32. Pitavy-Souques, "Blazing," 548.

33. Pitavy-Souques argues something along these lines in her fine essay, "A Blazing Butterfly: The Modernity of Eudora Welty," *passim.*

34. Derrida, *Speech and Phenomena*, 63.

35. Derrida, *Of Grammatology*, 154, 298.

36. Danièle Pitavy-Souques, "Technique as Myth: The Structure of *The Golden Apples*," in Prenshaw, ed., *Eudora Welty*, 150.

37. Eudora Welty, *Short Stories* (New York: Harcourt, Brace and Co., 1949), 10.

38. Jane Marcus, "Still Practice, A/Wrested Alphabet: Toward a Feminist Aesthetic," in Benstock, *Feminist Issues in Literary Scholarship*, 84.

39. Welty, *Short Stories*, 52.

Nine Stories:

J. D. Salinger's Linked Mysteries

RUTH PRIGOZY

From its publication in April 1953, through the heyday of "the Salinger industry" in the 1960s, and intermittently through the 1970s and 1980s, J. D. Salinger's *Nine Stories* has proven an unusually seductive text for critical theorizing.[1] Indeed, even those most devoted to Salinger studies, after the first burst of scholarly enthusiasm, welcomed a moratorium on further efforts to interpret Salinger's *oeuvre*, including this collection for which there apparently could be no final word. What is most striking, after thirty years of critical attention, are the contradictory, even antipodal responses to each of the collected stories. At the heart of *Nine Stories* is a mystery, perhaps epitomized by the "monstrous vacuole" that the narrator sees below the nose of the Laughing Man.[2]

Further, within each story there lie other mysteries, some trivial, some profoundly complex, but all defying easy solutions. To search for a unifying principle in *Nine Stories* is to admit that the individual stories must be bent and shaped to conform to a preconceived pattern. But these stories stubbornly resist such attempts. The clue to the cryptic nature of the collection lies in the Zen koan epigraph that subtly instructs the reader to forgo the effort to devise a too logical scheme linking the individual works that follow. Whatever linkage we may find in the stories derives as much from what is *missing* as from similarities of subject, structure, voice, symbolism, character, milieu, and other literary elements that provoke interpretation. In story sequences, as J. Gerald Kennedy has noted, "recurrent features may disclose differences as readily as similarities."[3] But Salinger's mysteries, finally, disgorge further mysteries, so that whatever unifying pattern we may have discovered (perhaps to render the experience of reading *Nine Stories* less disturbing) simply crumbles into those cigarette ashes that the author so obsessively describes.[4] And perhaps the mysteries in *Nine Stories* account for its continuing appeal as much as does its enormous readability.

The stories are thus characterized as much by discontinuity as by those deceptive surface similarities for which Salinger initially won critical and popular attention: brilliant mimicries of postadolescent speech, accurate depictions of upper-class, sophisticated New Yorkers, memorable evocations of childhood sensitivity and adolescent pain, and repellent glimpses into the "phony" world of material plenty and spiritual waste. Yet each story suggests another dimension beyond the narrative, a realm that exists beyond the silence of the Zen koan. John Wenke sees the Zen koan epigraph as a clue to the collection as a whole, discussing Salinger's interpretive openness and the vexing holes that appear in the narratives.[5] I would like to carry Wenke's argument a step further, by demonstrating how the unifying elements combine with the fragmenting mysteries that shadow each of the stories. Despite persuasive critical interpretations, such problems as the motive for Seymour's suicide, the cause of the Coach's failed love affair, or the impulse behind Teddy's pursuit of death, resound like the hollow echoes in the Marabar caves.[6]

The arrangement of the stories in the collection coincides with the sequence of their original publication as separate works. The first six, "A Perfect Day for Bananafish," "Uncle Wiggily in Connecticut," "Just Before the War with the Eskimos," "The Laughing Man," "Down at the Dinghy," and "For Esmé – with Love and Squalor," dating from January 1948 to April 1950, precede the publication of *The Catcher in the Rye*, and the seventh, "Pretty Mouth and Green My Eyes," was published in the same week in July as the novel. The last two stories, "De Daumier-Smith's Blue Period" and "Teddy," were published, respectively, in May 1952 and January 1953. Salinger would continue writing about characters who first appeared in this collection, the Glass family, in five later stories from 1955 through 1965.[7] He did not alter the publication sequence for the collection, and it is assumed that "De Daumier-Smith's Blue Period" was the first story he wrote after publication of *Catcher*. Although he published "Teddy" after he left New York for his permanent home in Cornish, New Hampshire, in January 1953, he had already made plans for the collection before his move. The immense popularity and immediate cult status among college students of *Catcher in the Rye* insured a wide audience for *Nine Stories*, but clearly readers were intrigued with the volume beyond their fascination with the novel.[8]

Salinger's title, *Nine Stories*, presents the initial interpretive challenge of the collection. Always interested in numbers (tantalizingly so in many instances), the author directs us only to the simple fact that nine stories have been grouped together.[9] We will never know why Salinger settled on such a spare title (think of F. Scott Fitzgerald's first collection, *Flappers and Philosophers*, or Hemingway's *In Our Time*, or Flannery O'Connor's *A Good Man is Hard to Find* for titles of first volumes designed to suggest their contents or to pique the reader's interest), but it is the first of the many puzzles pervading the sequence.

Less simple, but no less inscrutable than the title, the Zen koan epigraph reads: "We know the sound of two hands clapping, / But what is the sound of one hand clapping?" A koan is a problem that defies rational, intellectual solution, the answer having no logical connection to the question. The purpose of the koan for the Zen disciple, as Alan Watts explains, is to present "the central problem of life in an intensified form." For when we accept that there is no solution available through our traditional approaches to problems, we must stop trying, we must relinquish even our right to know and accept life as "free, spontaneous and unlimited." [10] The central fact of Zen, according to D. T. Suzuki, lies "in the attainment of 'Satori' or the opening of a spiritual eye." [11] Thus, at the outset, Salinger presents the reader with a paradox that throughout the book, grows insistent: The stories delineate the path from spiritual death to spiritual enlightenment (satori) at the same time that they exemplify the uselessness of imposing *any* pattern, through logical analysis, on this random collection of fiction. This contradiction persists throughout *Nine Stories*, producing a multiplicity of critical responses.

Although Salinger collected the stories in their order of publication, there are connections, illuminating juxtapositions, and incremental repetitions that suggest a more subtle arrangement. The individual titles, with the exception of the last story, derive from the texts they introduce; they are puzzling, intriguing, and literarily unique, in sharp contrast to the title of the volume. These individual titles refer to stories within the stories, or italicize a crucial moment, or allude to place or time. The title "Teddy," for example, proves as cryptic as the story it precedes and the psyche of the child it names.

The arrangement of the stories also illustrates what Kennedy describes as "purposive juxtaposition," where "the differential relationship between two conjoined narratives . . . generates supplemental meanings distinguishable from those of the collection as a whole." [12] Thus, the first two stories are linked by references to place and by similarity of character. The last two are connected by repetitive language, and "For Esmé" and "Pretty Mouth" may be said to find their complementarity in the contrast between redemption and betrayal in love. The third story, "Just

Before the War," offers yet a third alternative to the two that precede it in its offering the possibility of emotional openness and compassion. And the questions raised by "The Laughing Man" are linked with those raised by "Down at the Dinghy" and "For Esmé." The following analysis of structuring devices of *Nine Stories,* culminating in questions that elude conclusive interpretation, should clarify the method by which Salinger constructs the linked mysteries of these collected stories.

As in many similar collections, the subjects, characters, and milieus of *Nine Stories* bear many superficial similarities. Four reflect the war, although only in "For Esmé" is there a wartime setting; in the other three, it serves as a catalyst for emotional distress. All but one of the stories ("Pretty Mouth") focus on either very young children or adolescents. All of them concern the plight of sensitive outsiders alienated by a society unable or unwilling to recognize and value their special qualities, their unique sensibilities. Three stories dramatize the relationship between a very young child and a parent or surrogate parent, providing suggestive glimpses into the psychic needs of both. The overriding subject of each story, directly or indirectly, is death – physical, emotional, or spiritual. Clearly, some kind of death is the price Salinger's characters pay for their inability to adapt to a hostile world.

Many of the characters, then, resemble Flannery O'Connor's misfits, although Salinger's are distinguished by minor physical imperfections or quirky behavior, rather than by the cartoonish grotesqueries of O'Connor. Indeed, Salinger's characters are appealing, rather than repellent, in their uniqueness. Seymour is pale, with narrow shoulders and a sickly look, but he is also witty and perceptive; Ramona is pitiable in her homeliness and her need for love and companionship; Eloise is cold and unfeeling, yet even she, reduced to tears by missed opportunities, evokes reluctant sympathy. And a few of the characters find the strength to transcend the banalities and petty cruelties of their world (Boo Boo Tannenbaum, Esmé, Ginnie) to find meaning in a connection to another sensitive hungry soul. Beyond their special gifts, personalities, and desires, Salinger's protagonists prove exceptionally intelligent and occasionally brilliant (Seymour, Teddy, Sergeant X). The major characters show keen insight into others; what they fail to understand they nevertheless question, repeatedly and persistently ("De Daumier-Smith's," "Teddy"). Those questions become as important for the reader as for the characters and enhance the sense of mystery and openness that marks these stories. Further, Salinger's important characters are unusually verbal. Like O'Connor he captures accurately the speech patterns and cadences of his own world, here an educated, often intellectual environment, enlivened by the vitality of adolescent verbal excesses. Like Holden Caulfield in *Catcher*, the characters in *Nine Stories* assume a life of their own, (partly, too, because of the stories' lack of closure). It seems entirely fitting that Salinger was moved to continue the saga of a few of them, the Glass family, in his later stories.

The local references in *Nine Stories* clearly indicate a recognizable fictive world: New York City predominates, from the opening line in "A Perfect Day," set in Miami, but alluding to "ninety-seven New York advertising men" (3). In "The Laughing Man," the precise geography of the city forms a substructure for the double-layered story as does the east side of Manhattan for the dramatized encounters of "Just Before the War." Whether the characters are on vacation, on a ship, in a foreign country, or in a Connecticut suburb of the city, the sensibility of Salinger's world is firmly established by its references to the sophistication, polish, manners, and locales associated with the New York City of Salinger's educated upper middle class. Similarly, the temporal signs point to the post–World War II era, not only in stories that refer directly to the war, but also in those stories that capture the characteristics of the period: the sense of estrangement from the past, the reflection of Reisman's "lonely crowd," the adolescent angst seemingly rekindled after the traumatic events of the previous decade, and above all the precise evocation of the era that pondered men in gray flannel suits, their pursuit of thoroughly materialistic ends belying the expressed efforts of the war years to find meaning in a democratic society. Salinger is not a sociological writer, but as surely as in those books that sought to explain what had happened to us materially and spiritually after our wartime victory, *Nine Stories* heralds that period in our nation's history that has been since characterized as frighteningly conformist, spiritually bankrupt, and intellectually adrift – the American 1950s.

In its structural patterns, self-reflexive buried stories, and insistent symbolic motifs, as well as in Salinger's use of narrative voice and evocative language, *Nine Stories* illustrates the cryptic, elusive design of its linked mysteries. Each story, moreover, presents its own challenges.

"A Perfect Day for Bananafish" is divided into two sections, with a brief concluding epilogue. The major divisions dramatize the conversations of two sets of characters, first Muriel Glass and her mother, then Seymour Glass and the child, Sybil (a brief interlude with Sybil and her mother heightens the atmosphere created by the first section and prepares the reader for the Sybil/Seymour meeting). The last section, Seymour's return to his hotel room and stunning suicide, conveys a finality that the preceding events belie. Within the story, as elsewhere in the volume, lies a riddle, or more precisely, a series of riddles, all of which suggest diverse interpretations of Seymour's action: Muriel's mother's concerns about the trees, "that business with the window," remarks to "granny," "what [Seymour] did with all those lovely pictures from Bermuda," the bananafish story, Seymour's playful yet cryptic remarks about his nonexistent tattoo, his injunction to the woman on the elevator not to stare at his toes, his teasing colloquy with Sybil about the color of her bathing suit and other matters of interest to her, and even his faintly ominous control of the child's raft. Further, Salinger's insistent use of numbers, six in particular, invites speculation while defying resolution. After the opening paragraphs that define Muriel with withering precision, the ensuing dialogues reveal the essence of his characters, yet provide possibilities for alternative readings.[13]

Salinger uses a variety of narrative voices and perspectives in the collection. In "A Perfect Day" the narrator (whom some believe is Buddy Glass) is casually omniscient, relinquishing dispassionate objectivity to remark with cruel accuracy, "She was a girl who for a ringing phone dropped exactly nothing. She looked as if her phone has been ringing continually ever since she had reached puberty" (3). The narrative voice is familiarly conversational, blending effortlessly into two lengthy dialogues. The opening story establishes immediately the tone of the volume, an inviting informality, a series of conversations between people we might ourselves know, a perfect mimicry of the cadences and inflections of contemporary speech of his upper-middle-class city dwellers. Indeed, Salinger's language is perhaps the most consistent, recognizable element in *Nine Stories;* it is a unique voice, whether conveyed by authorial omniscience, first-person narrative, or the precise transcription of telephone conversations. That language is a clue to the deeper structure of the fictions is most evident in the first story. After the Muriel/mother dialogue, the second section begins with Sybil's prescient words to *her* mother, "See more glass." With the child's mystifying request, repeated again to her mother and then to Seymour Glass, the reader is covertly instructed to look for the hidden import of the Seymour/Sybil repartee. At the same time, Salinger alerts his readers to the multiplicity of meanings contained in even the simplest assertion.

The next story, "Uncle Wiggily in Connecticut," is structured by time and place, its three sections occurring on a winter afternoon in a wealthy Connecticut suburb. That time is a major issue becomes apparent as Eloise and Mary Jane, her guest, recall their past college days, leading Eloise to recount the tragic event in her past that has corroded her present life as suburban wife and mother. As the two women drink from afternoon into evening, Eloise shows increasing nastiness, exacerbated by the tearful revelation of her lover's violent and senseless death. She expresses her unhappiness in cruel and insensitive remarks to and about her child, in a brusque drunken response to her husband's telephone call (rejecting her maid's request that her husband be allowed to spend the night because of the bad weather), and in a furious heaving of one of her daughter's galoshes over the bannister. Eloise's violent and tragic story repeats itself in her daughter Ramona's imaginative life: The child kills her imaginary companion, Jimmy Jimmereeno. The emotional ending of the story – Eloise's refusal to countenance Jimmy's replacement, Mickey Mickeranno, her tears that wet the lenses of Ramona's glasses, her kiss for the sleeping child, and her final pitiful plea for reassurance that she once was a "nice girl" – fail to alleviate the pervasive bitterness of the narrative tone.

As in "A Perfect Day," the narration is informally omniscient, with an opening description that cruelly mimics the banality of Mary Jane's speech and the bitchiness of Eloise's response to Mary Jane's verbal mistake ("Merrick"): "*Merritt* Parkway, baby" (19). Eloise is immediately identified as someone who does not allow anyone to escape her criticism. Linguistic patterns are again both subtle and obvious: Eloise never addresses Ramona by name, and she is consistently critical and irritable as when she takes the child's galoshes off: "Gimme your foot . . . Sit down, first, please. . . . Not *there* – *here*. God!" (34). Eloise censures and corrects; she is unresponsive, indeed blind, to her daughter's obvious loneliness and misery. Ramona's eyes, her glasses and myopia, are linked by contrast, with Sybil's unknowingly wise misuse of Seymour's name. Salinger's language again points the reader toward meanings that lie beneath a very detailed and visually explicit surface. Here again the key moments revolve around an adult and a child and stand in sharp contrast to the affectionate exchange between Seymour and Sybil. The juxtaposition of these two stories reinforces the importance Salinger attaches to relations between adults and children.

Although "Just Before the War with the Eskimos" is not linked in the way that its two predecessors are, this two-part story with a brief epilogue nevertheless offers an oblique commentary on what we have already perceived as insensitive responses to extreme suffering. Through the central consciousness of an adolescent girl, Ginnie, Salinger offers a perspective that suggests the redemptive power of compassion. The buried stories here concern her friend Selena's "goofy" brother Franklin's unrequited love for Ginnie's sister, Joan, and his ambiguous relationship with his unpleasant, certainly homosexual friend, Eric. The two major scenes, which take place within an hour in Selena's apartment, reveal Franklin's hopeless ineptitude at life along with his desperate need for human connection (expressed by the sandwich he insists on giving Ginnie) and Eric's intangible yet faintly sinister hold over his friend. The previous stories lead one to expect despair, but this story, primarily through the narrative voice that reflects Ginnie's sustained central consciousness, offers the distinctly redemptive possibility of an unexpected and generous response to a thoroughly unattractive, deeply suffering soul. As different as this story is, it connects to the other two by Salinger's suggestive use of glasses and eyestrain, implying that vision, no matter how difficult to attain, is at the heart of his characters' often ineffectual struggles. Ginnie unconsciously shares Holden Caulfield's dream of rescuing children before they fall off a cliff; Franklin may have already fallen, but like the dead Easter chick it took her three days to dispose of some years earlier, she must save his sandwich and, in so doing, perhaps save him.

Salinger's language is particularly notable in this story; Franklin and Ginnie's loose slang dominates the first section, and Eric's revelatory italicized declamations define his orientation in the second. Throughout, the reader is treated to the observations, clearly through Ginnie's eyes, of a myriad of repellent, often physical details, as when she watches Eric "scratch his ankle till it was red. When he began to scratch off a minor skin eruption on his calf with his fingernail, she stopped watching" (46). Salinger defines his misfits consistently by unattractive physical qualities or behavior, like Ramona's repeated scratching herself and picking her nose.

The fourth story, "The Laughing Man," departs from the first three in narrative structure and voice. Told in four parts from a first-person perspective with minimum dialogue by an adult looking back to a defining moment in his youth, the story also marks the most self-reflexive fiction in the collection. On several occasions, the narrator comments on the difficulty of telling a story, of remembering important details that should not be omitted from his account of the Chief and the boys, the Chief's continuing narrative about the Laughing Man, and the buried

mystery of the Chief's broken love affair with Mary Hudson. The narrator thus assures the reader that "the Chief's physical appearance in
1928 is still clear in my mind" (57), and later, referring to the story of the
Laughing Man, he asserts, "I'm not saying I will, but I could go on for
hours escorting the reader – forcibly, if necessary – back and forth across
the Paris–Chinese border" (61). Self-consciously he directs the reader
to the story's lingering mystery: "I had no idea what was going on between the Chief and Mary Hudson (and still haven't, in any but a fairly
low, intuitive sense)" (70). Actually, in this complex work, three levels of
narrative develop: the flashback, the Chief's relationship to Mary Hudson, and the story of the Laughing Man, which the Chief tells in install-
ments for the delectation of the boys who spend their afternoons with
him either in sports or in visits to Manhattan museums. As in "Just Before the War," the narrative voice is intimate, deeply involved in the
events witnessed. And in both, a revelation of adult pain intrudes pierc-
ingly upon adolescent confusion. Here, however, the narrator tells the
story of the Chief and the Laughing Man to make sense of something
deeply felt, but only dimly comprehended, years ago. In so doing, he
recaptures the actual voice of his younger self. The story of the Laughing Man is closely allied to events in the lives of the Chief *and* of the
narrator whose identification with the older man is certainly that of a
son. And both stories, the Laughing Man's and (by implication) the narrator's, suggest thwarted expectations of the family.

The location of "The Laughing Man" within the collection directs
the reader to the problem of storytelling. So unlike the preceding three
stories, it illuminates Salinger's exploration of the craft of fiction, and at
the same time offers the reader a less tense, less hyperbolic glimpse of
suffering and struggle. The language is informal and indirect, with conversations recalled rather than enacted: "I asked her if she had a
cold. . . . I told her I didn't have anybody in left field. I told her I had a
guy playing center field *and* left field. There was no response at all to
this information" (70). The end of the Chief's romance and the violence
with which he concludes the story of the Laughing Man profoundly
affect the narrator. The elusiveness of both tales, with their shattering
finales, adds a tragic dimension to this affectionate memoir of an unforgettable episode of his youth.

The next story, "Down at the Dinghy," returns to the earlier Salinger
strategy of presenting a situation through revealing dialogue. Told in
four parts by a narrative voice resembling that of the first two stories, it
also centers on relationships between adults and children. Yet unlike "A

Perfect Day" and "Uncle Wiggily," the key relationship – between mother Boo Boo Tannenbaum and her son Lionel – reveals the affection and understanding of a parent for her child; but structurally it resembles "Just Before the War" in its relatively strong narrative closure and its unity of time and place. The informally omniscient narrator, as in "A Perfect Day," offers with relaxed objectivity a peculiar and certainly puzzling description of Boo Boo: "Her joke of a name aside, her general unprettiness aside, she was – in terms of permanently memorable, immoderately perceptive, small-area faces – a stunning and final girl" (77). Salinger's descriptive prose often contains similarly cryptic lines that reinforce the puzzles developed by the narrative pattern. Like the Chief, Boo Boo creates a fantasy world for Lionel wherein she is the admiral calling her crew with a bugle, but the buried story in this narrative is the mystery of Lionel's repeated running away from his loving, sensitive family.

Dialogue in "Down in the Dinghy" occurs first between two employees of the Tannenbaums, revealing the author's skill at mimicking lower-class inflections and idioms to illustrate their ignorance and bigotry, and then between the mother and son, which recalls Seymour's light bantering with Sybil. Here too, language assumes importance beyond its referential meaning. Just as Sybil's three words suggest deeper implications, the too-obvious meaning of Mrs. Snell's description of Daddy as "a big – sloppy – kike" (86), which Lionel hears as "kite," suggests an adult world that this intuitive child cannot forever flee.

The subsequent story, "For Esmé – With Love and Squalor," connects with "The Laughing Man" as a self-conscious act of storytelling, the first-person narrator addressing the reader with disarming directness. We learn that indeed, it has been written for a specific reader – Esmé – and that this story fulfills a promise the narrator made to her six years earlier during the war. Placed between "Down at the Dinghy" and "Pretty Mouth," "For Esmé" assumes even greater importance than its length and complex narrative structure imply. The stories that precede and follow are dramatic, unified in time and space, whereas "For Esmé" employs two narrative voices (we learn why the voice shifts to omniscient narrator in part four) and recalls several actions occurring over a two-month period six years earlier, first in England, then in an army barracks, and later in New York City where the narrator now lives and writes his story for Esmé.

The opening of this six-part story introduces the narrator, whose voice is assured, ironic, humorous, and confiding. His description of his

wife as "a breathtakingly levelheaded girl" and his almost imperceptible
dislike of his mother-in-law, "Mother Grencher," stir an interest in the
story he tells "to edify, to instruct." Several elusive stories inform the
narrative he writes for Esmé, some of which concern the narrator's psychological and emotional breakdown, Esmé's recovery from her own
war wounds, and the importance of the Goebbels book to the low-level
Nazi official who has left it in the house where Sergeant X (the narrator), who arrested her, finds it. Finally, there is the unspoken question of
the life the narrator has been living for the past six years. All of these
stories are buried within the central narrative that links his meeting with
Esmé, his breakdown and inability to function after leaving the hospital,
his alienation from his insensitive fellow soldiers, and finally, the gift
from Esmé that restores his hope – and his ability to sleep. An additional
layer of narrative complexity lies in the language, especially in Esmé's
letter, which reflects with total accuracy the inimitable pattern of her
conversation with the soldier in the tea shop on a memorable afternoon
in Devon. Like other conversations between adults and children in the
collection, theirs is marked by the child's utterly serious demeanor, yet
it is unique in the expression of her obvious insecurity, her appealing
misuse, yet clear love, of language (including French), and above all her
brave efforts, through words, to surmount the stunning loss of her father
in the war. The bond of loneliness between Esmé and the narrator is
apparent, and both treat little Charles like indulgently appreciative parents. Before Esmé returns to ask him to write an "extremely squalid
moving story" (103), the narrator has confessed that her leaving the tea-
room "was a strangely emotional moment for [him]" (102). Esmé's parting words, "I hope you return from the war with all your faculties intact" (103), direct the narrator, as well as the reader, to the story he will
now write for Esmé.

   At this point, the narrator self-consciously begins his narrative,
changing the voice from first person to omniscient third person, but
with the admonition to the reader not to trust the narrator's objectivity.
He says, "I'm still around, but from here on in, for reasons I'm not at
liberty to disclose, I've disguised myself so cunningly that even the clev-
erest reader will fail to recognize me" (103). He is, of course, immediately recognizable as Sergeant X, and his "reasons" become one of the
buried stories in the narrative. The narrator also tells his reader that *this*
is the way to tell a story.

   We learn that the young man has not come through the war with his
faculties intact (104) and that he is now pondering the Nazi's inscription

in the Goebbels book, "Dear God, life is hell" (105). His response, to inscribe Dostoevski's "'What is hell?' I maintain that it is the suffering of being unable to love," is undecipherable, so complete is the loss of his "faculties." The penultimate section, his conversation with Corporal Z, or Clay, who quotes his girlfriend's letter offering psychological banalities about X's condition, serves as a sharp contrast to the final section when he receives Esmé's gift of her father's watch and reads her formal, precise, infinitely moving letter. Salinger maintains the omniscient narrative voice until the last line of the story, when the narrator speaks directly to Esmé, and by indirection to us, revealing in Esmé's own words the effect of that moment on the broken soldier. "For Esmé" is a long, ambitious, complex narrative that picks up several structural and narrative patterns from previous stories but adds a degree of closure that, although not resolving the questions that remain, makes the experience of reading it enormously pleasurable. Paradoxically, "A Perfect Day," which raises more questions than it can handle, and "For Esmé," which at least on the surface satisfies a reader's desire for a well-made story, remain Salinger's most popular short stories.

The next story in sequence, "Pretty Mouth and Green My Eyes," seems startlingly unlike those that precede and follow it. Both "For Esmé" and "De Daumier-Smith's" are long, multilayered, primarily first-person narratives that draw the reader into the emotional and spiritual conflicts of their protagonists. "Pretty Mouth" is a richly dramatized account of an adulterous affair between a young married woman and her older lover, who are interrupted by two phone calls from the woman's husband who is trying to locate her. The narrative voice is once again cruelly objective, noting apparently trivial details of the couple's activities while the two men are talking. After the opening passage describing the couple with unsparing precision, the ringing telephone and the gray-haired man's efforts to answer it, the rest of the story portrays, through dialogue, a sordid affair, morally squalid lives, and a brief, touching memory – the buried story – of the husband's idealized love. The pathetic second telephone call that reveals the latter's efforts to salvage his pride leave the older man stunned and perhaps angry at himself, and the reader is repelled by this brutal revelation of spiritual waste. "De Daumier-Smith's Blue Period" is constructed in ten parts, with a first-person narrator whose reliability, unlike that of the narrators of "The Laughing Man" and "For Esmé," is distinctly questionable. His narrative voice is insecure and anxious, his imagination given to fevered excursions into fantasy, his responses to situations unexpected or exaggerated. He experiences the pain of facing adulthood after the painful loss of his mother, and he feels sexually jealous of his stepfather.

That he dedicates his story to his late stepfather indicates, however, that he has at last accepted his past, left behind his "blue period," and feels compelled to acknowledge his debt to the man with whom he was engaged in an inner, secret conflict years earlier when they discovered that they were "both in love with the same deceased woman" (133). Indeed, the story, like "For Esmé," is a repayment of a debt by someone who owes his current ability to function (in whatever way he does – his present condition is not made clear in either story) to the person to whom the story is dedicated. Unlike the former soldier in the earlier story, this narrator feels the urgency of correcting a wrong in telling his story: "It's a matter of life and death" to describe his late stepfather as "adventurous, extremely magnetic, and generous," having "spent so many years laboriously begrudging him those picaresque adjectives."

The opening paragraph thus suggests that the story will describe the young man's coming to maturity, which indeed it does, but in such a veiled, convoluted way that critics have differed widely in their interpretations.[14] Once again, Salinger's narrator returns to the past, to 1928 when he was eight years old, to recount the traumatic events that left him a lonely, alienated, sensitive young man. (In this story, as in "Laughing Man" and "Down at the Dinghy," the missing or elusive father figure is the source of disturbance to a child.) In the third part of the story, set in New York's Ritz Hotel in 1939, he finds the advertisement in a Quebec newspaper that will ultimately lead to his psychological and even spiritual regeneration.

The narrative momentum of the story gradually increases after the initial leisurely descriptions of Quebec and the Yoshotos, the couple who run Les Amis Des Vieux Maîtres for whom he is employed as instructor. Parts six, seven, and eight are sharply defined by the narrator's anxiety over a three-day period after he has written to one of his students, Sister Irma, whose work has strangely touched him. The intricately structured narrative reaches its climax in the narrator's real or imagined moment of spiritual illumination – the transmutation of apparatuses (irrigation basins, a truss) in an orthopedic-appliance shop into a "shimmering field of exquisite, twice-blessed, enamel flowers" (164). The unique experiences of De Daumier-Smith raise, however, a number of unanswered questions: what does he see? what prompts his conclusion that "everybody is a nun"? and (perhaps, the most important question contained in his letter to Sister Irma) why does he remember as "pregnant with meaning" the moment at seventeen, when ecstatically happy after a long illness and walking toward Avenue Victor Hugo in Paris, he "bumped into a chap without any nose" (160)? These mysteries connect with experiences within the story, yet questions linger even after the most convincing interpretation. Perhaps because of the openness of the body of the story, Salinger imparts a rare degree of closure as the narrator describes his return to normalcy signified by his reuniting with his stepfather, the apparent resolution of his sexual conflicts (he spends the summer "investigating that most interesting of all summer-active animals, the American Girl in Shorts," 164–5), and the fate of the art school and his pupils.

Salinger once again signals at the outset that language uncovers buried meanings. The narrator recalls a significant incident in New York City when he was nineteen, his "badly broken-out forehead" signifying his difficult late adolescence, when a bus driver says to him, "All right, buddy . . . let's move that ass." For the young man, it is the word "buddy" that deeply disturbs him, and that same word is the linguistic link with the last story, "Teddy," where in the first line a father cruelly mimics his son, using "buddy" as a disparaging epithet.

Despite its verbal and thematic connections to "De Daumier-Smith's Blue Period," the concluding story, "Teddy," is nevertheless the stunning complement to the first story, "A Perfect Day." They are constructed similarly (although "Teddy" is much longer and more philosophically suggestive) and both end in sudden, shocking deaths of the major characters. Indeed, it can be argued that the ending of "Teddy" is another suicide, for if the child *knows* the future and is aware that the swimming pool is empty, then his insistence on meeting his hateful little sister at the pool is certainly an act of self-destruction. Like "A Perfect Day," the opening sections describe through dialogue Teddy's materialistic, selfish, and insensitive parents, and his younger sister Booper, whose words reveal her resentment and rage. The narrative voice remains distant and objective, save for a typical Salinger interpolation when Teddy gives his father a look of inquiry, "whole and pure" (167). Language serves as a thematic link in the first two sections which take place in the family's stateroom. Mr. McArdle repeats his initial rhetorical threat with variations, addressing Teddy by the scathing and impersonal "buddy": "I'll exquisite day *you*, buddy, if you don't get down off that bag this minute" (166) and "I'll *Queen Mary you*, buddy, if you don't get off that bag this minute" (169). The husband and wife exchange remarks that are cruel, even violent: "I'd like to kick your goddam head open" (168), he tells her. His use of "god" and "Jesus" to curse his wife relates to Teddy's rejection of Christianity in favor of Eastern religion, specifically the Vedantic reincarnation and the rejection of emotion in pursuing spiritual advancement. The emotional level of the first section is thus connected to Teddy's need to be released from a world that finds spiritual sustenance in an expensive leather suitcase, a Leica camera, and the paraphernalia of everyday existence. Teddy *is* a prodigy, and his replies to the young teacher, Nicholson, reveal his intellectual sophistication and youthful intensity. The last sections of the story, like those in "De Daumier-Smith's," concern time: Teddy is intent on meeting Booper at the pool at precisely 10:30 a.m., and he tries to extricate himself from Nicholson's insistent curiosity. The interchange between Nicholson and Teddy provides Salinger with the opportunity to develop the Vedantic approach to spiritual purity, and at the same time to create suspense over Teddy's fate. The last lines, narrated through Nicholson's consciousness, are matter-of-fact, in stark contrast to the horror of Teddy's death and Booper's shriek after she has pushed him into the empty pool. Among the unsolved problems in "Teddy" are the haiku poems, his journal, the origin of Booper's hatred, and above all, Teddy's gift of foreknowledge. "Teddy" provides the perfect bookend to the collection, his death the mystery linked with Seymour's suicide and the many other instances of emotional and spiritual death that pervade the sequence.[15]

The preceding analysis of structural patterns, voice, language, and story arrangement suggests that the occasional links hardly unify the whole collection. Indeed, although Salinger uses repeated symbolic motifs to familiarize the reader with his fictional world and major concerns, they fail to offer a basis for a unified or conclusive interpretation. In addition to the pervasive symbolism contained in references to vision; to repellent physical characteristics and behavior; to cigarettes, ashes, and ashtrays; and to changing seasons, the collection is most suggestive in its symbolic allusions to Dantesque motifs that reinforce the primary conflict in the collection between the material world, a modern "Inferno," and a spiritual realm fitfully imagined but given a degree of shape and substance in the last two stories. An early Salinger critic noted that most of his work "is about those who think they are in hell, a place where the soul suffers according to its qualities, and without escape."[16] In Eastern thought there is no eternal hell, and Salinger's characters, looking for escape from this world, find it either in sleep ("For Esmé") or in an afterlife that offers eternal surcease from pain.

Dantesque motifs include references to the trees (Dante's Wood of the Suicides) that figure as the "whirly woods" of "A Perfect Day" and reappear in the following story set in the same Connecticut location. Seymour's pallor recalls the "death-pale" of Dante's suicides, as does the description of Sergeant X looking like "a goddam corpse." Dante's hell is reflected not only in the "life is hell" inscription on the Goebbels diary but in the popular culture Salinger evokes. As in *Catcher*, the author's favorite expletive is "hell!" familiar enough in contemporary speech, but symbolically suggestive in the context created by the first story. Muriel reads a magazine article, "Sex is Fun – or Hell," surely a clue to the psychosexual conflicts within most of Salinger's male characters. The tigers in "A Perfect Day" suggest the *Inferno*'s female hellhounds; and the repeated allusions to the extreme heat in that story, followed by the deathlike cold of the next, suggest Dantesque allusions to extremes of temperature. "Pretty Mouth and Green My Eyes" has also been linked to Dante's *Inferno*, not only through the repeated religious expletives and the fire and ashes, but also through the characters' resemblance to Dante's Paolo and Francesca.[17] If Salinger's Manhattan is hell, a hell of unleashed materialism, then for the tortured souls who inhabit the city, the search for a serene spiritual existence perforce becomes central to their efforts to find meaning where none apparently exists. This, then, is the spiritual level of *Nine Stories*, and it evolves naturally out of the brilliant depiction of a modern urban hell.

Does the search for a way out of hell or for meaning in a spiritual realm create, however, a firm structure linking the stories in the collection? The vexing mysteries raised by individual stories are, if anything, more insistent than any thematic link we may perceive. Indeed, the mysteries that linger after the last story are themselves the meanings that elude us throughout the collection. There have been many brilliant and intricate speculations and interpretations, but these enigmas provide the final link among the *Nine Stories*. I have previously alluded to the questions that remain after Seymour's and Teddy's deaths and the Chief's broken relationship, but they barely hint at the accumulating questions that suggest an ineffable narrative dimension that itself functions much like a Zen koan. They concern the symbolism of the bananafish story; the recurrent patterns of numbers; Eloise's careful placement of Ramona's glasses *lenses down;* her true feelings for her daughter; the source of her sorrow; the nature of Franklin's relationship with Eric; the importance of Franklin's misery to Ginnie; the allegory in the story of the Laughing Man; the meaning of Lionel's flights; the relationship between Boo Boo and her husband; the significance of the Nazi woman's inscription on the Goebbels book; the Sergeant's relationship with his wife; the effect of Esmé's invitation on his marriage; the impulse that led the husband in "Pretty Mouth" to poeticize his wife's eyes; the noises in the Yoshoto's room; the quality of Sister Irma's painting; the connection between the narrator's dentist and Father Zimmerman, who share the same name. Finally, the last story may contain a clue to the meaning of the entire work, but we can never be certain: Teddy may be the psychologically scarred child of cruelly insensitive parents, or he may be a true guru who achieves satori by relinquishing his material being.

I am not suggesting that these mysteries are utterly insoluble. They have, in fact, spawned the Salinger industry. But they pose questions that remain even after the most thorough explication has apparently tied up all the loose ends. They suggest the openness of life itself; they suggest the puzzles that Salinger and we well know lie at the heart of all human existence. No attempt to explain *Nine Stories* can erase its mysteries. That is why it is a classic, as fresh today as it was on publication, forty years ago.

NOTES

1. George Steiner, "The Salinger Industry," in *Salinger: A Critical and Personal Portrait*, ed. Henry Anatole Grunwald (New York: Harper & Row, 1962), 82.

2. J. D. Salinger, *Nine Stories* (1953; rpt. New York: Bantam, 1964), 59. Subsequent parenthetical references to Salinger's *Nine Stories* will correspond in pagination to this edition.

3. J. Gerald Kennedy, "Toward a Poetics of the Short Story Cycle," *Journal of the Short Story in English* 11 (Autumn 1988): 11.

4. Two of Salinger's favorite recurring motifs are cigarette ashes and the ashtray. In 1961 Alfred Kazin criticized the excesses of the Salinger industry: "Someday there will be learned theses on *The Use of the Ashtray in J. D. Salinger's Stories;* no other writer has made so much of Americans lighting up, reaching for the ashtray, setting up the ashtray with one hand while with the other they reach for a cigarette." See Kazin, "'Everybody's Favorite,'" in *Salinger: A Critical and Personal Portrait*, 45. James Finn Cotter, acknowledging Kazin's caveat, nevertheless explicates the religious import of Salinger's ashtrays in "Religious Symbols in Salinger's Shorter Fiction," *Studies in Short Fiction* 15 (Spring 1978): 129.

5. John Wenke, *J. D. Salinger: A Study of the Short Fiction* (Boston: Twayne, 1991), 32.

6. Although most commentary on *Nine Stories* has been devoted to individual stories, there have been three major discussions of the collection as a short story sequence, by Wenke (cited earlier), Paul Kirschner, and Warren French. Kirschner finds a "completed pattern" (76) emerging from the collection; French notes that "one develops a sense of an interconnectedness among [the stories], of a progression based upon the slow and painful achievement of spiritual enlightenment . . . of successive stages that a soul would pass through according to Vedantic teachings in at last escaping fleshly reincarnations." See Kirschner, "Salinger and His Society," *Literary Half-Yearly* 12 (Fall 1971): 51–60; 14 (Fall 1973): 63–78; and French, *J. D. Salinger Revisited* (Boston: Twayne, 1988), 63–4.

7. All were published first in the *New Yorker:* "Franny," 29 January 1955, 24–32, 35–43; "Raise High the Roof-Beam, Carpenters," 19 November 1955, 51–8, 60–116; "Zooey," 5 May 1957, 32–42, 44–139; "Seymour, An Introduction," 6 June 1959, 42–52, 54–111; "Hapworth 16, 1924," 19 June 1965, 32–113. All but the last story have been collected.

8. *Nine Stories* rose to ninth position on the *New York Times* bestseller list, and remained among the top twenty for three months, a remarkable record for a collection of short stories. The English publisher Hamish Hamilton feared the title would prove a handicap and persuaded Salinger to permit a change. The volume appeared as *For Esmé — with Love and Squalor, and Other Stories* (1955), without the Zen epigraph, and despite the title change, did not achieve the readership of the American edition. Today, *Nine Stories,* like all of Salinger's collected stories and novel, is available in mass-market paperback and sells steadily. See Ian Hamilton, *In Search of J. D. Salinger* (New York: Random House, 1988), 135–6.

9. These stories were selected from twenty the author had already published in such mass magazines as *Saturday Evening Post, Collier's, Good Housekeeping, Esquire,* and the *New Yorker,* as well as in the prestigious small circulation journals, *Story* and *University of Kansas City Review.* The selection reflects Salinger's correct perception of his skills: These are his most polished, skillful, and sophisticated fictions. That all but two originally appeared in the *New Yorker* led many early critics to the conclusion that Salinger's work was in part shaped by the editorial demands of that magazine. That conclusion is too simple; Salinger was already a skilled magazine writer by the time the first of the nine stories had been published. The high standards, editorial receptivity, and general ambience of the *New Yorker* provided Salinger with the ideal outlet for his fiction.

10. Alan W. Watts, *The Spirit of Zen* (New York: Grove Weidenfeld, 1958), 75.

11. D. T. Suzuki, *Essays in Zen Buddhism: First Series* (New York: Grove Weidenfeld, 1961), 37.

12. Kennedy, 16–17.

13. Although early readings of the story almost uniformly saw Muriel as a cold, materialistic woman, whose insensitivity leads Seymour to suicide, recent criticism has looked more charitably upon her and has seen his action as a far more complex response to his spiritual dilemma.

14. See, for example, the discussions by French, 80–3; Wenke, 56–60, who notes the narrator's "diseased imagination" and describes the story as the "most odd and

disjunctive" in the collection (59); and Frederick L. Gwynn and Joseph Blotner's fine analysis of the Oedipal conflict in the story in *The Fiction of J. D. Salinger* (Pittsburgh: University of Pittsburgh Press, 1958), 33–40.

15. The ending of "Teddy" illustrates the varying degrees of narrative closure in the volume. "A Perfect Day" and "Teddy" are the most open, perhaps because the endings do not settle any of the questions they raise. The muted endings of "The Laughing Man" and "Uncle Wiggily" also resist closure, and "Pretty Mouth" ends abruptly, but there is no resolution for any of the characters. The other four stories, "Just Before the War," "For Esmé," "Down at the Dinghy," and "De Daumier-Smith's," are the most structurally complete, with the strongest degree of narrative closure, yet the questions within these stories are no less insistent than in those that remain open-ended.

16. Donald Barr continues: "Ten people have read and enjoyed the *Inferno* for everyone who has read the *Purgatorio* or the *Paradiso*. It is fun; like looking at real estate, it gives us a sense of our own possibilities. But Salinger's hell is different. It is hell for the good, who can feel pain, who really love or hope to love." See his "Saints, Pilgrims and Artists," in *Salinger: A Critical and Personal Portrait*, 174.

17. John Hagopian, " 'Pretty Mouth and Green My Eyes': Salinger's Paolo and Francesca in New York," *Modern Fiction Studies* 12 (Autumn 1966): 353.

Cheever's Shady Hill:
A Suburban Sequence

SCOTT DONALDSON

Over the course of the previous half century, Vladimir Nabokov observed in November 1971, "the greatest Short Stories have been produced not in England, not in Russia, and certainly not in France, but in [the United States]." As examples, Nabokov went on to cite half a dozen personal favorites, with John Cheever's "The Country Husband" (1954) leading the list.[1] Two years later, John Leonard declared his belief that "Cheever is our best living writer of short stories," adding that this view was not commonly shared.[2] With the publication of *The Stories of John Cheever* in 1978, however, everyone sailed their hats in the air. What the critics neglected to discover earlier, reading Cheever's stories singly in the *New Yorker* or in his smaller collections, suddenly became clear in the wake of this whopping assemblage of sixty-one stories. In fact, Cheever now deserved recognition, according to Stephen Becker, as "one of the two or three most imaginative and acrobatic literary artists" in the world.[3]

One reason it took the critical establishment so long to respond to Cheever was his propensity toward short rather than long fiction. He himself addressed the question of story versus novel on several occasions during the 1950s, a decade that ended with the publication of his *The Wapshot Chronicle* (1957), a loosely organized episodic novel, and *The Housebreaker of Shady Hill and Other Stories* (1958), a coherently constructed story sequence. Simply for economic reasons, he understood that he must write novels. He also knew that a novel could do more than earn money: It could attract more serious attention than a book of stories. Circumstances proved the point. *The Wapshot Chronicle* won the National Book Award, and stayed in print for decades. *The Housebreaker of Shady Hill* generated some of the worst reviews of his life and soon disappeared from the bookstores.

Cheever was forty-five and had been writing stories for a quarter of a century before *Chronicle*, his first novel, was published. Many of his earliest stories were extremely brief, little more than sketches, and he omitted from his 1978 collection everything he wrote before the end of World War II. After the war he quickly found his stride as a writer of short stories, producing such excellent examples as "The Enormous Radio" (1947), "Torch Song" (1947), and "Goodbye, My Brother" (1951).[4] In 1951, he moved from Manhattan to suburban Westchester County, first to settle in Scarborough (until 1961) and then in nearby Ossining. There he began soaking up the atmosphere and discovering the trials of the characters who would populate *Shady Hill*, while struggling to complete the novel that had long been promised to his publisher. In effect he wrote *Shady Hill* and *Chronicle* at the same time, between 1953 and 1957. At the beginning of that period, Cheever publicly stated his preference for the short story. The novel, he felt, depended upon a stable social ambience rarely encountered in modern life. As a result, it was an artificial form, "unless you're living in Army installations or in a community that's fairly anachronistic." The short story, on the other hand, was "determined by moving around from place to place, by the interrupted event,"[5] and so ideally suited the unsettled nature of contemporary existence. Stories also carried a kind of concentrated energy that the novel, with its sustained length, could hardly match.

By 1958, after the publication of both *Chronicle* and *Shady Hill*, Cheever apparently changed his mind. He was still "interested in the short story form," he acknowledged, but generally it was better suited to "young writers, who are more intense, whose perceptions are more fragmentary."[6] Yet whether he was writing a novel or a story, Cheever felt acutely the confusion of modern life. Some reviewers of *Chronicle* took him to task for not supplying a linear plot, but such plotting, he believed, would be false to the chaos he witnessed everywhere around him. In his "The Death of Justina" (1960), for example, the narrator begins with a reflection on the purpose of fiction. "Fiction is art and art is the triumph of over chaos (no less)" yet it was terribly easy for the artist to go wrong in an environment where "even the mountains seem to shift in the space of a night."[7] Cheever's task, as Robert A. Morace has succinctly expressed it, was to "write about such a world in a way that will take account of the incoherence without succumbing to it."[8] Nowhere did he succeed more brilliantly than in *Shady Hill*, a book about people who inhabit an outwardly manicured but internally hangnailed community.

Considering that it included four of his best stories – the title story, "O Youth and Beauty!" (1953), "The Country Husband," and "The

Five-Forty-Eight" (1954) – *Shady Hill* was very badly reviewed. With few exceptions, reviewers criticized the stories for a presumed lack of moral depth, for appealing too directly to the comfortable upper-middle-class readership of the *New Yorker* (where seven of the eight stories originally appeared), and above all for their focus on a suburban milieu. Some damned him with snide praise. He was the "Dante of the cocktail hour" or "the poet of the exurbs" foolishly trying to invest the lives of "the country-club set" with significance. The general assumption was that those people, and the communities where they chose to reside, were dull, conformist, wealthy, and unworthy of fictional representation. Whatever miseries befell suburbanites might produce sadness, but never tragedy. As Richard Gilman expressed it, "Cheever's women are always loved for their blondeness or bosom line and his men because they are lithe. They have a nostalgic need for mountains (not high), sailboats at twilight and tennis with new balls." As against the stereotype of the spoiled and immature suburbanite lodged in Gilman's head, it hardly mattered that Cheever never created a character with an interest in tennis, whether with new balls or old, and that several of the protagonists of *Shady Hill* face financial crises. Apparently working from the same preconceptions, the distinguished critic Irving Howe labeled Cheever a "toothless Thurber" who "connive[d] in the cowardice of contemporary life." Herbert Mitgang in the daily *New York Times* offered a rare exception to this pattern of disparagement. *Shady Hill*, he wrote, presented "a diagnosis of a particular form of community life, at once striving and brave, melancholy and humorous." But the critical consensus, as articulated by Robert Kirsch, was that Cheever should "say goodbye to Shady Hill for a good long time." The place and its inhabitants were not worthy of his "unquestioned ability."[9]

Considering the prevailing climate of scorn for the suburbs, it is not surprising that so few of our best writers have chosen to focus their attention in that direction. In effect, demographic lag operates in our fiction. Up until 1925 or so, most major American writing concentrated its gaze on rural or small-town settings, though the nation itself was rapidly urbanizing. Then, during the last half century, the fictional scene shifted to the cities, while one-third of a nation was deserting to the suburbs. One of the writers who followed that migration was John Cheever, and it was the most natural thing in the world that he should begin to write about the people and events he encountered there. With the publication of *Shady Hill* in September 1958, he became fixed in the public mind as a chronicler of suburban life. For the previous two decades he had been writing about city dwellers, and he later went on to write about American expatriates in Italy and the inmates of Falconer prison. Nonetheless, for better or worse, he was categorized as the John Cheever who wrote those "Connecticut" (actually Westchester, though Shady Hill or Proxmire Manor or Bullet Park might just as well have been stops on the New Haven line as on the Hudson) stories for the *New Yorker*.[10] What was not generally recognized was the depth and sophistication of his understanding of what went on in those communities.

As well as anyone, Cheever knew that such places sometimes deserved derision for their materialism and conventionality. "God preserve me," says Charles Flint in "The Trouble of Marcie Flint" (1957), "from women who dress like *toreros* to go to the supermarket, and from cowhide dispatch cases, and from flannels and gabardines. Preserve me from word games and adulterers, from basset hounds and swimming pools and frozen canapés and Bloody Marys and smugness and syringa bushes and P.T.A. meetings." Yet the narrator of the story, who may speak for Cheever himself, objects at first that "there was absolutely nothing wrong with the suburb from which Charles Flint was fleeing," then retreats to the position that if there was anything wrong, "it was the fact that the village had no public library."[11] In the title story of the collection, housebreaker Johnny Hake defends the community. It is true, he admits, that "Shady Hill is open to criticism by city planners, adventurers, and lyric poets, but if you work in the city and have children to raise, I can't think of a better place."[12] Yet as a man driven to thievery to keep his suburban home, Johnny's opinions are somewhat compromised.

Manifestly, Cheever felt a degree of ambivalence about the manners and mores of suburbia. Thus he sarcastically described the compulsive *joining* of Shady Hill as "a regular Santa Claus's workshop of madrigal singers, political discussion groups, recorder groups, dancing schools, confirmation classes, committee meetings, and lectures on literature, philosophy, city planning, and pest control."[13] (Note the wonderful descending ladder of lecture topics.) At the same time he regarded the suburbs as representing "an improvisational way of life" adopted by many as a refuge from the expense of living in cities and the difficulty of raising children there. In such new communities tradition meant less, and it seemed to him that there was "more vitality, more change" in the suburbs than in the cities.[14] Above all he was not willing to dismiss the denizens of suburbia as unworthy of fictional representation. He does not demand that we identify with Shady Hill's Johnny Hake or Cash

Bentley or Francis Weed, but he does expect us to care about what happens to them, for in their particular distress they take on a measure of universality.

Cheever was "often labelled a writer about suburbia," as John Updike wrote in a memorial reminiscence, yet only he "was able to make an archetypal place out of it, a terrain we can recognize within ourselves, wherever we are or have been. Only he saw in its cocktail parties and swimming pools the shimmer of dissolving dreams; no one else satirized with such tenderness its manifold distinctions of class and style, or felt with such poignance the weary commuter's nightly tumble back into the arms of his family."[15] "Satirized with tenderness": Just so, for the cement that binds *Shady Hill*'s stories into a coherent group is not merely their common setting but the faintly ironic, far from judgmental, tone of the storyteller.

The Housebreaker of Shady Hill and Other Stories might have been subtitled *Suburbia and Its Discontents.* There are only eight stories, and in each of them – save one – one kind of demon or another lies in wait beyond the well-tended lawns and handsome facades of upper-middle-class homes in Westchester County. The male characters commute to work in New York and feel a sense of dislocation caused by incessant traveling. They are weighed down with debt, addicted to drink, themselves adulterous or suspicious of their wives' faithfulness, and – as in the poignant "O Youth and Beauty!" – overcome by nostalgia for the glories of the past. Yet no matter how painful their troubles or vexatious their daily existence, almost all of them conspire in the pretense that everything is perfectly all right.

As willing partners in this communal hypocrisy, the citizens of Shady Hill are skeptical about the Crutchmans, who not only seem to be, but actually are, entirely contented with their lot. The Crutchmans are the central figures of "The Worm in the Apple," a brief and tellingly ironic story Cheever wrote at the last minute especially for *Shady Hill* and placed at the midpoint of his collection to bind together the seven other tales. "The Crutchmans were so very, very happy and so temperate in all their habits and so pleased with everything that came their way that one was bound to suspect a worm in their rosy apple," the story begins.[16] Larry's ship had been sunk in the war and surely he must suffer from nightmares, people speculate. Or, they think, Helen had too much money: Larry might quit his job, play golf, and take to drink. But no, "Larry seemed to have no nightmares and Helen spread her income among the charities and lived a comfortable but a modest life" (108). Perhaps they were sexually unsatisfied, then. Was Helen, with that "striking pallor," a concealed nymphomaniac? And what about Larry? "Everyone in the community with wandering hands had given them both a try but they had all been put off." What could explain such constancy? "Were they frightened? Were they prudish? Were they monogamous?" (109).

The Crutchmans have two children who are not spoiled by their money and turn out well. But why, people wonder, only two children and not three or four? And how to account for the apparent pleasure Larry took both in his work and in the activities of Shady Hill?

> Larry went to his job each morning with such enthusiasm that you might think he was trying to escape from something. His participation in the life of the community was so vigorous that he must have been left with almost no time for self-examination. He was everywhere: He was at the communion rail, the fifty-yard line, he played the oboe with the Chamber Music Club, drove the fire truck, served on the school board and rode the 8:03 into New York every morning. What was the sorrow that drove him? (108)

Finally, the narrator proposes the alternative that there might be no worm in the Crutchmans' apple at all, that the worm might instead be "in the eye of the observer who, through timidity or moral cowardice, could not embrace the broad range of their natural enthusiasms and would not grant that, while Larry played neither Bach nor football very well, his pleasure in both was genuine." In any case the Crutchmans continue to entertain their friends and read books and remain euphoric as they age. Larry gives up the fire truck but continues his other activities, and – so the story ends – "they got richer and richer and richer and lived happily, happily, happily, happily" (112).

This ending prefigures the closing lines of Cheever's novel of suburbia, *Bullet Park* (1969), where the youth Tony Nailles is rescued from a would-be assassin by his father and their everyday life resumes. "Tony went back to school on Monday and Nailles – drugged – went off to work and everything was as wonderful, wonderful, wonderful, wonderful as it had been." [17] Similar though they may seem, the two endings depend on different kinds of irony. In *Bullet Park*, Nailles's drugged happiness is clearly suspect, and the quadruple repetition works to undercut what is stated. In "The Worm in the Apple," however, the Crutchmans *are* happy, and the irony of the repetition is directed at the end, as throughout the story, against those Shady Hill observers who will not credit the Crutchmans' contentment or will only acknowledge it as the consequence of their wealth.

It is predictable that the residents of Shady Hill should think this way, for they are beset – many of them – by financial woes. It is not easy to afford the green lawns and good schools and weekend parties of their suburban environment. If only they had more money, they would be perfectly happy, or so they think. Specifically, financial troubles provide the donnee of the first two stories in the book, "The Housebreaker of Shady Hill" and "O Youth and Beauty!" Johnny Hake of "Housebreaker" comes from a privileged background. "I was conceived in the Hotel St. Regis, born in the Presbyterian Hospital, raised on Sutton Place" (3), he tells us in the opening paragraph of this first-person narrative. At thirty-six, he and his wife Christina and their children live in a handsome house in Shady Hill with a garden and a place to cook meat outdoors. Sitting there on summer nights with the kids, looking down the front of Christina's dress or up at the stars, he feels a thrill, and that, he supposes, "is what is meant by the pain and the sweetness of life" (3). Then through no fault of his own, Johnny is fired and for six months is out of work. In desperation – he had never yearned for anyone the way he yearned for money, he realizes – he breaks into Carl Warburton's house and steals his wallet, which contains just over nine hundred dollars.

Johnny's conscience is immediately awakened. On the way into town the next morning, he consigns himself to the sorry company of the bank robbers and embezzlers he reads about in the paper. He begins to see thievery everywhere. At a restaurant, a stranger lifts a thirty-five-cent tip left by a previous customer. At a brokerage house, his friend Burt Howe offers to let him in on a lead-pipe cinch of a deal. "It's a steal," Burt tells him. "They're green, and they're dumb, and they're loaded, and it's just like stealing" (15). Earlier he had ignored such examples of greed, but now he longs for redemption. He experiences what Robert Coles calls "a visionary moment"[18] as he rides home on a peaceable spring evening. "It seemed to me that fishermen and lone bathers and grade-crossing watchmen and sand-lot ballplayers and lovers unashamed of their sport and the owners of small sailing craft and old men playing pinochle in firehouses were the people who stitched up the big holes in the world that were made by men like me" (19). But he does not go in the company of those ordinary honest people who do not care about money. Instead he becomes depressed and embittered. He quarrels with his wife. The natural world that once gave him such joy now appears to be the locus of desolation. In his extremity, he schemes to break into the house of the Pewters, neighbors who drank so heavily that even a thunderstorm wouldn't rouse them once they'd gone to bed. As it happens, he encounters only a gentle rain as he walks toward their house at three in the morning: "There was a harsh stirring in all the trees and gardens . . . and I wondered what it was until I felt the rain on my hands and face, and then I began to laugh" (28). The rain miraculously sets him straight, and on the spot he abandons his career as a thief. The next day, in what may seem too convenient a coincidence, the same man who fired him asks him to come back to work, with a healthy advance. And that night, after "taking some precautions about fingerprints," he sneaks back into the Warburtons' and places an envelope containing nine hundred dollars on their kitchen table (30).

The tale of Johnny Hake's financial distress ends happily enough. In fact, his venture into crime seems to have made him morally more discerning.[19] For Cash Bentley in "O Youth and Beauty!" it is a very different story. He is not aptly named, for he has suffered business reversals and has never owned an elegant motor car. In fact, he and his wife Louise barely scrape along. The drawer of their hall table is stuffed with unpaid bills, and at night Louise talks in her sleep. "I can't *afford* veal cutlets," she says, with a sigh.[20] The Bentleys relieve the drabness of their lives at the parties of their friends – the Beardens, the Farquarsons – on Alewives Lane. At the end of these parties, in what has become almost a ritual, a well-muddled Cash rearranges the furniture and goes hurdling over it. He is forty years old, with dim prospects for the future, but in his youth he had been a track star and when he hurdles the furniture it is as if he were recapturing the triumphs of the past.

But Cash is no longer young, and one night he trips and falls and breaks his leg. As his recovery drags on, he grows discontented. His senses repeatedly remind him of mortality. The meat in the icebox has spoiled, and he cannot shake off the rank odor. Up in the attic, "looking for his old varsity sweater," he walks into a spider web that nearly gags him. On a New York side street, he sees an old whore "so sluttish and ugly that she looked like a cartoon of Death." The faded roses Louise brings in from the garden give off "a putrid, compelling smell" and he dumps them into a wastebasket (40). Without his race to run, the parties no longer amuse him. He is rude to his friends, and irritable around Louise.

The climax comes on a summer weekend when Shady Hill is bathed in "placid golden light," and the scent of the new grass and trees is invigorating, not depressing (41). Apparently revived, Cash once again hurdles the furniture on Saturday night. On Sunday he returns from a party at the Farquarsons: "Oh, those suburban Sunday nights, those Sunday-night blues!" the narrator comments. Louise has stayed home, and is upstairs busily "cutting out of the current copy of *Life* those scenes of mayhem, disaster, and violent death that she felt might corrupt her children. She always did this." After a while, she hears Cash moving the living-room furniture around, and he calls her down to fire the starting pistol. Eager to run his race, he neglects to tell her about the safety. "'It's that little lever,' he said. 'Press that little lever.' Then, in his impatience, he hurdled the sofa anyhow. The pistol went off and Louise got him in midair. She shot him dead" (46).

The Lawtons in "The Sorrows of Gin" (1953) belong to the same heavy-drinking party set as the Bentleys, and it is their drinking – particularly that of "Mr. Lawton," who unlike his wife Marcia is not referred to by a Christian name – that the story explores. The tale is told from the point of view of their young daughter Amy, whose unsophisticated account adds a measure of pathos. It soon emerges that the Lawtons neglect their daughter in order to pursue their social rounds. Often, their evening martinis lead them out of the house for further imbibing, while Amy is left to have dinner alone. In a particularly suggestive section, Amy describes the effect of the cocktail hour on her father. He does not reel around like a circus clown, she observes. On the contrary, his walk is if anything steadier than usual, except that "sometimes, when he got to the dining room door, he would miss it by a foot or more." [21] And he keeps putting his drink down, forgetting where, and making himself another as a replacement. These confusions do not seem to bother Mr. Lawton at all, and no one says anything about them, but he is extremely judgmental about similar faults in others. Thus he commands Amy not to overdo by taking too many nuts from the tray she is passing to guests and berates her for misplacing her raincoat.

His most hypocritical burst of moral piety, however, is reserved for the cooks and gardeners and babysitters who, he is certain, have been drinking his liquor in vast quantities. Here Amy is partly at fault, for in an attempt to moderate her parents' drinking she has taken to pouring the contents of gin bottles down the drain. The Lawtons lose one wonderful cook because she actually does get drunk, though only on her day off. "I'm lonely, and I'm afraid, and it's all I've got" (92), she confesses. Mr. Lawton summarily fires her. Then they lose the next cook because of a gin bottle Amy has emptied. "Everybody is drinking my liquor," Mr. Lawton roars, "and I am God-damned sick and tired of it!" (94). Finally, the Lawtons leave Amy with a gossipy old babysitter for a party, and when they return at two in the morning, her father discovers that another bottle of gin has been drained. "You must be stinking, Mrs. Henlein," he tells the babysitter, who in her indignation threatens to call the police. "I'm over at the Lawtons'," she shouts into the receiver. "He's drunk, and he's calling me insulting names, and I want you to come over here and arrest him!" (100–1). Awakened by the uproar, Amy "perceived vaguely the corruption of the adult world," but she is frightened too, because she knows she is to blame for the argument, and decides to run away. This plan does not succeed, for the stationmaster recognizes her and calls her father when she tries to buy a ticket. Mr. Lawton drives over to collect his daughter. Why should she want to travel? he wonders in conclusion. "How could he teach her that home sweet home was the best place of all?" (104).

The final three stories in *Shady Hill* – "The Five-Forty-Eight," "Just Tell Me Who It Was" (1955), and "The Trouble of Marcie Flint" – all deal with adultery, and in the first of these Cheever creates a moral monster of such darkness as to make Mr. Lawton pale. An executive in New York, Blake has enjoyed a series of sexual conquests, while carefully avoiding any consequences. In fact, "most of the many women he had known had been picked for their lack of self-esteem" (119–20). That seduction is, for him, a way of exerting his power over others is underlined by his behavior toward his wife and son. One evening he came home to Shady Hill tired and hungry, only to find that his wife Louise had not prepared supper. In cruel retaliation, he drew a circle around a date two weeks hence on the kitchen calendar. "I'm not going to speak to you for two weeks," he told Louise, and though she wept and protested, it was to no avail, for she was no longer beautiful in his eyes and "it had been eight or ten years since she had been able to touch him with her entreaties."[22] Similarly, when his son Charlie befriended the Watkins boy, Blake took steps to break off the relationship. Mr. Watkins was, after all, only a commercial artist who had long dirty hair and sometimes wore sandals.

It is with a mixture of satisfaction and dread that we follow the course of the story, during which Blake is confronted by Miss Dent, a former secretary he had slept with one night, ordered personnel to fire the next day, and refused to see ever since. Bent on revenge, she follows him from his office to the train station, and though he thinks he has escaped her by ducking into the men's bar, she is on the five-forty-eight when he boards. During the ride up the Hudson, it develops that she is quite mad, that she means to do him harm, and that she has a pistol to do it with. The trip is one of terror for Blake. He keeps hoping that someone will notice his predicament, but no one does. Miss Dent's pistol keeps him quiet, while she debates whether or not to kill him. At Shady Hill, she marches him off into the soggy lowlands along the river and makes him kneel and put his face in the filth. "Now I feel better," she says. "Now I can wash my hands of you" (134). And so he is spared, though justly humiliated.

Blake's tyranny is not to be forgiven, or atoned for, by the degradation Miss Dent visits upon him. He will continue to exploit other people, in all likelihood, yet Cheever invites us to identify with him at least in one respect. Blake is offended by Mr. Watkins's unconventional garb partly because he himself "dressed – like the rest of us – as if he admitted the existence of sumptuary laws. His raincoat was the pale buff color of a mushroom. His hat was dark brown, so was his suit. Except for the few bright threads in his necktie, there was a scrupulous lack of color in his clothing that seemed protective" (120–1). Despicable as he is, Blake is almost pitiable in his attempt to secure protection through dun-colored clothing. And in that attempt, he is "like the rest of us," or at least like the rest who live in Shady Hill.

The end of "The Trouble of Marcie Flint," the final story in the book, provides a case in point. Sexual jealousy, not dominance, is central to this story. Marcie Flint has been unfaithful to her husband Charlie – he is often away on business trips – with the civic-minded, but otherwise unappealing, Noel Mackham. To keep busy while her husband is traveling, Marcie gets elected to the village council. There, one night, Mackham makes a plea for a public library. His words carry little weight, however, for he lives in the Maple Dell development, "the kind of place where the houses stand cheek by jowl, all of them white frame, all of them built twenty years ago, and parked beside each was a car that seemed more substantial than the house itself, as if this were a fragment of some nomadic culture" (169). Marcie feels sorry for Noel, whose proposal is rejected out of hand, and invites him back to her house for a drink. "Perhaps," she says, "we could get the library project moving again" (177). That they cannot do, for the rest of the council is adamantly opposed. Besides, as her old friend Mark Barrett tells her when he hears about Noel's visit, most of them think that "Mackham is a meatball" (182). This only makes Marcie pity Mackham more, however, and when he next comes by and clumsily pulls off his rubbers, she is helpless to resist him.

As honest as she has been unfaithful, Marcie tells her husband about her lapse. In response, he packs his suitcase and goes off to "Torino, where the girls love peanut butter and the world is a man's castle" (165). But as Charlie sails across the Atlantic, a foghorn begins to sound and his resolve weakens. He will catch a plane in Genoa, he will fly back to his dear sweet Marcie, he "will shelter her with the curve of [his] body from all the harms of the dark" (185).

Implicit in Charlie Flint's decision is the assumption that Shady Hill's residents – excluding those unfortunate enough to live in Maple Dell – *can* escape the dark. Cheever's stories make it abundantly clear that they cannot, that money and drink and sex will turn their rosy apple rotten. *Shady Hill* collectively demonstrates that you can't shut out trouble by willing it away or pretending it doesn't exist, by wearing drab clothes or excising accounts of unpleasantness from magazines. "The Country Husband," the best story in the book, most powerfully communicates this point.

"It goes without saying," Cheever remarked in a 1958 interview, "that the people in my stories and the things that happen to them could take place anywhere."[23] A significant difference, though, is that in the suburbs of Cheever's fiction, these people try very hard to ignore even the possibility of suffering. In Proxmire Manor, the setting for "The Death of Justina" and a community that strongly resembles Shady Hill, a local zoning ordinance decrees that it is illegal to die in Zone B. When Aunt Justina passes on, her relatives are advised to "put her in the car and drive her over to Chestnut Street, where Zone C begins."[24] The survivors lack moorings. They exist in a state of perpetual rootlessness deriving from their eternal commuting and frequent continent hopping. "The people of Bullet Park intend not so much to have arrived there as to have been planted and grown there," Cheever writes in his 1969 novel, but there is nothing organic or indigenous about their way of life. Bullet Park like Shady Hill and Proxmire Manor is what the sociologists call a final suburb, one whose residents have, presumably, arrived. But in due course many of them will be forced to leave, accompanied by "disorder, moving vans, bank loans at high interest, tears, and desperation" (4–5).

At thirty-four pages by far the longest story in *Shady Hill*, "The Country Husband" is (as Nabokov commented) "really a miniature novel beautifully traced, so that the impression of there being a little too many things happening in it is completely redeemed by the satisfying coherence of its thematic interlacings."[25] There are indeed a great many things going on: love, war, joy, sorrow, and the community's repudiation of bad manners, bad news, and both past and future. The story begins with Francis Weed on his way back from a business trip to Minneapolis. The plane that carries him makes a crash landing in a cornfield not far from Philadelphia, but no one is hurt. "It's just like the Marne," a fellow passenger says, but there is no sense of comradeship among the survivors as among soldiers. Later that day, Francis catches his regular evening train from New York to Shady Hill, and tells fellow commuter Trace Bearden about the close call. Trace, unimpressed, continues to read his newspaper.

Surely, one thinks, his tale will find a receptive audience when he reaches his Dutch Colonial home in Shady Hill. "Late-summer sunlight, brilliant and as clear as water," brightens the living room. "Nothing here was neglected; nothing had not been burnished" (51–2). Yet this "polished and tranquil" environment has been transformed into a war zone – one of the interlocking motifs Nabokov singled out – by his fractious children, and no one is interested in hearing about the accident. Henry, Louisa, and Toby exchange blows and accusations, while his wife Julia equably ignores the chaos and lights the candles for dinner. She asks Francis to go upstairs and summon their eldest child Helen to the table. He "is happy to go; it is like getting back to headquarters company." Helen says she "doesn't understand about the plane crash, because there wasn't a drop of rain in Shady Hill." At dinner, frustrated, Francis announces that "[he] was nearly killed in a plane crash, and [he] doesn't like to come home every night to a battlefield." It is *not* a battlefield, Julia objects, and dissolves in tears. "Poor Mummy," Toby says (53–4).

Afterward, Francis smokes a cigarette in the back garden and takes in the sights and sounds of the neighborhood. There he encounters Jupiter, the Mercers' black retriever. Jupiter is a nuisance "whose retrieving instincts and . . . high spirits were out of place in Shady Hill." He goes where he pleases, "ransacking wastebaskets, clotheslines, garbage pails, and shoe bags," and lifting steaks off the barbeque. From the way he is described – he has "a long, alert, intelligent, rakehell face," his eyes

gleam with mischief, and he holds his head high – it is apparent that
Jupiter is to be admired. Francis calls to him, but he bounds away, carrying the remains of a felt hat in his mouth (56).

The bulk of "The Country Husband" concerns Francis's infatuation
with Anne Murchison, a teenage babysitter who stays with the children
when the Weeds are out, which is often. One evening, during a dinner
party at the Farquarsons, Francis recognizes the maid as a young
Frenchwoman he had seen punished for consorting with the Germans
during the war. In a public ceremony, her fellow townspeople in Nor-
mandy had shaved her skull clean, stripped her naked, and jeered at
her. Francis decides not to tell anyone at the party, for "it would have
been a social as well as a human error. The people in the Farquarsons'
living room seemed united in their tacit claim that there had been no
past, no war – that there was no danger or trouble in the world." In such
an atmosphere, his memory would have been "unseemly and impolite" (58–9).

When they return from the party, Francis drives the sitter home. He
is expecting the same Mrs. Henlein who had been so grievously insulted
by Mr. Lawton for her supposed drinking; instead, the sitter is the remarkably beautiful Anne Murchison. Anne is crying, for her father is
an alcoholic. Unlike practically everyone else in Shady Hill she is willing
to talk about her troubles. She sobs on Francis's shoulder, gives him a
quick kiss good night, and he is smitten. In the morning he "washed his
body, shaved his jaws, drank his coffee, and missed the seven-thirty-one"
(63–4). As he waits for the next train, he insults boring old Mrs. Wrightson. The experience exhilarates him. It had been years, he realized,
since he "had enjoyed being deliberately impolite." For too long, he had
listened to fools and bores with as much attention as he gave the brilliant
and gifted, for that was what was expected of him. Now he felt a "brac-
ing sensation of independence," and – he thinks – he has Anne to thank
for it.

His passion for Anne, he knows, is both ridiculous – he is old enough
to be her father – and dangerous. The

> Moral card house would come down on them all – on Julia and the chil-
> dren as well – if he got caught taking advantage of a babysitter. Looking
> back over the recent history of Shady Hill for some precedent, he found
> there was none. There was no turpitude; there had not been a divorce
> since he lived there; there had not even been a breath of scandal. Things
> seemed arranged with more propriety even than in the Kingdom of
> Heaven.

Nonetheless, on his lunch hour he buys Anne a bracelet, and when he gets home in the evening, there she is. Stunned by her perfection, he "seized her and covered her lips with his, and she struggled but she did not have to struggle for long, because just then little Gertrude Flannery appeared from somewhere" (65–7).

Gertrude Flannery, like Jupiter, knows no boundaries and is hence an anomaly in Shady Hill: "garrulous, skinny, and unwashed, she drifted from house to house." You might find her on your front stoop in the morning, or on the toilet when you opened your bathroom door. She never goes home of her own free will, though people are always telling her to. That is what Francis tells her when she interrupts him and Anne. "Go home, Gertrude, go home and don't tell anyone, Gertrude," he says, giving her a quarter to seal the bargain. The Weeds are going out again, and during the course of the party Francis can think of nothing but where he should park the car when he takes Anne home. But Julia tells him to put the car in the garage, instead; she'd let "the Murchison girl" leave at eleven. Devastated, Francis realizes that he is to be spared "nothing . . . that a fool was not spared: ravening lewdness, jealousy, this hurt to his feelings that put tears in his eyes, even scorn" (67–9).

The jealousy is aroused the very next evening. First the Weeds, parents and children, are photographed for their Christmas card in absolute decorum. Then young Clayton Thomas stops by. He and his mother don't have much money, and Clayton has dropped out of college to get a job. They will probably move to New York, he says, in part because Clayton – who is tall and homely, with a deep voice and a judgmental streak – disapproves of Shady Hill's mores. At the club dance the previous Saturday night, he'd seen "Mr. Granner trying to put Mrs. Minot into the trophy case" and they were both drunk. Besides, he says, the community has no future. The only thing that people in Shady Hill care about is keeping out undesirables, and the only future will be "more commuting trains and more parties." That's not healthy, according to Clayton, and despite his youth and pretensions he is surely right. As he is leaving, Clayton tells the Weeds that he is engaged to Anne Murchison. The news strikes Francis "like a bitter turn of the weather" (71–3).

A nasty husband-and-wife dispute follows. Julia berates Francis for having insulted Mrs. Wrightson. She has invited everyone in the village to her anniversary party except the Weeds, and furthermore, as Shady Hill's official social gatekeeper, Mrs. Wrightson can keep their daughter

Helen from being invited to the assemblies. Francis tries to defend himself – "I have very good manners" and "I've got to express my likes and
dislikes" – but this only makes Julia angrier, and eventually Francis
strikes her. Immediately contrite, he tries to dissuade her from packing
and leaving. In a plaintive complaint, he blames what has gone wrong
between them on the incessant gregariousness of Shady Hill. "Julia, I
do love you, and I would like to be as we were – sweet and bawdy and
dark – but now there are so many people" (74–5). She decides to stay,
for he needs taking care of.

At the office the following day, Francis has a phone call from Trace
Bearden asking him to recommend Clayton Thomas for a job. He can't
do that, Francis says, "the kid's worthless." It is a gratuitously cruel act,
and its very wickedness makes Francis aware that he is lost, in trouble,
with only bleakness ahead. He calls a psychiatrist and demands an ap-
pointment that very day. When he arrives at the doctor's office, a policeman is on hand to frisk him down. Once inside, he starts to tell his old
sad story: "I'm in love, Dr. Herzog."

Dr. Herzog advises him to pursue a hobby, perhaps woodworking. A
week or ten days later, in our last glimpse of Shady Hill, Francis Weed –
his last name a clue that like Jupiter and Gertrude he is an outsider[26] –
is happily building a coffee table in the cellar. Neighbor Donald Goslin
is worrying Beethoven's "Moonlight Sonata," as he does every night,
and the housemaid at the Goslins is writing a letter to Arthur Godfrey.
The Weeds' son Tony dives from bed to floor in his space suit, "landing
with a thump that is audible to everyone in the house but himself."
Someone tells Gertrude Flannery to go home. The Babcocks' door flies
open, and Mr. Babcock, nude, pursues his naked wife behind their protective hedge. Mr. Nixon shouts at the squirrels in his bird feeder. "Rap-
scallions! Varmints! Avaunt and quit my sight!" A miserable cat, dressed
up in a doll's dress and hat, wanders into the garden. Julia calls to the
pussy, but she slinks off in her skirts. "The last to come is Jupiter. He
prances through the tomato vines, holding in his generous mouth the
remains of an evening slipper. Then it is dark; it is a night where kings
in golden suits ride elephants over the mountains" (82–3).

"The Country Husband" ends then, with a two-page burst of joy-
fulness. All of those described manage to assert their independence –
even their eccentricity – against the community's unwritten standard of
conventionality. The descriptions fairly glow with pleasure. Cheever
himself liked to quote aloud the final sentence about kings and elephants crossing the mountains. But how appropriate was this ending,

like the lyrical conclusion of "The Housebreaker of Shady Hill," to the sordid subject matter of these stories: a suburbanite falling in love with his teenage babysitter, another stealing his neighbor's wallet in the dead of night? In another writer's hands, the contrast would seem hopelessly sentimental, but Cheever's verbal magic carries the day. That Francis Weed takes up woodworking is not enough to convert Shady Hill into an earthly paradise, except that for the space of one golden evening Cheever makes it so.

The enduring impression that *Shady Hill* leaves is one of ambiguity. The author "seems to be suspended," as R. G. Collins comments, "between a tragic pessimism and a raptured expectancy; . . . he seems to be listening for the angels, as the earth smoulders beneath him." [27] On the one hand, the stories perceptively present the sorry spectacle of a community trying to shut out any vestige of trouble. The task was both foolish and futile, for as Cheever was to observe a few years later, "the characters [of fiction] have become debased and life in the United States in 1960 is Hell." [28] On the other hand, he wished to affirm the light that relieved the dark. As Joan Didion wrote in 1961, Cheever's stories represent nothing less than "a celebration of life." [29] Denying the existence of evil would not make it go away, as the residents of Shady Hill are persistently reminded. Yet magic could also strike even in such a *banlieue*, even in such an homogeneous, upper-middle-class, conformist, WASP suburb as Shady Hill. Cheever insists – *Shady Hill* insists – on having it both ways.

NOTES

1. Vladimir Nabokov, "Inspiration," *Saturday Review of the Arts* 1 (January 1973): 32.
2. John Leonard, "Cheever to Roth to Malamud," *Atlantic Monthly* 231 (June 1973): 112.
3. Stephen Becker, "Excellence Level . . . Astounding," *New Orleans Times-Picayune*, 9 November 1978, sec. 5, 10.
4. For an enlightening analysis of Cheever's development in this period, see James O'Hara, "John Cheever's Flowering Forth: The Breakthroughs of 1947," *Modern Language Studies* 17 (Fall 1987): 50–9.
5. Quoted in Harvey Breit, "In and Out of Books," *New York Times*, 10 May 1953, 8.
6. Quoted in Rollene Waterman, "Literary Horizons," *Saturday Review* 41 (13 September 1958): 33.
7. John Cheever, "The Death of Justina," *The Stories of John Cheever* (New York: Knopf, 1978), 429.
8. Robert A. Morace, "From Parallels to Paradise: The Lyrical Structure of Cheever's Fiction," *Twentieth Century Literature* 35 (Winter 1989): 509.

9. The reviews cited are Richard Gilman, "Dante of Suburbia," *Commonweal* 69 (19 December 1978): 320; Paul C. Wermuth, *Library Journal* 83 (15 September 1978): 2,438–9; Irving Howe, "Realities and Fictions," *Partisan Review* 26 (Winter 1959): 130–1; Herbert Mitgang, "Books of the Times," *New York Times*, 6 September 1978, 15; and Robert Kirsch, "Cheever Paints Pallid Exurbia," *Los Angeles Times*, 21 September 1978, part V, 7.

10. Cheever's treatment of suburban themes is a topic I have examined previously. See Scott Donaldson, "The Machines in Cheever's Garden," *The Changing Face of the Suburbs*, ed. Barry Schwartz (Chicago: University of Chicago Press, 1976), 309, and *John Cheever: A Biography* (New York: Random House, 1988), 170.

11. John Cheever, "The Trouble of Marcie Flint," *The Housebreaker of Shady Hill and Other Stories* (New York: Harper & Brothers, 1958), 165, 167, 185.

12. Cheever, "The Housebreaker of Shady Hill," *Shady Hill*, 12.

13. Cheever, "Marcie Flint," *Shady Hill*, 166–7.

14. John Callaway, interview with John Cheever, 15 Oct. 1981, *Conversations with John Cheever*, ed. Scott Donaldson (Jackson: University Press of Mississippi, 1987), 245.

15. [John Updike], "Notes and Comment: The Talk of the Town," *New Yorker* 58 (12 July 1982): 27–8.

16. Cheever, "The Worm in the Apple," *Shady Hill*, 107–12.

17. John Cheever, *Bullet Park* (New York: Knopf, 1969), 245.

18. Robert Coles, *The Call of Stories: Teaching and the Moral Imagination* (Boston: Houghton Mifflin, 1989), 151.

19. Financially, the story worked out well for Cheever, too. MGM bought film rights for $40,000; the money enabled the Cheever family to spend a year in Italy.

20. Cheever, "O Youth and Beauty!" *Shady Hill*, 35–6.

21. Cheever, "The Sorrows of Gin," *Shady Hill*, 96–8.

22. Cheever, "The Five-Forty-Eight," *Shady Hill*, 121–2. This story won the University of Illinois Benjamin Franklin Magazine Award for the best short story of 1954.

23. Quoted in Waterman, 33.

24. Cheever, "The Death of Justina," *Stories*, 433.

25. Nabokov, 32.

26. The inappropriateness of Weed's name to his place of residence is noted by Robert A. Morace, "John Cheever," *Dictionary of Literary Biography*, vol. 2: "American Novelists Since World War II" (Detroit: Gale Research, 1978), 91.

27. R. G. Collins, "Fugitive Time: Dissolving Experience in the Later Fiction of Cheever," *Studies in American Fiction* 12 (Autumn 1984): 175.

28. Quoted in Robert Gutwillig, "Dim Views Through Fog," *New York Times Book Review*, 13 November 1960, 68.

29. Joan Didion, "A Celebration of Life," *National Review* 10 (22 April 1961): 255.

John Updike's Olinger Stories:
New Light Among the Shadows

ROBERT M. LUSCHER

In his essay "Why Write?" John Updike recounts a childhood pastime that involved drawing assorted objects on a sheet of paper and then connecting them with lines "so that they all became the fruit of a single impossible tree." Such an activity, Updike continues, may be "as deep . . . as the urge to hear a story from beginning to end, or the little ecstasy of extracting resemblances from different things"; both playful and artistic, this childhood pleasure recurs when he fashions "several disparate incidents or impressions into the shape of a single story."[1] Essential to creativity, the connecting impulse not only recalls childhood happiness but also produces meaningful fictional patterns that link past and present, a central concern in Updike's writing, especially at the time *Olinger Stories* was published. As his fictional locale undergoes a shift from the rural Olinger of his youth to suburban Tarbox, the search for continuity in, and connection with, a receding past assumes increasing thematic importance and achieves formal realization in the gathering of the Olinger stories into a single volume whose composite structure reflects the splintered recall of the past as well as the attempt to fashion a new order that counters time's erosion.

Updike's description of the connective or pattern-making faculty relates to the complementary forces that unite all works of fiction: linear or diachronic unity – the force behind narrative continuity – and associative or synchronic unity, a looser but still powerful mode of coherence. The connecting impulse, of course, is not confined to the single story; it manifests itself in longer narratives as well, especially the short story sequence, an increasingly popular intermediate form between the novel and the miscellaneous collection that Updike employs in four volumes of short fiction: *Olinger Stories: A Selection* (1964); *Bech: A Book* (1970); *Too Far to Go: The Maples Stories* (1979); and *Bech Is Back* (1982). Although the thematic rationale for the form differs in these collections, they all depict discontinuous lives in which the forces creating separation – from the past, from one's spouse, or from creativity – exist in a dynamic tension with the continued struggle for reintegration.

This modern conflict finds its structural analogue in the short story sequence, a paradoxical form composed of independent narrative units in which both synchronic and diachronic aspects of the connecting impulse work to overcome the separateness of its components. Unlike the novel, whose narrative impetus subordinates its chapters to the dictates of plot, the story sequence is characterized by a more even balance between linear progression and associative links. The main lines uniting the independent fictions into a continuous, developing sequence are drawn when the author assembles the volume's stories. Yet the reader's perception of the work's overall pattern, less rigid than a novel's causal and temporal narrative spine, ultimately provides the unifying framework that works against the grain of discontinuity. Across the gaps created by the closure of each story, a more intricate set of connections can emerge from the "little ecstasies" the reader successively experiences weaving the volume together with a complex network of crossreferences arising from the interplay between recurrent images, characters, settings, and themes. Although any short story collection by a single author remains open to perceptions of intertextuality, story sequences such as Updike's possess a greater degree of intertextual resonance; furthermore, more miscellaneous volumes usually lack an overall pattern.

Whereas the Bech books and the Maples stories are predominantly unified by their focus on a recurrent central protagonist, *Olinger Stories* is more loosely held together by setting and by a composite protagonist. These other volumes may thus bear greater formal resemblance to the novel, although they never achieve – nor were meant to achieve – "novelhood." Over the course of *Too Far to Go*, the Maples are pulled apart and brought together numerous times by the forces of love, habit, time, and boredom; as Updike remarks in the book's introduction, "The musical pattern, the advance and retreat, of the Maples' duet is repeated over and over again, ever more harshly transposed." [2] For his first Bech volume, Updike purposefully chose the nondescript label "Book," to discourage expectations of novelistic unity:

> It began as a single story which was quite successful and it almost seemed to call out for the kind of "redux" I later gave Rabbit. . . . The last couple of stories in Bech were written, of course, with a book in mind. They were composed to round out – "fill in" might be a better term – the book as such, but basically Bech is a set of short stories, not a novel. . . . The whole texture of the book was that of short stories. [3]

While presenting further exploits of the protagonist, each Bech story retains its separate identity, providing a different texture from a novel with chapters that develop a relatively unbroken ongoing narrative. The composing process Updike describes also highlights the distinction between this "book" and a novel. He has stated that his novels are written with a loose rein but progress steadily toward some resolution: "an echo and a kind of click at the end."[4] Although the first Bech volume concludes with Bech entering a literary version of heaven (the writer's academy), its fitful development is merely rounded out by this final story; the gaps and discontinuities provided by each subsequent story's closure ultimately undercut the novelistic closure Updike describes.

Bech: A Book falls neatly into the last of Forrest Ingram's three categories of story sequences, each governed by a different compositional process: "Linked stories may have been *composed* as a continuous whole, or *arranged* into a series, or *completed* to form a set."[5] *Olinger Stories* comes closest to being an arranged sequence, since ten of the eleven stories have been culled from previous collections. Yet the addition of an explanatory foreword and the previously uncollected "In Football Season" as the concluding story suggests that *Olinger Stories* was to some degree completed. Furthermore, since Updike himself recognizes in his Pennsylvania fiction "a kind of running, oblique coherence,"[6] the collection's connective links may manifest an implied, but never formally acknowledged, compositional purpose – an Olinger "redux." Updike's recycling of two character names may signal an underlying coherence, but his choice not to rename the others when the stories were gathered maintains the separateness of the protagonist's various incarnations, thus creating a patchwork portrait while at the same time universalizing the experience.

Whatever creative strategies the author employs, the short story sequence's fundamental unity depends on the number and types of strategies that create coherence. However, because *Olinger Stories* gathers work published in previous collections, it is usually dismissed as an anthology – often omitted altogether from reviews of Updike's career – and seldom discussed independently or in depth.[7] Yet *Olinger Stories* is much more than a miscellany of twice-told tales that happen to concern the same place. Nor is it a set of stories assembled because their author is obsessed with his own autobiography – a common criticism of Updike's fiction.[8] Its variety and loose coherence make this early work an excellent illustration of how an author may exploit the story sequence's connections to create a volume that is much more than the sum of its parts.

Both the sense of place and the repeated character type – a maturing "local boy," as Updike calls him[9] – raise the volume beyond anthology status to a unique aesthetic whole that unfolds progressively and provides ample opportunity for harmonizing the stories with the connecting impulse Updike recognizes as crucial in the kindred endeavors of art and play.

Initially, however, Updike expressed reservations about creating a volume of previously published Olinger stories:

> My other collections were still amply for sale, and an anthology derived from them, especially by me, seemed fussy. In the matter of arranging stories, I think the order in which they have been written is the most natural and normally useful. A more pointed arrangement, seeking to reveal some inner consistency, could not help point up inconsistencies of detail. Further, not all of the stories whose spiritual center is Olinger took place there. And further still, the book would be slim. (vi)

Even if Updike originally thought of the volume as an anthology, the process of assembling the stories seems to have produced other ideas that led to an arrangement more creative than one that follows the order of composition. By formally assembling all but one of his Pennsylvania stories ("Home" is omitted), Updike brings out their implicit unity, characterized by Sanford Schwartz as "one long tale of a provincial teacher's son ... who grows up knowing that he will never be a true prince. . . . What he settles for is a priestly, in-between role."[10] As the saga of a "priestly" artist's departure and imaginative return, the story sequence can thus include stories set elsewhere that hark back to Olinger and attempt to mediate between past and present.

As Updike admits, autobiography may indeed be the "submerged thread" that unites a number of his works,[11] but more essential to the unity of *Olinger Stories* are the fictive strategies that weave the volume together – of which setting may be the most important. Updike's hometown of Shillington – the subject of such "barefaced reminiscence" as his memoir "The Dogwood Tree" – and Olinger, which more closely resembles "a town in a fable" (190) are undeniably related, but Olinger is ultimately the fictive ground of imagined pasts contemporaneous with his own. Olinger, Updike explains in his foreword, is "audibly a shadow" of the real Shillington (v), one whose very name emphasizes the town's call to linger. Like the shadow of the dogwood tree mentioned in his memoir, Olinger remains fixed in his narrator's memories, a dark shadow ready for retrospective illumination. For both Updike and the narrators of the volume's later stories, Olinger reinvokes a distant and somewhat idealized time and place, raised to a symbolic dimension.

Contrasting the fictional Olinger of his early short stories with his hometown, Updike states: "Shillington is a place on the map and belongs to the world; Olinger is a state of mind, of my mind, and belongs entirely to me" (v). Though striking a proprietary note, Updike's corrective distinction between reality and the art it inspires warns the autobiographical critic against formulating simple correspondences between the two. It also provides a clue to the volume's unity: In *Olinger Stories*, Updike maps out an emotional and intellectual state allied with a particularized, recurrent fictional setting. In contrast, *The Centaur*, Updike's Olinger novel, delineates a place in which the underlying mythic dimension overtly blends with a realistic narrative to emphasize the heroic struggle inherent in daily living. In the novel, Olinger is turned "explicitly into Olympus"; however, in the Olinger stories, the town is realistic on the surface but assumes the fabulist's qualities of a personal myth. Olinger in many ways resembles William Faulkner's Yoknapatawpha County, that postage stamp of soil of which its creator is "sole owner and proprietor." Yet although Faulkner continued to populate his fictional county, Updike has departed fictionally from Olinger, leaving it as a point of reference for his later fiction – one of the "stages in my pilgrim's progress, not spots on the map." [12]

On one level, *Olinger Stories* memorializes the past, but its form differs radically from Updike's other attempts to use his early experience as a point of departure for fiction. His initial extended treatment of his Pennsylvania youth turned into a six-hundred-page manuscript entitled "Home," which Updike called "good exercise" but then abandoned. [13] His first novel, *The Poorhouse Fair*, though inspired by the razing of a decaying poorhouse near his hometown, is a memorial gesture of a different sort, involving older characters and a vaguely futuristic New Jersey setting. Though the subsequent novels, *Rabbit, Run* and *The Centaur*, are set in Pennsylvania, they trace the life of characters enmeshed in the compromises that maturity and responsibility involve. Only in the Olinger stories, independently but steadily composed from 1954 to 1962, does Updike directly explore the source of youthful memories that evoke the constant wish to return to a simpler time and to reconstruct the small town as the spiritual center essential in shaping an artistic consciousness similar to his own.

In *Olinger Stories*, the discontinuity of the short story sequence emphasizes the fragmentary nature of the attempt to recall the past, yet Updike's assembly of disparate lives into a prototypical saga of maturation illustrates that a coherent order can be rescued. Each character in the early stories struggles in isolation to transcend Olinger; after that feat is accomplished, those now outside strain to connect themselves anew to that halcyon rural past. The literary and spiritual kinship that emerges between these protagonists when their stories become one story suggests a further connectedness that they themselves do not perceive. Thus, *Olinger Stories* fosters reader awareness of the opposition inherent in the modern consciousness: the divisions between humans separated from their origins and the yearning to transcend these distances and reestablish connection, despite a persistent awareness of fragmentation.

Retracing the transitional segment of the local boy's life produces a string of disjunct but related events, which is, the form suggests, perhaps the only way the past can be truly apprehended in an era of rapid social change. The volume begins with more traditional epiphanic stories, which are appropriate to Olinger's accessibility and unexpected gifts, but concludes with different forms – the montage and the lyric – which indicate the need for a new vision adequate for recovery of the receding past. Such a shift reflects the change Gordon Weaver sketches in the short story form during the modern era:

> As traditional social structures and attitudes crumble, as moral defini-
> tions are challenged by the hard realities of American experience in the
> aftermath of World War II, forms alter to accommodate new visions or
> old ones in a state of flux. The neat sequence of chronological narration
> gives way to fragmentation and distortion; the rounded depiction of mi-
> lieu and character is reduced to a narrow – though no less telling – slice
> or a vague presence."[14]

The protagonist's movement from Olinger coincides with this era of crumbling social structures and moral definitions in flux. Once he leaves Olinger, he nostalgically yearns for its simplicity and protectiveness, yet in his unsheltered condition he is forced to discover new modes of perception that – although fragmentary or narrow – arrest loss. Since most of the volume's stories culminate in an epiphany that caps the experience and creates closure, its overall "story" (in the sense of E. M. Forster's use of the term as implying a noncausal series of events) unfolds erratically. Although *Olinger Stories* is arranged in chronological order, this chronicle of a prototypical boyhood's significant moments achieves continuity in a nonlinear fashion. As Jerome Klinkowitz observes, the volume cyclically repeats a consistent narrative scheme: "A young, sensitive protagonist is by spatial displacement led into a reordering of personal judgment." [15] The complementary emphases on place and character serve as the fundamental unities of this reimagined past; in addition, a common tone and theme, repeated minor characters, and recurrent motifs (e.g., visions of the abyss) produce coherence. Above all else, Updike's quest in creating *Olinger Stories* is to give the past wholeness, but at the same time to recognize that only fragmentary recall is ultimately possible. As the past continues to recede, the short story becomes one mode of recapturing incidents and rebuilding lyric moments; in the context of the erosion of meaningful patterns, the short story sequence enables the writer to preserve an interconnected whole in a new provisional order whose discontinuous form recognizes the reality of fragmentation even as it seeks to overcome it. Although finally a piecemeal recovery, the short story sequence asserts the possibility of rediscovered and new connections; when these discrete incidents are juxtaposed, their tension produces new light among the shadows of the past.

Although the volume's foreword could be mistaken for a justification, its most important function is to orient the reader geographically and thus set the stage for the reader's assembly of the related characters' lives. Although the details Updike presents here and within the stories themselves lend Olinger verisimilitude, he also cloaks the town in mystery and universality. Like the preface to *The Scarlet Letter,* Updike's foreword places the subsequent action midway between the actual and imaginary, on a proverbial middle ground: "The town is neither young nor old, poor nor rich, backward nor forward. It is beyond the western edge of Megalopolis, and hangs between its shallow hills enchanted, nowhere, anywhere" (viii). Though easily located on a fictional map and characterized by concrete details such as its box factory and small hosiery mill, Olinger nonetheless retains a mythic and universal aura.

As Robert Nadon argues, Olinger embodies "a literal and figurative middle ground" between the rural and urban milieux that surround it. [16] Not a pastoral Eden, it is nonetheless more recently closer to that condition than larger cities, "haunted – hexed, perhaps – by rural memories" (viii), Updike notes. Olinger is already at least at one remove from pure innocence; most often it is portrayed as a simpler essence, balancing contrary forces rather than embodying a pure state. Still, "there's a kind of magic that is very hard to attach to later impressions that you voluntarily attach to the first one," Updike remarks. "The world is more wonderful to you. The people look bigger. The smells are sharper. The sights are more vivid. Also a child sees a relatively unguarded world. The things around him aren't defending themselves against him."[17] The youth in Olinger has an easy relationship with the material world, an open door that closes gradually as he matures.

Although Olinger may be taken for granted as "simply the world" by Updike's younger characters, in retrospect it gains a special quality as a time of "incoherent generosity" (vii), a source of self-consciousness, and a crucial stage in character formation. As Shillington did for Updike, Olinger stands as "the calm point that in [his] subjective geography is still the center of the world"[18] for his protagonist. However, what Olinger *becomes* for the local boy is perhaps more important than what it actually was to him; as in Sherwood Anderson's *Winesburg, Ohio*, the town becomes a background on which to paint his dreams and reestablish connection with a receding past.

Anderson's short story sequence, on which Updike wrote an essay in 1984, is perhaps the volume closest in spirit to *Olinger Stories*. Both volumes not only form a loose bildungsroman but also share a concern with the effect of place on character. This basic "topographical unity," as Valerie Shaw terms it, creating as it does an inclusive sense of realism, embodies "a tendency which persisted throughout the nineteenth century and into the twentieth."[19] *Winesburg* is the successor to unified regional collections such as Garland's *Main-Travelled Roads* and Jewett's *The Country of the Pointed Firs* and forerunner of such story sequences as Hemingway's *In Our Time*, Steinbeck's *The Pastures of Heaven*, Faulkner's *Go Down, Moses*, Welty's *The Golden Apples*, and Updike's *Olinger Stories*. In these works, spatial unity displaces causal and temporal unity as the basic principle of organization. In addition, place becomes more than a common stage for the action; like a recurrent character, it interacts with and influences characters' lives. Updike observes that Anderson's "wide-eyed eagerness" opened Michigan to Hemingway and Mississippi to Faulkner;[20] less directly, but in both a spiritual and a formal sense, perhaps Anderson opened Pennsylvania to Updike.

Updike's canvas is less expansive than Anderson's, yet both works examine small-town life in transitional eras, somewhat wistfully but with a critical eye unclouded by pure nostalgia. As Updike notes in "Twisted Apples," "*Winesburg, Ohio* describes the human condition only insofar as unfulfillment and restlessness – a nagging sense that real life is elsewhere – are intrinsically part of it."[21] Although the early local boys in Olinger are likewise bothered by similar doubts, the older characters, seeing the past recede, suspect that "real life" may have bypassed them, leaving its residue in memories of Olinger; like *Winesburg*'s narrator, the narrators of the last three Olinger stories comb the past to rediscover the "nagging beauty [that] lives amid this tame desolation."[22]

Both story sequences involve departure and retrospection, but with a crucial difference: *Winesburg,* an extended backward glance at many related lives, culminates in George's departure, whereas the "local boy" of Olinger, incarnated as John Nordholm, departs physically just past the collection's midpoint. Still, both works testify that their authors and departing characters never truly leave the past behind. Winesburg's grotesques, as Updike notes, "seem one enveloping personality"; in a similar but less consistently repeated pattern, the parents in *Olinger Stories,* destined to remain in or near Olinger, represent the potential entrapment that the young artist will escape.

For Updike, *Olinger Stories* becomes a "ceremony of farewell" similar to the final drive David Kern makes in the segment "A Traded Car" of the volume's penultimate story. Updike has stated his determination "to leave the state [of Pennsylvania] fictionally" after *Of the Farm,*[23] a novel set not in Olinger but in nearby Firetown; in that novel, a visit to the Olinger supermarket is the only incursion into the fictional realm that becomes, for its author, "a closed book" when *Olinger Stories* is assembled:

> [My doubts] succumbed to the hope that a concentration of certain images might generate new light, or at least focus more sharply the light already there. . . . I bind these stories together as one ties up a packet of love letters that have been returned. Olinger has receded from me. Composition, in crystallizing memory, displaces it, and the town and the time it localizes have been consumed by the stories bound here. Not an autobiography, they have made one impossible . . . , and I offer this book in the faith that it is a closed book. (vi)

Even though Updike has not rewritten the history of Olinger, he has, by binding his semiautobiographical "love letters" into a sequence that traces a local boy's maturation and nostalgic returns to Olinger, created a volume that offers readers a new aesthetic experience. For Updike, *Olinger Stories* may be a closed book; for his readers, however, it opens new possibilities for discovering light among the shadows of his previous fiction.

In his foreword, Updike guides the reader toward yet another significant connection: the unifying central theme. In the conclusion to "Packed Dirt," David Kern, when asked about the point of his stories, flatly replies "I don't know. . . . I wish I did" (171). Updike, in contrast, responding to a query about "the point" of "Friends from Philadelphia," states: "The point to me is plain, and that is the point, more or less, of all the Olinger stories. *We are rewarded unexpectedly.* The muddled and inconsequent surface of things now and then parts to yield us a gift" (vii). In retrospect, Updike discerns (as Kern finally does as well) a thematic thread that unites his distinct imaginings: Olinger is the realm of grace. Although this theme is not slavishly repeated in every story, an epiphanic access to the world is characteristic of the early stories, though not every gift the world offers is an unmixed blessing. Often these gifts either frustrate the characters or, in their ambivalence, sow the seeds of maturity that will push the local boy forever from the relative innocence and accessibility that Olinger seems to embody.

This theme of unexpected rewards is also pertinent to the volume's form. In their new aesthetic contexts, the stories provide the reader with moments when the narrative surface of a particular story parts to reveal a connection with an image or incident at some other point in the sequence. The recognition of such surprising coherence provides insights about the work's aesthetic wholeness that resemble the unexpected rewards Updike's characters experience. For instance, Updike's discovery that "the boy who wrestles with H. G. Wells and murders pigeons is younger than the one who tells Thelma Lutz she shouldn't pluck her eyebrows" yields the insight that "we age unevenly, more slowly in society than in our own skulls" (ix). Thus the mere arrangement can give rise to unexpected insights into character development. Furthermore, Updike's realization that "optically bothered Clyde Behn seems to me a late refraction of that child Ben who flees the carnival with 'tinted globes confusing his eyelashes'" (ix) draws an imagistic similarity that provides continuity between stories. Thematically, this connection suggests the cyclical nature of life's confusion; the context of the action differs, but such similarities depict the ongoing struggle for clear vision. In connecting these incidents, Updike becomes his own ideal reader, associative faculties bristling with attention, indicating how the collection should be read.

Although the Olinger stories possess a common theme and other interconnections that provide coherence, their sequential arrangement is the basis of their dynamic unity. Since Updike chose not to revise in creating this loose bildungsroman, there are some obvious constraints on the order, such as the protagonist's age. The stories (relative order of composition noted in parentheses) fall into roughly three groups: first, stories of early youth and adolescence: "You'll Never Know Dear" (8), "The Alligators" (2), "Pigeon Feathers" (7), and "Friends from Philadelphia" (1); second, stories of impending departure: "Flight" (5), "A Sense of Shelter" (6), and "The Happiest I've Been" (3); and third, returns, both physical – "The Persistence of Desire" (4) – and imaginative, in first-person retrospective narrations that blend past and present: "The Blessed Man of Boston, My Grandmother's Thimble, and Fanning Island" (9), "Packed Dirt, Churchgoing, A Dying Cat, A Traded Car" (10), and "In Football Season" (11).

Since Updike arranged his first two collections in order of composition, his reorderings are easily noted: In the first group, he alternates two stories from *Pigeon Feathers* with two earlier ones from *The Same Door* so that the stories progress from simple rejection to more self-consciously managed crises; in the second group, the oldest character, John Nordholm in "The Happiest I've Been," was Updike's earliest, and the stories set at Olinger High were written later; the last group retains the order of composition, showing Updike, like his narrators, further from the past. Overall, the arrangement finally approximates the contours of a maturation that sometimes dips rather than rises steadily. Also evident is an increasing complexity of vision as the local boy becomes an outsider peering in, knowing that each successive journey into the past (in the form of such stories) contains a certain indulgence and costs more as he matures, but affirming that the hard-earned reward – the capture of fleeting memories – is worth the cost it takes to preserve them.

In the first story, "You'll Never Know, Dear, How Much I Love You," ten-year-old Ben's attempt to lose his fifty cents at the local carnival calls forth Olinger's inherent protectiveness. Ben's excitement dissipates quickly when he sees through the commercial facade; nonetheless, he wants to become this world's willing victim. His innocence becomes a commodity to be spent; like the fifty-cent piece, it "must be broken, shattered into tinkling fragments, to merge in the tinsel and splinters of strewn straw" (5). Losing his money, Ben feels, would allow him "to sail away like a dandelion seed" from a world that may conceal "a treacherous stratum under this mud and straw" (6). Such metaphors of flight and hidden horror will be echoed in other Olinger stories, though Ben's fleeting perception does not disturb him greatly during his attempt to escape the enchanted circle of childhood. Yet when the carnival operator returns Ben's money – minus a dime – Ben cannot accept this partial return as the price of his lesson; the lost dime becomes "a tiny hole through which everything in existence i[s] draining" (8), and Ben makes a confused retreat. He wants the world to play by his rules: to be either glamorous or corrupt, not ambivalent. Ironically, the returned money represents the unexpected reward of a protective, loving summer world – the one for which those beyond Olinger will yearn.

The protagonist in the first two stories, Updike states, is "a pure Olinger child" (ix), though the locale is not explicitly named until "The Alligators," in which young Charlie's romantic disappointment is juxtaposed with the first story's concluding lesson: "Thus the world, like a bitter coquette, spurns our attempt to give ourselves to her wholly" (9). Like Ben, Charlie wishes to enter a closed world, but he too remains an outsider, unable to gain the social acceptance he craves. As pure Olinger children, neither boy is allowed to rise above his world, but both are exposed to experiences that hint at greater ambivalence and disappointment beyond.

In "Pigeon Feathers," physical separation and metaphysical doubt suddenly widen the distance from Olinger for fourteen-year-old David Kern. Such a chronological leap, of course, is one advantage of the story sequence: Already in the volume's third story, the local boy resides a small distance outside of Olinger, still capable of return, although an experience of cosmic dread shakes the foundations of his formerly unquestioned childhood faith. Just as the move has "upset, displaced, rearranged" the Kerns' furniture and routine, reading H. G. Wells's denial of Christ's divinity disturbs David's religious certainty so much that he experiences "an exact vision of death." Qualitatively different from the way Ben feels about his lost dime, this vivid premonition of extinction sends David desperately searching for new supports with which to build a "fortress against death." Neither his mother's pantheism, his father's perfunctory Protestantism, the minister's vague analogies, nor the diversions of Olinger, however, can satisfactorily block David's persistent "invitations to dread."

Only after he kills the pigeons fouling the old Olinger furniture in the barn does David receive an unexpected affirmation from an unlikely source: the dead pigeons, whose intricate beauty "robed him in this certainty: that the God who had lavished such craft upon these worthless birds would not destroy his whole creation by refusing to let David live forever" (50). Despite the leap of faith David makes, we should, as Robert Detweiler suggests, be attentive "to the possible irony in the whole performance."[24] Allen Dow's later reference in "Flight" to the cyclical recurrence of "steep waves of fearing death" (73) about once every three years suggests that David's affirmation of faith is perhaps provisional and will need support as the local boy moves further in time and space from Olinger. Like John Nordholm in the next story, "Friends from Philadelphia," David, despite his apparent sophistication, is only a step or two beyond the pure Olinger child, momentarily triumphant until the next inevitable encounter with ambivalence. When he returns as narrator and mature artist near the volume's end, he cannot rely on unexpected rewards and must take a more active role in shaping the means for countering loss and death.

In the volume's middle stories, separation from Olinger becomes more imminent. Dutiful John Nordholm, who remains immune to adult irony in "Friends from Philadelphia," gives way to Allen Dow, who retrospectively examines a crucial emotional separation from Olinger in "Flight." Struggling with his mother over his local girlfriend, Allen becomes "a bit more of a man but not quite enough," Updike states, and discovers "the irremediable grief in just living, in just going on."[25] This sensitized state represents a plateau none of the local boys has yet achieved, far above Nordholm's unwitting return with the expensive wine or Charlie's mild romantic disappointment in "The Alligators." The volume's next story, "A Sense of Shelter," is an appropriate midpoint: The local boy, poised to leave Olinger, retreats for the last time into a protective shell, harboring illusions of the future he will begin in "The Happiest I've Been." In the latter story, John Nordholm returns as narrator, portraying the "simultaneous sense of loss and recapture" that Updike remarks he experienced when writing the story.[26]

"Home," which depicts the beginnings of reassimilation when the local boy returns from Oxford with wife and child, could have followed "The Happiest I've Been,"[27] but Updike omits it altogether, choosing instead a more striking juxtaposition and a larger gap in time. If Nordholm's prolonged farewell to Olinger represents a high point in the local boy's happiness, then the verbal echo of Clyde Behn's subsequent declaration in "The Persistence of Desire" that "Happiness isn't everything" (132) rationalizes the inability to regain that state. Yet the last third of the volume contains stories showing that such desire does persist, though its satisfaction is elusive and unstable, and a return to the past can raise more discontent than it ultimately satisfies. Clyde's persistent yearning, as Donald Greiner observes, is "misguided because it fails to help him validate his past in order to reaffirm his present."[28] Instead, he attempts to redo his past after seven years of separation, and the concluding epiphany, in which he becomes "a child again in this town, where life was a distant adventure, a rumor, an always imminent joy" (135), appears to be an illusory escape.

More constructive than Clyde's physical return is the process depicted in the next two stories: imaginative linkings of the past with the present in which the narrators dramatize the very process that underlies the assembly of *Olinger Stories*. "The Blessed Man of Boston, My Grandmother's Thimble, Fanning Island" is, Updike claims, a "montage of aborted ideas,"[29] yet such a disclaimer should not undercut the story's status as a unified experimental work. The narrator, a "would-be novelist," fuses a triptych of images from aborted works into a coherent work of another order, much as a short story sequence is created. Most successful in resurrecting details from his grandmother's life, he laments his failure to write a narrative "all set sequentially down with the bald simplicity of intrinsic blessing, thousands upon thousands of pages, ecstatically uneventful, divinely and defiantly dull" (137) – the Proustian equivalent of capturing the pure Olinger state in prose. His desperation is heightened by a modernist consciousness of flux:

> Picking up that thimble . . . I felt at my back that night a steep wave about to break over the world and bury us fathoms down. For I feel the world is ending, that the mounting mass of people will soon make a blackness in which the glint of silver will be obliterated; it is this imminent catastrophe that makes it imperative for me to cry now, in the last second when the cry will have meaning, that there once was a woman whom one of the continents in one of its square miles caused to exist. (148)

This extended meditation, however, does not become a story in its own right but rather a part of a larger tale, woven into a montage much like *Olinger Stories* itself.

Whereas the narrator of "The Blessed Man" is frustrated by his inability to produce exhaustive literary catalogues of halcyon days, David Kern, reappearing as the narrator of "Packed Dirt, Churchgoing, A Dying Cat, A Traded Car", is content with the montage as a way of connecting past and present. Ten years older, with four children, Kern (now a writer) has moved to New England but still looks back to Olinger as his spiritual center. His montage of recollections is a cyclical journey, wearing a new path through the obstructive rubble of adult life with forays into his past. Updike's comments on the story's composition shed further light on his narrator's motives and accomplishments:

> If the story is dense, it is because there was a pressure of memory and worry upon it; as these farflung images collected at my typewriter, a bigger, better kind of music felt to be arising out of the compression. . . . I seemed to understand at last Proust's remark about the essence of the

writer's task being the perception of connections between unlike things. The themes here interwoven – and there is a good deal of conscious art in this farraginous narrative, and more fiction than may meet the eye – had long been present to me: paternity and death, earth and faith and cars. But I had not seized them so directly before.[30]

As distance in time from Olinger increases, so does the "pressure of memory and worry" that spurs the local boy's attempt to counter loss. Yet the connecting impulse and associative memory allow Kern to re-travel past incidents and create a new coherence, one that also weaves together many persistent themes and motifs of *Olinger Stories*. "Packed Dirt" not only harmonizes its four diverse elements but also produces an even "bigger, better kind of music" with echoes of the volume's preceding stories.

Kern's achievement in this story closely resembles that of *Olinger Stories* as a whole. Like "Packed Dirt," *Olinger Stories* is a "farraginous narrative" – composed of a mixture of materials. However, these materials are not confused or jumbled; instead they possess a conscious thematic and imagistic logic. On a smaller and more compressed scale, then, "Packed Dirt" mirrors the structure of the short story sequence, though it seems more composed than arranged, with obvious links, such as the repeated motif of the path, embedded to promote coherence. *Olinger Stories*, on the other hand, like the settlement of Fanning Island in the previous story, relies more on "accidents" as "the generating agency beneath the seemingly achieved surface of things" (151).

All four segments of this story in some way allude to Kern's father or to fatherhood; the final sketch, "A Traded Car," contains what may be his last visit with his sick father. Thus, the story serves as a foil to "Flight," in which Allen Dow attempts to come to terms with the memory of the emotional parting with his mother. Various images of packed dirt, such as the path worn by children's feet that makes Kern "reassured, nostalgically pleased, even . . . proud," also unite the story. Associated with the small town, youth, and the reassertion of human will on the environment, these "unconsciously humanized intervals of clay" evoke his own childhood, "when one communes with dirt down among the legs, as it were, of presiding fatherly presences" (154). The children's instinctive reassertion of a path through the dirt piled by machines is another in the series of unexpected rewards; it stirs memories that establish continuity with his own past and reasserts Olinger's characteristic "repose of grace that is beyond willing" (156).

The second segment, "Churchgoing," is overtly tied to the first when

Kern compares the "creeds and petitions" of the church service to
"paths worn smooth in the raw terrain of our hearts" (156). Faith, as an
avenue linking man with the spiritual, is another path that Kern sometimes finds blocked. Nonetheless, the church itself offers a "hushed shelter . . . like one of those spots worn bare by a softball game in a weed-
filled vacant lot" (159). The verbal echo of an earlier story title suggests
that, like William Young, Kern seeks "A Sense of Shelter," though in
this case it only can be experienced weekly. Churchgoing also evokes
memories of shared experience with his father, who is more involved in
the duties than the mysteries of religion; meanwhile, David's mother
remains home, reading Santayana and Wells without the disturbing
result faced by her son in "Pigeon Feathers." For the older David,
churchgoing functions as a conscious expression of "belief [that] builds
itself unconsciously," like the paths of packed dirt, keeping at bay the
"nihilistic counterpoint beyond the black windows" (158) – the intermit-
tent fear of death that recurs in the last segment of this story. Only
abroad, in a church on a Caribbean island, does he experience any lifting of the spirit – not from the service itself but from a view of the sea.

An observation about receiving "supernatural mail on foreign soil"
provides continuity between "Churchgoing" and "A Dying Cat," which
chronicles the weird coincidence of death and birth. Sent home from
the British hospital during his wife's prolonged labor, Kern humanely
attends to a dying cat, which he initially mistakes for a baby. Like the
dead pigeons in "Pigeon Feathers," the cat seems to relay a message –
"Run on home" – which rings appropriate later in life, when he travels
home to visit his father in the hospital. More of a transitional episode,
this section evokes the repeated themes of death, displacement, and
the return.

The final section, "A Traded Car," chronicles a more significant "ceremony of farewell": the narrator's final trip in his soon-to-be-traded first
car. The car, whose hood is likened to "the thorax of a broad blue baby,"
is symbolically linked with an epoch of his life, and its trading marks a
passage, one that he memorializes through a journey back to his Pennsylvania origins. Confronted with his father's illness and his own dread,
Kern realizes that there is only one answer: "run on home" in a quest
to banish his fear of death, just as Clyde Behn returns to Olinger "to
meet his disconsolate youth" (122) and confront the persistence of desire.

Kern's immersion in the Pennsylvania milieu becomes a temporary
tonic as he journeys south from the bleak New England spring to his
home state's more "authentic spring." Recalling youthful visits to a

nearby museum, he observes that "the world then seemed an intricate wonder displayed for [his] delight with no price asked" (176). Such unguarded accessibility, characteristic of Olinger's "incoherent generosity," has since vanished with maturity and responsibility. In the Alton library, Kern looks in books for date imprints that might indicate when he read them, instead of looking for the books he has written: "They were not me. They were my children, mysterious and self-willed" (175). Although his works in essence guarantee immortality, Kern seeks assurance through continuity with his past. Ultimately, he draws strength from both the locale and his father's apparent truce with death.

Kern's departure recalls a similar one by John Nordholm in "The Happiest I've Been," but his age and the impending car trade make it clear that this is a departure in a new key. In contrast to Nordholm's sunrise departure to Chicago, twilight descends for Kern at the New Jersey border; although he must return north in darkness, he now does so able to face his own dark forebodings. Whereas Nordholm feels a new sense of control at the wheel, because others are trusting him, Kern trusts the car, soon to be part of his past, to guide him back to his present, reconciled to change but conscious of the need for some "ceremony of farewell" to mark the passage. Through his art, he has recaptured the elusive past, clearing a pathway to it that may be traveled perpetually. These montage stories emphasize how the reconstruction of halcyon days by an outsider may produce not a seamless narrative but rather a form that successfully patches together a series of smaller, more focused attempts to assail the same theme.

The volume's coda, "In Football Season," is also a ceremony of farewell, providing the volume with closure that readers might find pessimistic if they are not attentive to the fact that the story itself, as well as the entire volume, has successfully immortalized Olinger in art. The lyric meditation of an outsider, it symmetrically balances the volume's first story, where young Ben seeks access to another realm beyond youthful innocence, unaware that once beyond it he will be haunted by his inability to return. The narrator of this final prose poem, no longer able to find the "air of permission" so pervasive in his youth, nonetheless captures a fragment from that time through sheer verbal art. Although "In Football Season" closes the book on Olinger, its concentration of rich sensory images counters loss, illustrating, as Updike states in his poem "Shillington," that "the having and the leaving go on together."[31]

Updike's sequence celebrates a region and a time when connectedness was stronger than the present, yet it retrospectively studies the impulse toward independence that leads ultimately to fragmentation and the yearning to preserve receding memories. The creation of *Olinger Stories* affirms that art may be one of the last refuges in a modern culture whose pace of change continues to escalate, more rapidly erasing vestiges of the past. In assembling such a sequence of rescued moments from an imagined past, the artist creates a drama about its recapture, colored by nostalgia yet at the same time serving as a ceremony of farewell. Despite the gaps in this reconstruction, a scheme of connection augments the moments of lyric capture, affirming that these now disconnected characters share a common spiritual center. Juxtaposition of the stories thus generates new light among the shadows of the past and affirms a connectedness to a place and an era. As a progressive ceremony of farewell, *Olinger Stories* evokes a concentrated series of significant moments that memorialize the past in a form that is the basis for new connections and retrospective illumination, even as it admits that these moments may be no more than fragments shored against the ruins.

NOTES

1. John Updike, *Picked-Up Pieces* (New York: Knopf, 1975), 34.
2. John Updike, *Too Far to Go: The Maples Stories* (New York: Random House, 1979), 10.
3. Charlie Reilly, "A Conversation with John Updike," *Canto* 3 (1980): 160–1.
4. Alvin P. Sanoff, "Writers 'Are Really Servants of Reality,'" *U.S. News and World Report*, 20 Oct. 1986, 68.
5. Forrest L. Ingram, *Representative Short Story Cycles of the Twentieth Century: Studies in a Literary Genre* (The Hague: Mouton, 1971), 17.
6. Charles Thomas Samuels, "The Art of Fiction XXLIII: John Updike," *Paris Review* 12 (1968): 84–117; repr. *Writers at Work: The Paris Review Interviews, Fourth Series*, ed. George Plimpton (New York: Viking, 1975), 433.
7. Although Donald Greiner, "John Updike," *American Novelists*, ed. James J. Martine, vol. 1, *Contemporary Authors Bibliographical Series* (Detroit: Gale, 1986), 347–8, correctly notes the genre of the Bech books and Maples stories as the "short story cycle" in this recent bibliography on Updike, he fails to accord *Olinger Stories* the same distinction. In his *The Other John Updike: Poems, Short Stories, Prose, Play* (Athens: Ohio University Press, 1981), 130, Greiner does refer to the volume as "the Olinger cycle" in the five pages he devotes to the work; half of this short chapter, however, concerns the final story, "In Football Season."
8. See, for instance Nadine W. Overall, review of *Olinger Stories: A Selection*, by John Updike, *Studies in Short Fiction* 4 (1967), 197, who concludes with the remark that Updike is "still tied to his *ego*-strings."

9. John Updike, *Olinger Stories: A Selection* (New York: Vintage, 1964), v. All subsequent quotations from *Olinger Stories* will be cited in the text by page number.

10. Sanford Schwartz, "Top of the Class," *New York Review of Books,* 24 Nov. 1983, 29.

11. Samuels, 433.

12. Samuels, 432.

13. Eric Rhode, "John Updike Talks to Eric Rhode about the Shapes and Subjects of His Fiction," *Listener* 81 (1969): 861.

14. Gordon Weaver, ed., *The American Short Story, 1945–1980: A Critical History* (Boston: Twayne, 1983), xv.

15. Jerome Klinkowitz, *Literary Subversions: New American Criticism and the Practice of Fiction* (Carbondale: Southern Illinois University Press, 1985), 63–4.

16. Robert Nadon, "Updike's *Olinger Stories:* In the Middle Landscape Tradition," *Perspectives on Contemporary Literature* 5 (1979): 62.

17. Sanoff, 68.

18. John Updike, *Assorted Prose* (New York: Knopf, 1965), 186.

19. Valerie Shaw, *The Short Story: A Critical Introduction* (New York: Longman, 1983), 158.

20. John Updike, "Twisted Apples," *Harper's,* Mar. 1984, 97.

21. Updike, "Twisted Apples," 97.

22. Updike, "Twisted Apples," 97.

23. Lewis Nichols, "Talk with John Updike," *New York Times Book Review,* 7 Apr. 1968, 34.

24. Robert Detweiler, *John Updike,* rev. ed. (Boston: Twayne, 1984), 50.

25. Samuels, 434.

26. John Updike, "The Artist and His Audience," *New York Review of Books,* 18 July 1985, 16.

27. Greiner, *The Other John Updike,* 116, remarks that Robert, the story's protagonist, is "David Kern grown up."

28. Greiner, *The Other John Updike,* 99–100.

29. John Updike, *Hugging the Shore* (New York: Knopf, 1983), 851.

30. Updike, *Hugging the Shore,* 852.

31. John Updike, *Telephone Poles and Other Poems* (New York: Knopf, 1969), 60.

Louise Erdrich's Love Medicine:
Narrative Communities and the Short Story Sequence

HERTHA D. WONG

Louise Erdrich's *Love Medicine* (1984)[1] is most often classified as a novel. In fact, if we have any doubts about its genre, the title page informs us: "*Love Medicine*. A Novel by Louise Erdrich." When asked what they thought about the fact that some reviewers of the "novel" insisted on labeling it a "collection of short stories," Erdrich and her husband-collaborator Michael Dorris were not particularly interested in the topic. "It's a novel in that it all moves toward some sort of resolution," explained Erdrich. "It has a large vision that no one of the stories approaches," added Dorris.[2] In addition, even though half of the fourteen chapters of the first edition had been published previously as short stories in literary journals or popular magazines,[3] Erdrich and Dorris insisted that they had adapted these individual stories significantly in order to create, extend, or enhance thematic, structural, and other literary connections. Erdrich, who describes herself as "a person who thought in terms of stories and poems and short things," credits Dorris's influence for how the "book became a novel."[4] "By the time readers get half way through the book," noted Dorris, "it should be clear to them that this is not an unrelated, or even a related, set of short stories, but parts of a larger scheme" (Wong, 212). Length, an expansive vision, and some sense of unity seem to inform their notion of what constitutes a novel.

It was surprising, then, to find little difference between the chapters of *Love Medicine* and the short stories published earlier. At least two of the seven published short stories, "Love Medicine" (which becomes the "Flesh and Blood" chapter in *Love Medicine*) and "Lulu's Boys," were essentially the same as they appeared in the novel, except no narrators or dates were announced as they are at the beginning of each chapter in the collection. In fact, added to two of the story titles, very likely by an editor, was the descriptive label: "a short story." Similarly, "Saint Marie" had only minor syntactic and word changes, but everything else was the same. In "Scales" the editing was more extensive, but still not substantial. In addition to minor alterations in word choice, phrasing, and punctuation, Dot's five-month pregnancy became a six-month pregnancy, and her baby boy was transformed into a baby girl. Although the gender switch is dramatic, it does nothing to unify the narratives in *Love Medicine*. Why, then, does Dorris say that at first they were "a series of stories," but in "the last several drafts we went back and tied them together" (Coltelli, 43)? The distinction between a collection of short stories and a novel remains somewhat elusive.

Certainly novels appeal to a larger market and generate greater prestige than short stories or poems. Perhaps the Erdrich–Dorris revisions refer simply to a Jamesian type of reenvisioning. Placing the short stories between the covers of a book encourages the reader to note their juxtaposition, association, and overall relation to one another. But what narrative theorists, particularly those focusing on the difficult-to-define "short story," have been postulating about *collections* of short stories complicates definitive notions of the genre and provides another vocabulary for this discussion. *Love Medicine* is neither a novel, if by novel we insist on a continuous and unified narrative, nor a collection of unrelated short stories. Nor is it a "short story composite," a "short story compound," or even an "integrated short story collection" since these definitions emphasize the autonomy of each story within a collection more than the particular dynamism created by their organization and juxtaposition.[5] The series of narratives in *Love Medicine* may very well be, though, what Forrest Ingram refers to as a "short story cycle" or what Robert Luscher calls "the short story sequence."

A short story cycle, explains Ingram, is "a set of short stories linked to each other in such a way as to maintain balance between the individuality of each of the stories and the necessities of the larger unit." In addition, the reader's experience of each story is modified by the experience of all the others. Ingram proposes a narrative spectrum with the "collection of unconnected stories" on one end, the novel on the other end, and the short story cycle balanced between them. Outlining the parameters of the short story cycle itself, Ingram delineates three basic types: a *composed* cycle (the most tightly structured), a series of linked stories "conceived as a whole from the time" of the "first story"; an *arranged* cycle (the most loosely structured), stories "brought together to illuminate or comment upon one another by juxtaposition and association"; and a *completed* cycle, stories formed into a set by adding, revising, and rearranging them.[6] Within Ingram's tripartite categories (problematically organized according to the process of composition, as J. Gerald

Kennedy notes), *Love Medicine* most closely resembles a completed cycle because Erdrich and Dorris neither planned the whole narrative network from the first story nor simply assembled and arranged a collection of stories, but added new stories and at least slightly revised earlier ones.

Whereas Ingram's framework highlights *Love Medicine*'s construction, Luscher's notion of "the short story sequence" may more fully delineate its structure, both the form constructed by the writer and that structure experienced (or co-created) by the reader. According to Luscher, "the short story sequence" is "a volume of stories, collected and organized by their author, in which the reader successively realizes underlying patterns of coherence by continual modifications of his [or her] perceptions of pattern and theme." Thus the reader becomes aware of "a network of associations that binds the stories together and lends them cumulative thematic impact."[7] Although it seems that similar claims can be made for chapters in a novel (and the reader's sequential experience of reading them), the distinction is that, unlike the chapters in a novel, each narrative unit can stand on its own. Its meaning is modified and enriched, however, in proximity to other stories.

But how can a short story sequence accommodate Native American narratives, which are often associated with a communal narrator and a nonlinear sense of time? The notion of a sequence assumes or imposes linearity on the inherent nonlinearity of multivoiced, achronological narrative. With no singular point of view or authoritative narrative voice to unify a collection of short stories, without a straightforward chronology to connect the narrative action over time, a sequence may not reflect the structure of many Native American short story clusters as precisely as it charts the experience of reading the collection, one story following another. The image of a web or a constellation of short stories[8] might more accurately reflect the cyclical and recursive nature of stories that are informed by both modernist literary strategies (for instance, multiple narrative voices) and oral traditions (such as a storyteller's use of repetition, recurrent development, and associational structure).

In numerous Native American oral traditions, the spider's web is a common image to convey the interconnectedness of all aspects of life. Just as one individual filament cannot be touched without sending vibrations throughout the entire network, one story, although it can be read in isolation from the others, cannot be fully comprehended without considering its connection to the others. Such an interrelationship is fundamental to oral traditions where a storyteller and an audience create a community, a "web of responsibility," as Henry Glassie calls it.[9] Many scholars have lamented (or at least noted) the loss of the intimacy of direct human contact when stories moved from storyteller to text, from voice to print, from cycle to sequence, from interactive to isolated experience. But many Native American writers have been engaged in a counter movement, recreating the spoken word in written form, suggesting (even rekindling) a relationship between writer/teller and reader/listener, and restoring voice to their histories and communities. In particular, Erdrich's story sequences chronicle the centrality of one's relationships, tenuous though they may be, with one's land, community, and family; and the power of these relationships, enlivened by memory and imagination and shaped into narrative, to resist colonial domination and cultural loss and to (re)construct personal identity and communal history on one's own terms.

The novel, in its construction of a multivocal unity from various modes of discourse, may be the fundamental expression of the pluralism embedded in language as Bakhtin suggests, but Native American oral traditions have long reflected such inherent polyvocality. Paula Gunn Allen has noted that many Native American traditional literatures have "the tendency to distribute value evenly among various elements," reflecting an "egalitarian," rather than a hierarchical, organization of society and literature. In such a narrative structure, "no single element is foregrounded."[10] This organization is particularly notable in *Love Medicine,* whose multiple narrators confound conventional Western expectations of an autonomous protagonist, a dominant narrative voice, and a consistently chronological linear narrative. In some indigenous oral traditions, "the presence in narratives of regularly occurring elements that are structured in definable, regularly occurring ways, employed to culturally defined ends and effects" is what determines a work's category.[11] That is, variable, but measured repetition of narrative features (in a specific cultural context), not chronology, character development, or a narrative voice (for a general reader) is what may sometimes shape a story type. But if we insist, for instance, on isolating a protagonist in *Love Medicine,* it would most likely be the community itself. For many Native American writers such a collective protagonist does not reflect fragmentation, alienation, or deterioration of an individual voice, as is often suggested by modernist and postmodernist explanations, but the traditional importance of the communal over the individual, the polyphonous over the monovocal.

Although nineteenth-century American and British novelists often experimented with multiple plots, they rarely expanded point of view, tending instead to unify the narrative action from a single narrative voice. With modernism, often associated with the disintegration of communities, and the consequent alienation and fragmentation of individuals, writers fractured multiple plots into multiple narrative voices as well. Such a breakdown, exacerbated for many indigenous people by colonialism, is reflected in some early Native American novels as well, but more in theme than in form. Closer to the detailed description of realism and the narrative fatalism of naturalism, than to the innovation of modernism, D'Arcy McNickle's (Cree/Salish) 1936 novel, *The Surrounded*, incorporated oral storytelling into the Western narrative model of conflict-crisis-resolution (in this case, resolution equalled surrender and destruction).

But particularly since the 1960s Native American writers have emphasized the possibility of reconciliation along with a degree of formal experimentation (most often by combining and juxtaposing Native American and European American traditions). Whereas McNickle used a standard Western singular, omniscient third-person narrator to tell the story of Archilde's alienation, contemporary Native writers often use multiple points of view. But ironically, despite a history of colonialism, Native use of multiple narrators often has little to do with alienation and loss and much more to do with the coherent multiplicity of community. What is experienced as loss of control, a breakdown of unified consciousness, an indeterminacy of language, by many non-Native Americans is a natural reflection of the interplay of difference for many Native people. After 500 years of adaptive survival, Native writers know how to entertain difference without labeling it "Other." The task, as Erdrich describes it, is to "tell the stories of the contemporary survivors while protecting and celebrating the cores of cultures left in the wake of the catastrophe." [12]

NARRATIVE COMMUNITIES AND INTRATEXTUALITY

Although each of the short stories in *Love Medicine* is inextricably interrelated to a network of other stories beyond its covers, the sequence of stories within the book has its own coherence, just as each story has its own integrity. Helen Jaskoski best describes *Love Medicine*'s structure as a "complex series of . . . tales, interlocking through recurrence of character and event and through variation of point of view." [13] The first edition of *Love Medicine* consists of fourteen stories (chapters) (actually fifteen, if you count June's story in the first section of chapter one as a separate short story, that is, as a story that can stand on its own), each narrated by a character in the first person (or, in some cases, several characters) or, less frequently, by a third-person omniscient narrator. A brief overview of the structure will help to clarify the following discussion. In general, the work is organized as the juxtaposed stories of eight narrators: Albertine Johnson, Marie (Lazarre) Kashpaw, Nector Kashpaw, Lulu Lamartine, Lipsha Morrissey, Lyman Lamartine, Howard Kashpaw, and a third-person narrator.[14] No new narrators were added to the 1993 new and expanded edition unless we consider Lulu Nanapush (the young Lulu who becomes Lulu Lamartine) as a new voice. But her voice parallels the young Marie Lazarre (who becomes Marie Kashpaw), highlighting the proliferation of subject positions (in this case, identities at different stages) as well as voices. (See Outline for an overview of narrative voices in *Love Medicine*.) Throughout the work these narrators and their unique voices, perspectives, and uses of language convey surprising revelations about other characters as well as themselves. Their stories, like their lives, are intimately interrelated.

Certainly *Love Medicine* was not designed for the short stories to be read randomly (although with a few exceptions that would be possible). There is clearly an intended narrative sequence, not organized chronologically so much as associationally, even though the book begins in 1981 and ends in 1984. After the first chapter, the action shifts back to 1934 and from there moves progressively up to 1984. Macroscopic unifying aspects of *Love Medicine* include a common setting (the flat, expansive farm and woodlands of North Dakota) and a set of narrators (Albertine, Marie, Nector, Lipsha, Lulu, Lyman, and Howard Kashpaw). On the microscopic or intratextual level, there are numerous connective devices, such as the repetition of the same event narrated from various perspectives, to consider as well. Patterned after spoken, as well as written, narrative voices, the characters tell and retell family and community stories from their particular points of view and in their own unique idioms, reflecting the polyphony of individual, family, and community voices and the subjectivity of personal and communal history.

Often, stories are embedded within stories. Family and community narratives are told and retold from different perspectives throughout the book so that the reader is forced to integrate, interpret, and reinterpret the narrative(s). For instance, Marie's story of how she met Nector on her way down the hill from the convent is juxtaposed to Nector's version of that event in the next section. Similarly, an anecdote about one of

June's childhood escapades (when the children almost hang her) is re-counted several times from varying perspectives. Marie, who balances on her "stool like an oracle on her tripod" in preparation for telling the story, begins: "There was the time someone tried to hang their little cousin."[15] When Zelda and Aurelia jump into the storytelling, the story dimensions shift and sway as they're pulled now from three narrative voices. A fourth is added when the mixed-blood Albertine urges them to move the story ahead: "Then [June] got madder yet . . ." (20) she prompts. Of course, none of these interpretive retellings is exactly the same, and according to Albertine who narrates the entire storytelling session (providing a fifth perspective that organizes the others), the story of June's hanging was at one time "only a family story," but becomes, after her death, "the private trigger of special guilts" (19). Later, in her own words, Marie, June's adoptive mother, tells the story of saving June from hanging, of punishing June for her insolence, and of learning of June's sadness, a deep, untouchable "hurt place" that was "with her all the time like a broke rib that stabbed when she breathed" (68). Often such narratives are told in isolation, each person nurturing his or her own private interpretation of events. Finally, it is only the reader who hears all the stories and can attempt to link them to a larger significance.

In addition to the incremental repetition of personal and community stories from various points of view, several repeated images, water, for example, create a structural connectivity. The recurrent imagery of wa-ter appears most often in the form of rivers (or lakes) and is associated with a series of oppositions: Water can join or separate, cleanse or kill, save or erode. Flood imagery is used to describe Nector's sexual union and emotional release during his affair with Lulu. "I was full of sink-holes, shot with rapids," Nector remembers. "Climbing in her bedroom window, I rose. I was a flood that strained bridges" (100). But water also obstructs. After the violent sexual encounter between Albertine and the troubled Army veteran Henry Junior, the third-person narrator de-scribes the gulf separating them. From Henry's perspective, it seemed "as if she had crossed a deep river and disappeared" (141). The flood of exuberant passion transforms into the river of separation.

As well as uniting or separating, rivers can cleanse or kill. Nector seeks to purify himself of his adulterous affair with Lulu by diving naked into the cold, deep lake, hoping to feel "a clean tug in [his] soul" before he returns home to his wife, Marie (103). But while Nector achieves at least a temporary purification by immersing himself in water, Henry Jr. gains a permanent watery relief from his haunted life. Jumping into the flood-swollen river, Henry Jr. announces calmly, "My boots are filling," before he goes under. Alone on the shore, his brother Lyman, senses "only the water, the sound of it going and running and going and running and running" (154).

Similarly, rivers can save or erode. When Nector poses for the rich white woman who paints a picture of him jumping naked off a cliff "down into a rocky river," he imagines fooling her, letting the current pull him safely to shore (91). But later, just as water erodes rock, time erodes Nector. "Time was rushing around me like water around a big, wet rock," Nector explains. "The only difference is, I was not so durable as stones. Very quickly I would be smoothed away" (94). Such an erosion of self is shared by Marie. When she thinks of "small stones" on "the bottom of the lake, rolled aimless by the waves," she sees "no kindness in how the waves are grinding them smaller and smaller until they finally disappear" (73).

Although not necessarily related to each other, two associated aspects of water imagery appear in the form of fishing and bridges, which, like rivers, serve either to unite or divide. Lipsha's voice is "a steady bridge over a deep black space of sickness" (35); heart-damaged Henry Jr. builds a dangerous and impassable "bridge of knives" (135), trying to impress Albertine with his bar tricks. Whereas Henry lacks a bridge back to a healthy life and ends up committing suicide, Lipsha drives across the bridge to return home.

Whereas bridges are structures built to help us pass from one place or state to another, fishing is a process of acquiring, pulling something back to ourselves. As an old and senile man, Nector fishes for thoughts in the depths of Lake Turcot, while the would-be martyr, Sister Leopolda, fishes for souls, hooking children together like a stringer of fish.[16] Water and its associated imagery, both negative and positive, dominate the book, providing a network of images and references that link character and action.

Although less persistently than water imagery, images of edges and boundaries recur also. Erdrich has described her own perspective as one she remembers developing as a child: lingering unnoticed on the outskirts of a group of grown-ups, hanging on the fringe of conversation. Similarly, Albertine remembers that, unlike other grown-ups, Aunt June never kept her on the "edge of conversation"; Albertine's mother's house is on "the very edge of the reservation"; and many of the characters are on the edges of society. Many characters are not only marginalized in white towns, but sometimes even in their own community. Being a perpetual onlooker (in both Native and non-Native communities) is often the situation of a mixed-blood Indian; and, says Erdrich, it is "the condition of a writer" (Wong, 211) as well. Such multiple marginality is reflected structurally in the proliferation and juxtaposition of individual voices (voices often not speaking or listening to each other) positioned between the covers of *Love Medicine*.

A final connective element is the variable repetition of humor, in this case, humor with a decided edge to it. As William Gleason has stated, "the humor in *Love Medicine* is protean. Laughter leaks from phrase, gesture, incident, situation, and narrative comment" and takes the form of "farce, slapstick, and outright joke-telling" [17] as well as sarcasm, tricksterism, and verbal shenanigans. Some of the humor is *verbal*, often based on malapropisms, such as Lipsha's account of God's deafness: the God who "used to raineth bread from clouds, smite the Phillipines, sling fire down on red-light districts where people got stabbed. He even appeared in person once in a while" (194). Some is *literary*, like Nector's description of the "famous misunderstanding" about *Moby-Dick*. When he explains to his mother that the book was the story of the great white whale, she thinks hard for a while and asks: "What they got to wail about, those whites?" (91)

But almost all of the humor is *political,* indirectly (like the first two examples) or directly, like Nector's description of the rich white woman who wanted him to pose for her painting, *The Plunge of the Brave*. "Remember Custer's saying?" Nector asks. "The only good Indian is a dead Indian? Well, from my dealings with whites I would add to that quote: 'The only interesting Indian is dead or dying by falling backwards off a horse'" (91). Similarly, after a bar fight with a particularly offensive racist, the tricksterish Chippewa[18] "outlaw," Gerry Nanapush, learns: "There is nothing more vengeful and determined in this world than a cowboy with sore balls. . . . He also found out that white people are good witnesses to have on your side, because they have names, addresses, social security numbers, and work phones. But they are terrible witnesses to have against you, almost as bad as having Indians witness for you" (162). Social criticism may be more palatable when it is delivered through humor. But perhaps, more importantly, humor can be a survival strategy or even an act of resistance. Laughing at oppression, "survival humor" as Erdrich calls it (Coltelli, 46), is recognizing and reformulating it on your own terms.

Even though such elements as a common setting, a set of narrators, juxtaposition of perspectives, recurring themes and images, and repeated humor provide an overall interconnectedness, most of the short stories can also function individually. At this point, one brief example will suffice. In the first section of Chapter 1, a third-person narrator tells about June Kashpaw's life in the "oil boomtown Williston, North Dakota," where she looks perpetually for the man who "could be different" this time (3). Here Erdrich introduces the water (in this case, snow) imagery, male–female relationships, Native American–European American interactions, the North Dakota landscape, and the impulse to return home to one's family and community. By the end of the section, "the snow fell deeper that Easter than it had in forty years, but June walked over it like water and came home" (6). The sense of closure (a concept so crucial to short story) seems evident here. June's story ends, albeit somewhat ambiguously, with her death. Death is the ultimate closure (at least from the perspective of an earth-bound body), yet June's death is used as the beginning of the entire series of stories.

The conclusion of this brief story opens the sequence of narratives to come. June's untimely death provides the occasion for the gathering of all the characters, her relatives. In fact, even though June dies on page six, she is what links each of the highly individual characters throughout. All of the characters (with the exception of the child Howard Kashpaw) remember June and define themselves, in some degree, according to their relationship to her. June is Gordie's ex-wife, Marie's unofficially adopted daughter, Albertine's aunt, King and Lipsha's mother, and Gerry's ex-lover. Even though she never narrates a word, June (or at least her memory) is a palpable absence and the most dominant character in the entire work. Just as readers interpret and reinterpret the linked stories, the characters construct and reconstruct June. The beginning also suggests the end. The final story concludes with Lipsha, who like his mother before him, travels across the water to return home.[19]

In fact, the structure of *Love Medicine* (in its original form) is somewhat chiasmic, the first and last stories thematically mirroring each other, the second and thirteenth echoing each other, and so on. Specifically, the first and final stories focus on homecomings, one failed, one successful. Stories two and thirteen both address Marie's spiritual condition: her early desire to be a martyred saint contrasted with her truly saintly behavior in forgiving and helping to heal her life-long rival, Lulu. The third and twelfth stories deal with Nector and Marie's relationship: its beginning when they meet on the hillside and its end as Nector chokes on Lipsha's love medicine meant to restore Nector's love for his wife. Stories four and eleven focus on memories of June: Marie muses about taking in June and Gordie hallucinates about June's return. The fifth and tenth stories share the vaguest connection, but both focus on Lulu's boys. The first introduces them and the latter develops the character of one son, Gerry. Stories six and nine mirror each other more clearly as Nector poses for the painting "The Plunge of the Brave" in one and Henry Jr. literally plunges to his death in the other. Finally, the seventh and eighth stories seem linked by an explosive combination of love and violence. In the first, Marie returns to the convent to see the crazed, would-be saint, Leopolda, and in the second, Albertine leaves home for the big city.

In the new and expanded 1993 edition, the roughly chiasmic structure breaks down. While the first and eighteenth, second and seventeenth, third and sixteenth, fourth and fifteenth, and ninth and tenth stories appear to have clear links, the sixth and thirteenth, seventh and twelfth, and eighth and eleventh do not. The first and final chapters remain the same as those in the 1984 edition; both focus on homecoming. The second and penultimate stories both present characters seeking a "better" life by adapting to colonial impositions, in particular, Catholicism and capitalism. Whereas Marie seeks sainthood by joining a convent fifty years later, Lyman Lamartine seeks wealth by planning to build a gambling casino on Indian land. The third and sixteenth stories are connected tenuously through the central figure of Nector. In the third story, Nector meets Marie (the woman he will marry), and the sixteenth concludes with a scene in which Lyman (Nector's son with Lulu) dances with Marie (Nector's wife) and, in the process, both (re)-connect to the now-deceased Nector. Stories four and fifteen both turn on the difficult relationship between Lulu and Marie. In the former, the young Lulu loses Nector to Marie and, in the latter, after a lifetime of rivalry, Marie assists Lulu. On the surface, stories five and fourteen address Marie's mothering (and to a lesser extent, her own need to be mothered). In the fifth story, Marie tries to form a relationship with her adoptive daughter, June (and, in the second section, gives birth with the help of her mother-in-law); and in the fourteenth, Marie attempts to save her birth son, Gordie, from alcoholism. Finally, stories nine and ten focus on running away. Albertine runs away to a new life in Fargo, and Henry Jr. runs away from a painful life by committing suicide. There is also a development from Henry Jr.'s debilitating war trauma to his self-destruction in the two narratives. As noted above, though, there seem to be few explicit connections between the other paired chapters. Mirrors turn into multiple refractions.

Overall, Erdrich's additions serve several purposes: to more fully develop certain characters (we hear more from Lyman Lamartine, for instance); to introduce new characters (like Rushes Bear who was merely
mentioned in the first edition); to fill in parts of the character's personal
histories (such as learning about Lulu as a young woman returning from
boarding school); to bring some of the characters up to the present of
the book (for example, the elderly Lulu's political activism and Lyman's
plans for Indian-owned gambling are emphasized); to include more
overt reservation politics as well as social commentary about the ongoing effects of over two hundred years of colonial rule (e.g., jobs – or the
lack of them – on the reservation, Indian gambling, alcoholism, poverty,
pressures to "sell out," and Native political activism generally); and to
cross-reference characters and incidents between and among *Love Medicine, The Beet Queen,* and *Tracks* (for example, adding the young Lulu's
voice provides a clear link to her story in *Tracks*). All of these help the
reader understand more about the relationships in *Love Medicine,* but,
more importantly, they help make clearer and more coherent connections to the planned tetralogy of narrative sequences overall. In the 1993
edition, the fact that these stories are "parts of a larger scheme" (Wong,
212) is made even more explicit.

NARRATIVE CONSTELLATIONS AND INTERTEXTUALITY

What I am particularly interested in here is not so much to insist that
Love Medicine is either a short story sequence or cycle rather than a novel,
but to consider how it fits into a network of stories, what we might call,
using Kennedy's image, "a constellation of narratives" – both Native
American and European American, family and community, oral and
written.[20] Just as many of the short stories within the narrative network
of *Love Medicine* shape and reshape themselves in relation to each other,
the work as a whole is part of a larger constellation of stories. "Intertextuality for Indians," claims Paula Gunn Allen, "is use of tradition" (Allen, *Spider,* 17), but these days tradition comes in variety packages. Erdrich retells family, community, and mythical narratives, continuing
traditions of oral storytelling. Family stories are particularly important
since traditionally for the Chippewa, family was seen as "the basic political and economic unit . . . and the primary source of personal identity."[21] "Sitting around listening to our family tell stories," Erdrich has
explained, "has been a more important influence on our work than
literary influences in some ways. These you absorb as a child when

your senses are the most open, when your mind is forming" (Wong, 204). Erdrich's grandmother, grandfather, father, and mother all told stories. But Erdrich has taken special care to note also that "some of [her] father's stories are just indelible" (Wong, 204). Both Chippewa and German-American family narratives, then, have influenced the book.

Even more important than family stories are community narratives, natural extensions of Chippewa familial and clan identity and of identity shaped by a small-town community. In fact, Kathleen Mullen Sands suggests aptly that the root of Erdrich's "storytelling technique is the secular anecdotal narrative process of community gossip." [22] For Erdrich and Dorris, community – with its attendant sense of place (geographical, cultural, and social) and personal identity – are irrevocably linked. "We both grew up in small communities where you were who you were in relation to the community," explained Erdrich. "You knew that whatever you did there were really ripples from it" (Wong, 204–5). Growing up, Erdrich's community included Turtle Mountain Reservation (which she visited) as well as the small town of Wahpeton, North Dakota. She is not recreating a "traditional" Chippewa community in writing as much as she is describing the vexed boundaries between the reservation and white towns. In fact, claims James Stripes, she is "inscribing revisionist histories of the cultural borderlands." [23] It is no accident that family histories, fragmented by the effects of colonialism, are continually retold by community tellers who attempt to reweave the familial, communal, and cultural narratives into a coherent pattern in the present. No one story is more important than any other; but each narrative has special significance for a specific context and listener (both within and outside of the book) and a unique meaning in its proximity to other stories. Each story, like each individual, although complete in itself, is reconnected to the whole through remembering and telling.

As well as family and community stories, Erdrich has incorporated some traditional mythical and contemporary Chippewa (and, to a certain extent, pan-Indian) narratives, characters, and images into her fiction. Nanabozho (variant spellings include Nanabush, Wenebojo, Nanabozho, and Manabozho), the mythical Chippewa Trickster who serves as a creator and culture hero, is one of the most dominant. The family name Nanapush echoes the Trickster's, just as the 250-pound Gerry Nanapush's antics in outwitting the police recall Trickster's mythical and hyperbolic escapades. [24] Another mythical figure is Missepeshu, the Chippewa water monster who is responsible for pulling attractive, young girls to the bottom of the lake.

Just as vital as her adaptations of Chippewa myth is her use of contemporary Native American and mixed-blood history, particularly evident in her stories about the Trickster-like Chippewa political activist Nanapush who spends half his life incarcerated for resisting European American law (which he distinguishes from justice). Nanapush's life, modeled after American Indian Movement (AIM) members, recalls the political activism of the 1970s. Because Erdrich moves "toward the historical novel and the family saga," as Robert Silberman notes, "she is able to touch upon economic and political matters" effectively.[25] Throughout the stories, there are references to political, historical, and legal policies (e.g., the General Allotment Act and the inequity of the U.S. legal system in general) that still shape Native peoples' lives. Similarly, Gordie's alcoholism is an all-too-familiar story in some Indian communities. In "Crown of Thorns," Erdrich deftly links Gordie's spiritual death by [fire]water to Chippewa tradition as the story ends with Gordie "crying like a drowned person, howling in the open fields" (188).

Beyond Chippewa history and oral traditions, Erdrich has been influenced by the Western literary tradition. Although the "entire literary canon" has been an influence, the impact of William Faulkner, whom Erdrich has referred to as that "wonderful storyteller" (Wong, 203), is dramatic and obvious. Like Faulkner's *Go Down, Moses*, for instance, *Love Medicine* emphasizes a collection of characters, often family or extended family members, and their interrelations in a specific community in a particular regional setting. Like Faulkner, Erdrich examines the effects of race, miscegenation, the haunting power of the past, and the ironic intersections of the comic and tragic. Like Faulkner, Erdrich uses multiple narrators who tell their own stories, many of which overlap, confirm, contradict, or extend the others. Although each short story is autonomous, each acquires a new significance in relation to the others. Similarly, like Faulkner's *As I Lay Dying*, *Love Medicine* begins with the death of a central female character, which initiates the actions and memories of the characters and, to a great degree, unifies the narrative sequence.

While Erdrich's fiction may seem like a direct descendent of William Faulkner's, it also arises from a literate tradition of Native American fiction. Both Pauline Johnson (Canadian Mohawk) and Zitkala-Sa (Sioux), also known as Gertrude Simmons Bonnin, for instance, wrote short fiction in which they grappled with the Indian issues of their day. Although *Cogewea, the Half-Blood* (1927) by Mourning Dove (Christine Quintasket), a member of the Colville Confederated Tribes of Washington State, was until recently considered "the first novel written by an American Indian woman," it may really be, as Paula Gunn Allen points out, "a long story composed of a number of short stories" (Allen, *Spider,* 17).[26] The reasons for Mourning Dove's short story format are clear. With little education or money, she had to support herself and her family by working long hours as a migrant laborer or housekeeper. "After backbreaking days in the orchards and fields," explains Jay Miller, the editor of her autobiography, "she would write for most of the night in a tent or cabin."[27] Little education and scant leisure time combined with a cultural familiarity with cycles or series of short narratives (rather than novels) contributed to the production of short stories by this early twentieth-century Native American writer.

Like Mourning Dove, Leslie Marmon Silko (Laguna Pueblo) has struggled with acquiring the "large expanses of time and peace" necessary for writing long fiction.[28] Like Erdrich, she has written novels, but in *Storyteller* she has also combined short narratives from multiple points of view into a story cycle or narrative sequence. But because, unlike *Love Medicine, Storyteller* has not been presented as a novel, the reader feels freer to select a narrative trail through the text, reading a poem here or a story there.[29]

Far from being unusual, then, Erdrich's short story sequence arises from both Native American and European American literary and oral traditions. Her work reflects the activity of many twentieth-century writers who emphasize multiple narrators, recreate oral narratives for the written page and for an expanded readership, and create and maintain community through literary discourse. Women writers of color, in particular, seem to have returned to local roots – family, community, and ethnicity – as sources of personal identity, political change, and creative expression. Telling one's story or the story of one's people as an act of self-definition and cultural continuance is a strong collective impulse. Jay Clayton has noted that the current emphasis on the theme of storytelling in fiction is "related to the emphasis in a postmodern society on local political struggles," rather than to a new conservatism. Storytelling can be "empowering" because it creates community and because stories are all we have to counter the "grand metanarratives" of history.[30]

But although the sequence of short stories in *Love Medicine* is connected to the network of oral and literate narrative traditions noted

above, they are part of another series of stories. In fact, this short story
cluster is one component, manifold though it may be, of a series of narrative sequences. Erdrich and Dorris planned a tetralogy of short story
sequences, the predominant imagery of each focusing on a different natural element. So far, three of the four have been published: *Love Medicine*
(in which the dominant imagery is associated with water), *The Beet Queen*
(air), and *Tracks* (earth). The fourth will focus on fire. Together these
works tell the multivoiced story of several generations of Chippewa,
mixed-blood, and European American relations in North Dakota. *Love
Medicine* (1984 and 1993) tells the story of Chippewa and mixed-blood
families on and near a reservation in North Dakota. Polyphonous community voices narrate the events of fifty years, 1934–84. An assortment
of narrators in *The Beet Queen* (1986) tells a somewhat parallel series of
personal stories from 1932–72, but focuses on European American and
mixed-blood Indian characters in the small town of Argus, North Dakota. In *Tracks* (1988) only two individuals, Nanapush and Pauline, narrate the history of Chippewa and mixed-blood families from 1912–24.
Deciding to write four works was no accident. Four, according to Erdrich "the number of completion in Ojibway mythology" (Wong, 211),
is a sacred number associated with the four cardinal directions, the four
elements, and the four seasons. Erdrich's narrative quartet is like a literary medicine wheel in which the personal, family, community, and
mythical narratives are made whole in precise relation to one another.

PARTICIPATORY NARRATIVE: READERS AND *LOVE MEDICINE*

Because the life of the story outside the text, the story the reader brings
to the text – what Susan Garland Mann refers to as "trans-story dynam-
ics" – is important; and because "stories become meaningful only within
particular acts of reading,"[31] a brief consideration of reader responses
to *Love Medicine* is in order. Certainly there is no monolithic readership.
Some reviewers and students have seen the characters overall as
poverty-stricken, alcohol-addicted Indians who are "durable," but desperate and ultimately "doomed." However, this is a simplistic recapitu-
lation of nineteenth-century stereotypes of the noble, but doomed Indian – a figure to be pitied or condemned, rather than understood.
What is often overlooked is the role of humor, love, and endurance, precisely what Erdrich portrays, as aspects of daily life and as modes of resistance to colonial conditions. Others have relished Erdrich's humor and
have seen the characters as complex and resilient humans (who cope with

problems all too common in some Indian communities). Still others have raised difficult questions about "authenticity" and appropriation.[32]

Recently, Catherine Rainwater has contributed an interesting analysis of reader responses to Erdrich's fiction. Noting "Erdrich's concern with liminality and marginality," Rainwater suggests that Erdrich's texts "frustrate narrativity," which "amounts to a textually induced or encoded experience of marginality" in the reader. Although this leads to a temporary disempowerment because the reader must "cease to apply the conventional expectations associated with ordinary narrativity," it results finally in a new kind of power, a new vision.[33] Rainwater aptly distinguishes the bicultural filaments from which Erdrich spins her narratives. But although this model makes perfect sense and may be true for many (or even most) readers,[34] it is based on two potentially problematic assumptions: that readers are non-Indians or, at the very least, not marginal themselves; and that Western conventions amount to "ordinary narrativity." What happens to a mixed-blood or Native reader? Does a reader who is comfortable with oral traditions, achronology, and extended kinship networks also experience such marginality? Is there always a degree of slippage between a text and its interpreter? Is it possible for a reader to be bi- or multiliterate, that is, to negotiate linguistic or cultural code switching with facility? Although it is impossible to imagine a model of narrativity that encompasses the infinite diversity of individual readers, these are particularly important and vexed questions to consider as we move to an increasingly pluralistic American literature.

Erdrich's work challenges Western-trained readers, but Western expectations of narrativity are actively confounded by writers like Leslie Marmon Silko, N. Scott Momaday, Maxine Hong Kingston, Amy Tan, Sandra Cisneros, Ana Castillo, and many others. Like Erdrich, they present a variety of voices from (multi)ethnic communities in interlaced sequences of short stories. Amy Tan writes a series of linked short stories about four sets of mothers and daughters, told from different points of view, emphasizing family and community, and spanning two cultures and generations. The short story collections of Sandra Cisneros offer diverse Chicana voices of Chicago and Texas, highlighting the influences of class, gender, and ethnicity. Ana Castillo playfully invites readers to select and vary the sequence of her epistolary short story sequence, *The Mixquiahuala Letters*. "Dear Reader," she writes in a prefatory note, "It is the author's duty to alert the reader that this is not a book to be read in the usual sequence. All letters are numbered to aid in following any one of the author's proposed options." Although she offers three options – *for the conformist, for the cynic,* and *for the quixotic* – she concludes: "For the reader committed to nothing but short fiction, all the letters read as separate entities. Good luck whichever journey you choose!"[35] Like Erdrich, all of these writers construct stories that create community and challenge readers to broaden their understanding of both narrative and community.

These contemporary short story networks are important means to promote each generation's education, to enhance personal and community renewal, to assist cultural continuity, in short, to insure survival. Narrative theorists have long noted the reflexive dynamism of storytelling. We tell and retell stories, our own and others. Today more overtly than ever, Native American writers raise questions about self-representation, about who controls the production and transmission of meaning. Many are actively wresting control of community stories and histories from anthropologists and academics. The contemporary impulse to remember and retell, not the continuous, unified narrative of the dominant history, but the discontinuous narratives of individual survivors, is part of what motivates writers like Erdrich and Dorris. In their short story sequence, they narrate (and in so doing, construct) not ethnographic artifacts, but living narratives derived from family and community. The "stories of the contemporary survivors" (Erdrich, "Where," 23), the network of individual stories recycled and reshaped, may, in fact, turn out to be an ongoing short story sequence, reconfigured perpetually by the writers and their readers, the tellers and their listeners.

OUTLINE OF NARRATORS IN *LOVE MEDICINE*

(Chapters added in the 1993 edition are unnumbered; the narrator added to Chapter 4 of the 1993 edition is italicized.)

CHAPTER	NARRATOR	YEAR
1. "The World's Greatest Fisherman"	1. 3rd person: June Kashpaw 2. 1st person: Albertine Johnson 3. 3rd person: anonymous 4. 1st person: Albertine Johnson	1981
2. "Saint Marie"	1st person: Marie Lazarre	1934
3. "Wild Geese"	1st person: Nector Kashpaw	1934
"The Island"	1st person: Lulu Nanapush	no date

CHAPTER	NARRATOR	YEAR
4. "The Beads"	1. 1st Person: Marie (Lazarre) Kashpaw	1948
	2. *1st Person: Marie (Lazarre) Kashpaw*	
5. "Lulu's Boys"	3rd person: Lulu (Nanapush) Lamartine	1957
6. "The Plunge of the Brave"	1st person: Nector Kashpaw	1957
7. "Flesh and Blood"	1st person: Marie (Lazarre) Kashpaw	1957
8. "A Bridge"	3rd person: Albertine Johnson	1973
9. "The Red Convertible"	1st person: Lyman Lamartine	1974
10. "Scales"	1st person: Albertine Johnson	1980
11. "Crown of Thorns"	3rd person: Gordie Kashpaw	1981
12. "Love Medicine"	1st person: Lipsha Morrissey	1982
"Resurrection"	3rd person: Marie (Lazarre) Kashpaw, Gordie Kashpaw, Marie (Lazarre) Kashpaw	1982
13. "The Good Tears"	1. 1st person: Lulu Lamartine	1983
	2. 1st person: Lulu Lamartine	
"The Tomahawk Factory"	1st person: Lyman Lamartine	1983
"Lyman's Luck"	3rd person: Lyman Lamartine	1983
14. "Crossing the Water"	1. 3rd person: Howard Kashpaw	
	2. 1st person: Lipsha Morrissey	1984
	3. 1st person: Lipsha Morrissey	
	4. 1st person: Lipsha Morrissey	

NOTES

1. The first edition of *Love Medicine* is the focus of this essay. The new and expanded edition of *Love Medicine* (1993) came out too late to consider fully here, but it does not

significantly change my reading of the work. Although there are eighteen chapters in the 1993 edition, they function in the same ways as the fourteen chapters of the 1984 edition.

2. Hertha D. Wong, "An Interview with Louise Erdrich and Michael Dorris," *North Dakota Quarterly* 55.1 (1987): 212; hereafter cited in the text as Wong.

3. The seven chapters of the 1984 edition of *Love Medicine* published as short stories include "Crown of Thorns," "Flesh and Blood," "Lulu's Boys," "The Red Convertible," "Saint Marie," "Scales," "The World's Greatest Fisherman." I examined "Flesh and Blood," published as "Love Medicine" in *Ms. Magazine*. 13.5 (1984): 74–84, 150; "Lulu's Boys," published in *Kenyon Review*, 6.3 (1984): 1–10; "Saint Marie," published in *The Atlantic Monthly*, 253.3 (1984): 78–84; and "Scales," published in *The North American Review*, 267.1 (1982): 22–7.

4. Laura Coltelli, ed., *Winged Words: American Indian Writers Speak* (Lincoln: University of Nebraska Press, 1990), 49; hereafter cited in the text as Coltelli.

5. For a fuller discussion of Silverman, J. Reed, and P. Reed and T. Alderman, who introduce these terms, respectively, see Robert M. Luscher, Susan Garland Mann, and J. Gerald Kennedy, cited in notes 7, 31, and 8, respectively.

6. Forrest L. Ingram, *Representative Short Story Cycles of the Twentieth Century: Studies in a Literary Genre* (The Hague: Mouton, 1971), 13–15, 17–18.

7. Robert M. Luscher, "The Short Story Sequence: An Open Book," in *Short Story Theory at a Crossroads*, ed. Susan Lohafer and Jo Ellyn Clarey (Baton Rouge: Louisiana State University Press, 1989), 148–9.

8. Paula Gunn Allen has written extensively about the significance of web imagery in Native American literature. See *The Sacred Hoop: Recovering the Feminine in American Indian Traditions* (Boston: Beacon, 1986). The idea of a constellation of short stories was suggested by J. Gerald Kennedy, "Towards a Poetics of the Short Story Cycle," *Journal of Short Story in English* 11 (1988): 9–25.

9. Henry Glassie, *Passing the Time at Ballymenone* (Philadelphia: University of Pennsylvania Press, 1982), xiii.

10. Paula Gunn Allen, *The Sacred Hoop: Recovering the Feminine in American Indian Traditions* (Boston: Beacon, 1986), 240–1.

11. Paula Gunn Allen, Introduction to *Spider Woman's Granddaughters: Traditional Tales and Contemporary Writing*, ed. Paula Gunn Allen (Boston: Beacon, 1989), 5; hereafter cited in the text as Allen, *Spider*.

12. Louise Erdrich, "Where I Ought to Be: A Writer's Sense of Place," *The New York Times Book Review*, 28 July 1985, 23; hereafter cited in the text as Erdrich, "Where."

13. Helen Jaskoski, "From Time Immemorial: Native American Traditions in Contemporary Short Fiction," in *Since Flannery O'Connor: Essays on the American Short Story*, ed. Loren Logsdon and Charles W. Mayer (Macomb: Western Illinois University Press, 1987), 59.

14. Albertine Johnson narrates sections 2–4 of chapters 1 and 10; Marie Lazarre (who becomes Marie Kashpaw) narrates chapters 2, 4, and 7; Marie's husband, Nector Kashpaw, narrates chapters 3 and 6. Lulu Lamartine (Nector's lover) and her son, Lyman, narrate one chapter each: chapters 13 and 9, respectively. Howard Kashpaw narrates only the first section of the final chapter. Lipsha Morrissey narrates

chapter 12 and the final three sections of chapter 14. Finally, a third-person narrator tells the story of June's death in the first section of chapter 1, explains Lulu's behavior in chapter 5, describes Albertine's experiences as a 15-year-old runaway in chapter 8, and details Gordie's breakdown in chapter 11. Four new chapters, or stories, are added in the new and expanded 1993 edition. The first, positioned between chapters 3 and 4 of the 1984 edition, is narrated in the first person by Lulu Nanapush (who becomes Lulu Lamartine); the second, placed between chapters 12 and 13, is narrated in the third person from alternating points of view: Marie (Lazarre) Kashpaw, Gordie Kashpaw, and Marie (Lazarre) Kashpaw. The final two new stories, both narrated by Lyman Larmartine (one in the first person, the second in third person) are placed together between chapters 13 and 14. In addition, a second section (narrated in the first person by Marie Kashpaw) has been added to "The Beads."

15. Louise Erdrich, *Love Medicine* (New York: Holt, Rinehart, & Winston, 1984), 19. Unless otherwise stated, all quotations from *Love Medicine* refer to this edition and are cited in the text.

16. Leopolda's attempts to hook children for God, grotesquely echoes, as Jaskoski has noted, "the New Testament passage in which the apostles are to become 'fishers of men' and 'catch' souls for heaven" (55) as well as the colonial imposition of Christianity on Native people.

17. William Gleason, "'Her Laugh an Ace': The Function of Humor in Louise Erdrich's *Love Medicine*." *American Indian Culture and Research Journal*, 11.3 (1987): 51–2.

18. In order to be consistent with Erdrich's usage, I will use the term Chippewa, rather than Anishinaabe or Ojibwa(y), throughout this essay.

19. For a discussion of how, in Native American fiction, the characters are always trying to go home, see William Bevis, "Native American Novels: Homing In," in *Recovering the Word: Essays in Native American Literature*, ed. Brian Swann and Arnold Krupat (Berkeley: University of California Press, 1987), 580–620.

20. To avoid oversimplification it is important to keep in mind that each of these communities of stories — family, community, Native American, European American — sometimes collapses into the others because they are not discrete categories and each has both an oral and a literate component.

21. Gerald Vizenor, *The Everlasting Sky: New Voices from the People Named the Chippewa* (New York: Crowell-Collier Press, 1972), ix.

22. Kathleen Mullen Sands, review of *Love Medicine*. *Studies in American Indian Literatures* 9.1 (1985): 14.

23. James D. Stripes, "The Problem(s) of (Anishinaabe) History in the Fiction of Louise Erdrich: Voices and Contexts," *Wicazo Sa Review*, 7.2 (1991): 26.

24. For a detailed consideration of how Erdrich retells Trickster tales and "fuses Chippewa Windigo stories with European romance and fairy-tale motifs and allusions to Christian practice and iconography" (55), see Helen Jaskoski, note 13.

25. Robert Silberman, "Opening the Text: *Love Medicine* and the Return of the Native American Woman," in *Narrative Chance: Postmodern Discourse on Native American Indian Literatures*, ed. Gerald Vizenor (Albuquerque: University of New Mexico Press, 1989), 113.

26. For an astute discussion of *Cogewea* as the first novel by a Native American woman,

see A. LaVonne Brown Ruoff, *American Indian Literatures: An Introduction, Bibliographic Review, and Selected Bibliography* (New York: Modern Language Association, 1990), 70. The collection of short narratives in *Cogewea* includes traditional oral narratives from the Colville, personal narratives adapted from Mourning Dove's life, and popular narratives from the dime-novel Western. All of these narratives were shaped and edited by Lucullus Virgil McWhorter, her literary advocate, and published as a novel.

27. Jay Miller, Introduction to *Mourning Dove: A Salishan Autobiography* (Lincoln: University of Nebraska Press, 1990), xi.

28. Anne Wright, ed., *The Delicacy and Strength of Lace: Letters Between Leslie Marmon Silko and James Wright* (St. Paul, MN: Graywolf Press, 1986), 91.

29. In many ways, Silko's *Storyteller* is more radical in its structure than *Love Medicine*. The narrative voices are manifold, arising from the mythical long ago, the historical past, and the present. Figures from Keres myth speak in their own voices, recalled and imagined, of course, by Silko, and through the contemporary narratives. The stories take on the forms of letters, poems, autobiographical accounts, myths, photographic images, and short stories.

30. Jay Clayton, "The Narrative Turn in Recent Minority Fiction," *American Literary History* 2.3 (1990): 378–9, 383.

31. Susan Garland Mann, *The Short Story Cycle: A Genre Companion and Reference Guide* (New York: Greenwood Press, 1989); Ian Reid, "Destabilizing Frames for Story," in *Short Story Theory at a Crossroads*, ed. Susan Lohafer and JoEllyn Clarey (Baton Rouge: Louisiana State University Press, 1989), 299. See also Wolfgang Iser, *The Act of Reading* (Baltimore: Johns Hopkins University Press, 1978).

32. For a discussion of students at Turtle Mountain Reservation who feared that, if not read with care, *Love Medicine* would "confirm ugly, dangerous stereotypes" of the "drunken Indian," see James McKenzie, "Lipsha's Good Road Home: The Revival of Chippewa Culture in *Love Medicine*," *American Indian Culture and Research Journal* 10.3 (1986): 53. Another controversy involves questions of appropriation. Were stories of community members on or near Turtle Mountain Reservation reshaped, but not enough to insure anonymity? Who is entitled to tell or write such stories? As the works of many contemporary indigenous writers attest, these are not rhetorical questions. But they are difficult questions to answer, particularly when many publishers and readers want each Native American writer to be a "representative" Indian (often based on non-Indian notions of what is "authentically" or "suitably" Indian). Certainly, the label "Native American literature" is too general to delineate precisely the varieties of Native languages, cultures, communities, and individuals.

33. Catherine Rainwater, "Reading Between Worlds: Narrativity in the Fiction of Louise Erdrich," *American Literature* 62.3 (1990): 406, 422.

34. This model is particularly suitable for applying to what often happens in introductory Native American literature classes in which many students, having little or no knowledge of Native cultures and contexts, feel temporarily lost or marginalized.

35. Ana Castillo, *The Mixquiahuala Letters* (Binghamton, NY: Bilingual Press/Editorial Bilingue, 1986).

BIBLIOGRAPHY

Allen, Paula Gunn. Introduction to *Spider Woman's Granddaughters: Traditional Tales and Contemporary Writing by Native American Women*, ed. Paula Gunn Allen. Boston: Beacon Press, 1989. 1–21.

The Sacred Hoop: Recovering the Feminine in American Indian Traditions. Boston: Beacon Press, 1986.

" 'Whose Dream Is This, Anyway?' Remythologizing and Self-Redefinition of Contemporary American Indian Fiction." In *Literature and the Visual Arts in Contemporary Society*, ed. Suzanne Ferguson and Barbara Groseclose, 95–122. Studies in Recent American History No. 2. Columbus: Ohio State University Press, 1985.

Bevis, William. "Native American Novels: Homing In." In *Recovering the Word: Essays in Native American Literature*, ed. Brian Swann and Arnold Krupat, 580–620. Berkeley: University of California Press, 1987.

Castillo, Ana. *The Mixquiahuala Letters*. Binghamton, NY: Bilingual Press/Editorial Bilingue, 1986.

Clayton, Jay. "The Narrative Turn in Recent Minority Fiction." *American Literary History* 2.3 (1990): 375–93.

Coltelli, Laura, ed. *Winged Words: American Indian Writers Speak*. Lincoln: University of Nebraska Press, 1990.

Erdrich, Louise. *Love Medicine*. New York: Holt, Rinehart & Winston, 1984.

Love Medicine. New and expanded ed. New York: HarperPerennial, 1993.

"Where I Ought to Be: A Writer's Sense of Place." *The New York Times Book Review*. 28 July 1985. 23.

Glassie, Henry. *Passing the Time in Ballymenone*. Philadelphia: University of Pennsylvania Press, 1982.

Gleason, William. " 'Her Laugh an Ace': The Function of Humor in Louise Erdrich's *Love Medicine*." *American Indian Culture and Research Journal* 11.3 (1987): 51–73.

Ingram, Forrest L. *Representative Short Story Cycles of the Twentieth Century: Studies in a Literary Genre*. The Hague: Mouton, 1971.

Jaskoski, Helen. "From the Time Immemorial: Native American Traditions in Contemporary Short Fiction." In *Since Flannery O'Connor: Essays on the Contemporary American Short Story*, ed. Loren Logsdon and Charles W. Mayer, 54–71. Macomb: Western Illinois University Press, 1987.

Kennedy, J. Gerald. "Toward a Poetics of the Short Story Cycle." *Journal of the Short Story in English* 11 (1988): 9–25.

Luscher, Robert M. "The Short Story Sequence: An Open Book." In *Short Story Theory at a Crossroads*, ed. Susan Lohafer and JoEllyn Clarey, 148–67. Baton Rouge: Louisiana State University Press, 1989.

McNickle, D'Arcy. *The Surrounded*. 1936. Albuquerque: University of New Mexico Press, 1978.

Magalaner, Marvin. "Of Cars, Time, and the River." In *American Women Writing Fiction: Memory, Identity, Family, Space*, ed. Mickey Pearlman, 95–112. Lexington: University Press of Kentucky, 1989.

Mann, Susan Garland. *The Short Story Cycle: A Genre Companion and Reference Guide.* New York: Greenwood Press, 1989.

Maristuen-Rodakowski, Julie. "The Turtle Mountain Reservation in North Dakota: Its History as Depicted in Louise Erdrich's *Love Medicine* and *Beet Queen.*" *American Indian Culture and Research Journal* 12.3 (1988): 33–48.

Miller, Jay. Introduction to *Mourning Dove: A Salishan Autobiography.* Lincoln: University of Nebraska Press, 1990. xi–xxxix.

Mourning Dove [Christine Quintasket]. *Cogewea, the Half-Blood: A Depiction of the Great Montana Cattle Range,* ed. Lucullus Virgil McWhorter. 1927. Lincoln: University of Nebraska Press, 1981.

Rainwater, Catherine. "Reading Between Worlds: Narrativity in the Fiction of Louise Erdrich." *American Literature* 62.3 (1990): 405–22.

Reid, Ian. "Destabilizing Frames for Story." In *Short Story Theory at a Crossroads,* ed. Susan Lohafer and JoEllyn Clarey, 299–310. Baton Rouge: Louisiana State University Press, 1989.

Ruoff, A. LaVonne Brown. *American Indian Literatures: An Introduction, Bibliographic Review, and Selected Bibliography.* New York: Modern Language Association, 1990.

Sands, Kathleen Mullen. Review of *Love Medicine. Studies in American Indian Literatures* 9.1 (1985): 12–24.

Silberman, Robert. "Opening the Text: *Love Medicine* and the Return of the Native American Woman." In *Narrative Chance: Postmodern Discourse on Native American Indian Literatures,* ed. Gerald Vizenor, 101–20. Albuquerque: University of New Mexico Press, 1989.

Silko, Leslie Marmon. *Storyteller.* New York: Seaver Books, 1981.

Stripes, James D. "The Problem(s) of (Anishinaabe) History in the Fiction of Louise Erdrich: Voices and Contexts." *Wicazo Sa Review* 7.2 (1991): 26–33.

Vizenor, Gerald. *The Everlasting Sky: New Voices from the People Named the Chippewa.* New York: Crowell-Collier Press, 1972.

Warren, William W. *History of the Ojibway Nation.* 1885. Minneapolis, MN: Ross and Haines, 1970.

Wong, Hertha D. "An Interview with Louise Erdrich and Michael Dorris." *North Dakota Quarterly* 55.1 (1987): 196–218.

Wright, Anne, ed. *The Strength and Delicacy of Lace: Letters Between Leslie Marmon Silko and James Wright.* St. Paul, MN: Graywolf Press, 1986.

From Anderson's Winesburg
to Carver's Cathedral:
The Short Story Sequence and the Semblance of Community

J. GERALD KENNEDY

If the sense of community "begins with, and is very largely supported by, the experience of interdependence and reciprocity," as Philip Selznick observes, then the modern short story sequence poses a provocative analogy to this basic social structure.[1] Assembling narratives about diverse characters to form a composite text, such collections curiously resemble the gathering of a group to exchange the stories that express its collective identity. Whether or not fictional protagonists narrate their own accounts, their juxtaposed experiences disclose connections that apparently link their lives to a larger scheme of order and meaning. The analogy between communities and story sequences becomes inescapable in works such as *The Country of the Pointed Firs, Dubliners, Tortilla Flat,* or *Olinger Stories* – all of which represent specific population groups or identified enclaves. Sherwood Anderson's *Winesburg, Ohio* epitomizes this local emphasis insofar as it maps a town and surveys its populace, yielding a panoramic view of its collective life. In a broad sense, the mixed voices and multiple perspectives in these self-conscious "narratives of community" expose the element of communal dialogue inherent in all short story sequences.[2]

Yet, as a written artifact, a product of print culture, the story sequence always assumes an ironic relation to the scene of communal narration that it obscurely simulates. In a much-quoted essay, Walter Benjamin has lamented the recent decline of "the art of storytelling" – the accumulation of narrative density through repeated recitation – noting that the modern short story has already "removed itself from oral tradition."[3] Much earlier, in *Sketches from a Hunter's Album,* Turgenev had depicted the same break with orality, projecting the short story writer's loss of community. His tale, "Bezhin Lea," describes a hunter-narrator who loses his way in the country and camps overnight with a group of peasant boys tending horses. Around the fire, the boys ward off their fears of the supernatural by telling weird stories that manifest shared beliefs and instinctive bonds. As a member of the educated, landowning gentry, the narrator enjoys the storytelling but takes no part in it; he remains an appreciative spectator, excluded from the swapping of tales, it would seem, by his sense of cultural difference. Quietly the next morning he departs for home, there to recover his place within polite society and literate culture where (we must assume) he will relate *his* story of the campfire – the text of "Bezhin Lea." But unlike the boys, he will compose the narrative privately for an invisible and anonymous audience, plying the silent medium of the printed magazine page.[4] The implied contrast between the boys' spirited fabulations and the solitary travail of Turgenev's narrator portrays the transition from oral folkways to literacy and mass culture as a loss of human presence – the ineluctable separation of storyteller and audience.

This condition of alienation that grounds the practice of the modern writer transforms the short story sequence – the gathered text as literary commodity – into something more than a commercial strategy or a formal exercise in arrangement. On some level, it also marks a social or cultural gesture, a tacit protest against the estrangement of writing, the crafting of texts destined for mechanical reproduction and impersonal dissemination. If we accept Frank O'Connor's view that the short story as a genre concerns itself fundamentally with the "Little Man," or with "outlawed figures wandering about the fringes of society," we may see the story sequence as an ironic convocation of misfits, outcasts, and other marginalized types, assembled partly in response to the writer's alienated position within the system of literary production.[5] The obscure or victimized figures populating the story sequence comprise an imaginary confederacy, a cast of loners and losers gathered to create the semblance of community in the face of the storyteller's irrevocable separation from a living audience.

Despite the many variations of content, arrangement, and structure implicit in twentieth-century story sequences, the genre embodies an insistently paradoxical semblance of community in its structural dynamic of connection and disconnection. The simultaneous independence and interdependence of stories in a sequence fosters a corresponding awareness of both the autonomy of individual stories and the elements that conjoin them.[6] We see characters as discrete entities inhabiting separate fictional spheres, yet we also recognize common themes and recurrent situations yoking the narratives. Rooted in the holistic assumptions of New Criticism, most theorizing about the sequence has underscored the formal unity implied by interdependence.[7]

Attention to textual discontinuities may, however, offer more productive insights into the cultural significance of the form.

As one's own experience confirms, the autonomy of stories in a sequence disrupts the reading process; there is no sustained plot or linear narrative, no inclusive narratorial perspective, only a disjunctive series of fictional scenes. Individual narratives trace the situations of figures whose lives seldom intersect; each story typically introduces new characters and fresh problems. While in some sequences individuals appear in more than one story, there is rarely the sense – common to the novel – of a fluid social order in which personalities interact from episode to episode across time. Even when characters recur, incidents overlap, or a single narrator presides, constituent stories tend to depict separate, completed actions in ways that novel chapters do not. The sequence typically offers no transitions, no narratorial bridges connecting one story to another. Instead, breaks or intervals between narratives produce a formal cleavage and impose a textual insularity. As we move from story to story, we experience a partitioning of fictional scenes.

These breaches remind us that (as noted above) characters in story sequences, unlike those in novels, rarely meet or become conscious of one another and thus remain unaware of the ways in which their situations may be similar. Ironically, sequences like *Dubliners* – in which characters inhabit the same locality – often evoke the sharpest sense of mutual estrangement; textual divisions correspond to absolute boundaries between one life and another. Figures who walk the same streets and whose stories appear side by side nevertheless remain oblivious to each other and unconscious of parallels between their own situations and those of other characters.

The discovery of connections instead remains the reader's function and enhances the pleasure of the text. Lacking a continuous narratorial presence, the sequence – like the decentered modernist novel – places the reader in a strategic position to draw parallels, to discern whatever totalizing meanings may inhere in the composite scheme. The aggregate text at last yields a global perspective of wholeness or collectivity that some readers would call the defining experience of the story sequence: the vision of unity or community. But this glimpse of connection, we must remind ourselves, forms a partial and problematic view, ordinarily achieved by the suppression of those fissures and incongruities that complicate the reading of the sequence and expose the gulf between one text and another. In a genre marked by formal breaks that relentlessly signal social differences or psychological distances, gaps between characters can never be entirely masked by the semblance of community.

The cultural implications of this discontinuity become clearer when we examine the critique of communal life initiated in *Winesburg, Ohio*. Anderson's influential collection, which provided a model for the story sequence as a modern form, portrays a small midwestern town in ways that seem at first glance to emphasize the significance of community. Anderson traces an imaginary geography, supplies an accompanying street plan, and situates successive narratives within a specific, articulated landscape to create the sense of grounded experience. Passing references to events like horse races, county fairs, or apple harvests fill in the picture of local life. The author also portrays characters who figure in several stories, creating the impression of an interconnected social order. He moreover links characters through George Willard, the young reporter who acts as intermediary between Winesburg and the odd figures inhabiting its margins. These "grotesques" believe that George personifies "the spirit of the town" and view him as an insider who "belongs" to the community, partly because the newspaper for which he writes, *The Winesburg Eagle*, serves as a nexus of communal identity.

The surface impression of a tightly-knit citizenry nevertheless proves deceptive. *Winesburg* follows the pattern of Edgar Lee Masters' *Spoon River Anthology*, reconstructing the secret life of a community through the confessions of individual denizens. One by one, George's informants disclose the frustrations, compulsions, and delusions that twist their private lives and alienate them from others. Gradually the reporter uncovers the terrible loneliness beneath the seeming normalcy and routine of Winesburg. Despite Anderson's connective strategies – juxtaposing complementary stories, repeating certain images (such as rooms or hands), and tracing the maturation of young George – the breaks between stories come to represent absolute rifts in the illusion of communal life. Each character seems isolated, sealed off from meaningful connection with the rest of the town, even while playing a public role.

Nowhere in *Winesburg* is this sense of dissociation more evident than in the self-consciously paired stories of Curtis Hartman, the anguished Presbyterian minister, and Kate Swift, the neurotic school teacher. In "The Strength of God," Anderson explores the sexual torment that surfaces when Hartman, during his devotions, observes in the "upper room" of the house next to the church a woman "lying in her bed and smoking a cigarette while she read a book."[8] Hartman gazes upon the "bare shoulders and white throat" of Kate Swift through a hole in a broken stained-glass window depicting Christ blessing a young boy. Significantly, the heel of the boy has been "nipped off," knocked out by the minister in a gesture that reveals his own Achilles heel. Consumed by sexual longing, Hartman prays for divine strength to resist temptation and for a time directs this desire toward his wife, who has "always been ashamed of passion." One night, however, he yields to compulsion and sees an unexpected image – a naked woman, weeping on her bed and pounding her fists into the pillow. Hartman has a revelation: "In the lamplight her figure, slim and strong, looked like the figure of the boy in the presence of Christ on the leaded window." In this androgynous scene, the transformation of female into male ironically turns the profane gaze into a sacred vision. The glimpse of Kate's private misery enables Hartman to smash the window so that it must be replaced, and he hastens out to tell a confused George Willard that he has "found the light" and that "God has manifested himself . . . in the body of a woman" (155).

Meanwhile Kate Swift is undergoing a crisis of her own. In "The Teacher," Anderson tells of the simmering relationship between Kate and the young reporter, who has been "stirred" to "lustful thoughts" by the belief that his teacher loves him. With unusual intensity Kate has urged George to live life and learn "what people are thinking about" rather than simply "fooling with words." In effect she wants him to guess her own concealed yearning, the unacknowledged sexual hunger that impels her effort to "blow on the spark" of the boy's genius. She later finds her mind "ablaze with thoughts of George Willard" and goes to the newspaper office on a snowy night, filled with "the passionate desire to be loved by a man" (165). Conveniently George feels himself "ready to play the part of a man," and at the decisive moment he embraces the teacher, who first falls against him and then beats his face "with two sharp little fists" before running away. In a connecting passage unusual in story sequences, Anderson's narrator remarks: "It was into this confusion that the Reverend Curtis Hartman protruded himself. When he came in George Willard thought the town had gone mad. Shaking a bleeding fist in the air, the minister proclaimed the woman George had only a moment before held in his arms an instrument of God bearing a message of truth" (165).

The suggestion that the town has "gone mad" gives the scene a comic twist; George's bewilderment seems complete when he later tries to figure out what has happened and lamely concludes that he has "missed something that Kate Swift was trying to tell [him]" (166). The young man has likewise missed Hartman's meaning, just as he has missed the multiple ironies inherent in the juxtaposed stories. The reader sees what the reporter cannot: that George and the minister have been sexually aroused by the same woman and that Kate, the object of male fantasy, suffers from an internal conflict between desire and propriety ironically similar to Hartman's own predicament.[9]

But despite the explicit linkage between "The Strength of God" and "The Teacher," the textual break between these stories signals an important separation of consciousness. While one might argue that the spectacle of Kate's suffering "redeems" Hartman by freeing him from the delusion that he alone experiences agony, he nevertheless remains oblivious to the nature of her anguish and (mis)reads the bedroom scene strictly in terms of his own spiritual dilemma. Likewise Kate seems blind to her own conflict and resists George Willard's passion because she cannot reconcile her erotic impulses with her public role. At the same time she remains unaware of the minister's voyeurism and his extravagant interpretation of her bedroom outburst. Ironically, at the very moment that Hartman decides to "seek other women" and to act upon his "carnal lusts," Kate too feels a craving for love. These neighbors never discover their mutual longing, however, and play out instead a script of neurotic sexual repression, each retreating into the prisonhouse of isolated consciousness.

The gap between their stories reflects the utter discontinuity between Hartman's frenzied sense of deliverance and Kate's abject despair. Between them there is no compassion, no communication, no sense of community. Both approach George Willard only to leave the reporter confounded. By splitting a potentially single narrative into two stories, Anderson accentuates the solipsistic quality of his characters' lives and prepares us for the realization that George reaches in the penultimate tale, "Sophistication." Here the reporter recognizes "the limitations of life" and – in the company of Helen White, the banker's daughter – he senses both "his own insignificance in the scheme of existence" and the inevitability of human solitude. He finally achieves the insight well summarized by Edwin Fussell: "The loneliness is assuaged – there is no other way – by the realization that loneliness is a universal condition and not a uniquely personal catastrophe; love is essentially the shared acceptance by two people of the irremediable fact, in the nature of things, of their final separateness."[10]

What is the apparent cause, however, of this "final separateness" that

undermines the idea of community in Winesburg? Why do the inhabitants of this town feel so profoundly estranged from each other? Following Fussell's logic, we may infer that such isolation is simply the ultimate
existential truth about human consciousness. But the collection itself ad-
vances other explanations. Several stories suggest that the repressive
tendencies of puritanical American middle-class life have alienated individuals from each other by inducing the sexual guilt that leads to denial
and frustration, to morbid secretiveness, or to derangement – conditions
impeding ordinary human interaction. So, for example, Alice Hindman
in "Adventure" runs naked in the rain, acting out her long-thwarted
craving for sexual release. Sick with desire, she accosts a baffled old
man, throws herself on the wet ground, and then retreats in shame to
her bedroom, barricading the door, not to protect herself from an external threat but to contain and control her frightening libido.

In "The Book of the Grotesque," however, the old writer (possibly
an aging George Willard) attributes psychic deformity – and consequent
estrangement – to monomania or obsession: Each person seizes upon a
"truth" that as a fixed idea becomes a "falsehood," a source of self-
delusion. These preoccupations remain rigorously private and incom-
municable, symptoms of eccentricity, despite the efforts of characters
like Dr. Parcival to translate their intimations into a warning. "Everyone
in the world is Christ and they are all crucified," Parcival tells young
George (57).

Other stories, though, depict inarticulateness itself as the principal
source of solitude. The inability of the grotesques to communicate the
deepest truths of their experience leaves them forever ridiculed, misunderstood, and exasperated by the inadequacy of language. In "Loneliness," Enoch Robinson's predicament is typical: "He knew what he
wanted to say, but he also knew that he could never by any possibility
say it" (169). Repeatedly the twisted figures of *Winesburg* express their
mistrust of words or their frustration at being unable to express their
sentiments; condemned to silence, each feels cut off from an imagined
community.

Recently Thomas Yingling has developed a new and provocative theory of alienation in *Winesburg*, arguing that Anderson situates the stories
in the late 1890s precisely to portray the "end of collective experience"
in America. Yingling suggests that the estrangement pervading the town
results less from puritan repression than from the "alienation from social
relations that occurs in an economy dedicated to commodity production."[11] Industrialism and mass production, though seemingly remote

from the life of Winesburg, have nevertheless wrought (as Anderson remarks in "Godliness") "a tremendous change in the lives and in the
habits of thought of our people of Mid-America" (70–1). Anderson suggests that local life has been contaminated by modernity largely through
the "badly imagined books," mass-circulation magazines, and innumerable newspapers spawned by a profit-oriented consumer economy.
These products of print culture have debased language and have filled
the minds of ordinary folk "to overflowing" with meaningless words and
trivial ideas (71). One such victim is Joe Welling (in "A Man of Ideas"),
who overwhelms his listeners and himself with "a tidal wave of words,"
making bizarre assertions ("the world is on fire") to explain the ideas
that obsess him (106, 110). Anderson's comment on the proliferation of
mindless books and articles places the obsessions of his grotesques – as
well as their verbal frustrations – in a suggestive context that associates
their alienation with consumerism and modernization. We may extend
Yingling's argument to infer that the debasement of language works
against the idea of community first by blocking communication
(through vacuous, idiosyncratic talk) and second by supplanting shared,
communal beliefs with absurd notions promulgated in pulp magazines
and tabloids.

As a budding wordsmith, George Willard occupies an oddly ambiguous position in this cultural process. He strives to build community by
passing along the stories the grotesques themselves are powerless to
communicate, but as a newspaper reporter, he himself is complicitous
in the circulation of meaningless language. Anderson satirizes his verbal
vacuousness in "An Awakening" when he depicts George uttering "big
words" to himself: "He said words without meaning, rolling them over
his tongue and saying them because they were brave words, full of
meaning. 'Death,' he muttered, 'night, the sea, fear, loveliness'" (185). In
a comment broadly applicable to the hunter-narrator in "Bezhin Lea,"
Yingling describes the divided role of the aspiring writer: "George Willard becomes the focus of collective experience and energy in a moment
of transition between an oral culture of proximity that is rapidly disap-
pearing and a print culture (the culture of exchange) rapidly instituting
itself as the agent of a 'larger' but less authentic culture of industrialism
and distance."[12] Though George himself endeavors to make connections and to restore some sense of community, we see that eventually he
must, like Turgenev's narrator, distance himself from indigenous orality
to engage in the life of writing. In "Departure," the reporter boards a
train that will carry him to the great, anonymous city where he will use

the details of local life as "a background on which to paint the dreams of his manhood" (247). George's desertion of the village is in fact symptomatic of an irreversible change in Winesburg itself, wrought by the seductive influence of material, metropolitan values. Ultimately, the breaks between Anderson's stories may be read as irreparable fractures in an oral culture already losing its cohesiveness through the intrusion of modern mass culture and its transformation of life and language.

In the influential study *Habits of the Heart,* Robert N. Bellah and his collaborators analyze a troubling clash in American culture between the philosophy of individualism and the ethics of community responsibility. Summing up a major result of this insidious, hidden conflict, the authors observe:

> Perhaps the crucial change in American life has been that we have moved from the local life of the nineteenth century – in which economic and social relationships were visible and, however imperfectly, morally interpreted as parts of a larger common life – to a society vastly more interrelated and integrated economically, technically, and functionally. Yet this is a society in which the individual can only rarely and with difficulty understand himself and his activities as interrelated in morally meaningful ways with those of other, different Americans.[13]

Ironically, as modern culture has attuned itself to the satisfaction of consumer needs through commercial and technological networks, individuals have felt increasingly less connected to a larger whole through shared beliefs and values. Or to restate the problem, the United States has achieved a complex, highly integrated infrastructure in support of a materialistic "good life" at the expense of the "larger common life," the sense of communal belonging that resides in local concerns and goals. This is but a contemporary version of the cultural predicament to which Anderson had alluded in "Godliness," and indeed the precarious semblance of community in American story sequences since *Winesburg* may function as a residual, ironic sign of the disintegration of communal life.

The crisis explored in *Habits of the Heart* – the problem of recovering a sense of connection in a "culture of separation" that has long celebrated individualism, personal success, and the headlong pursuit of happiness – forms the social context of Raymond Carver's *Cathedral* (1983), his last major story sequence.[14] The narratives in this collection mark an apparent shift in Carver's reading of postmodern American life; they seem to reflect (as the author insisted in interviews) a "more generous" appraisal of the possibilities of fellowship and communication in the late twentieth century.[15] In such stories as "A Small, Good Thing," "Where I'm Calling From," "Fever," "The Bridle," and "Cathedral," Carver appears to reaffirm the importance of communal relations and – against the alienation and escapism of bourgeois middle-class life – to project unexpected images of understanding, helpfulness, and compassion.

As such, *Cathedral* forms an ostensible contrast to the minimalist sequence preceding it, *What We Talk About When We Talk About Love* (1981). The earlier collection, which Carver himself conceded to be extreme in its truncation of dialogue and relationship, depicts the apparently irreversible loss of a "community of memory" – to borrow a key term from *Habits* (153). In the stories of *What We Talk About* there is no significant consciousness of past or tradition; banal characters live in the present moment, inhabitants of a suburban limbo of broken marriages and shattered lives. One brief reminiscence in "Gazebo" – when Holly recalls an "old farm place outside of Yakima" where she and Duane once stopped for water – betrays their own lack of roots. The gazebo on the farm represents a vanished communal life: "A real long time ago, men used to come around and play music out there on a Sunday, and the people would sit and listen" (28). Conspicuously lacking any commitments to community, the characters in *What We Talk About* also possess little sense of grounding in a specific place. In the title story depicting two couples drinking gin as they philosophize about love, Carver's narrator observes: "We lived in Albuquerque then. But we were all from somewhere else." The adverb "then" implies the subsequent relocation of four rootless characters whose stories betray the tenuousness of their personal attachments. While the collection includes a few actual place names, the stories could take place almost anywhere. William L. Stull has aptly remarked, "The setting of *What We Talk About* is indeed Hopelessville, U.S.A., the contemporary counterpart of Sherwood Anderson's *Winesburg, Ohio.*"[16] In the radical displacement and quiet desperation of his characters, Carver seems to complete the project initiated by Anderson, portraying the apparently irreversible disappearance of community in America.

To judge from recent critical reaction to *Cathedral*, however, one might conclude that the later sequence overturns this dire verdict with an optimistic, sanguine portrayal of life in the early eighties. Summing up the shift in *Cathedral*, Ewing Campbell hails its affirmative tone: "Truncations vanish; where once the narrative halted in emotional tumult, the story continues and equilibrium is restored. Despair becomes redemption; the alienated are reconciled. Hardboiled realism turns out to be allegory with a soft center."[17] Predictably, early criticism has focused on "A Small, Good Thing," a revised and expanded version of the story "The Bath," which had appeared in *What We Talk About*. The differences between the two narratives illustrate – perhaps a little too neatly – the change in sentiment ascribed to the author of *Cathedral*. In both stories a boy named Scotty suffers a traumatic head injury that leads to an agonizing hospital vigil for his parents; the accident occurs on the boy's eighth birthday, and the family's failure to pick up a cake from a surly baker leads to a series of disturbing telephone calls. But while "The Bath" accentuates uncertainty – Carver never specifies the boy's fate, and the parents never figure out who has been making menacing calls "about Scotty" – the longer narrative, "A Small, Good Thing," offers formal closure, portraying both Scotty's death and the parents' encounter with the baker, who after hearing about the tragedy offers sympathy, cinnamon rolls, and a patently sacramental loaf of bread. As Stull notes, the story ends in "forgiveness and communion," with the bereaved parents now listening compassionately to the lonely, alienated baker.[18]

The ritual of sensitivity at the end of "A Small, Good Thing" resembles similar moments of human connection elsewhere in *Cathedral*. "Where I'm Calling From" describes the routine at Frank Martin's "drying-out facility," where the narrator (a second-time visitor) eases his jittery nerves by listening supportively while another guest tells his story. In "Fever," Carlyle literally gets sick thinking about his breakup with Eileen (who has left her family to become an artist), and in the climactic scene, he confides in Mrs. Webster, the elderly babysitter, whose sympathy allows Carlyle to exorcise his grief and achieve closure on the marriage. A heart-to-heart conversation likewise ensues in "The Bridle" when the narrator (an apartment manager named Marge) gives a shampoo to Betty Holits, whose revelations about her dimwitted, bankrupt husband make Marge want to confess her own tribulations. This scene explains the mutual compassion signified at the conclusion: In vacating her apartment, Betty has polished the floor as a kindness to Marge, who thinks: "Wherever she's going, I wish her luck" (208). Similarly, in "Cathedral," Carver portrays a crass narrator-husband who achieves an unlikely rapport with his wife's house guest, a blind man named Robert. Despite his apprehensions and prejudices, the narrator's effort to draw a Gothic cathedral – with Robert's hand resting on his own – apparently develops respect for the blind man and (for the first time) a belief in the reality of what he cannot see.

These moments of sensitivity contribute to the view that, as a sequence, *Cathedral* depicts a resurgence of kindness and fellow feeling in the late twentieth century. But such a view oversimplifies the effect of the collection and ignores its critique of contemporary postmodern culture. Although Carver closes the volume with a trio of generally affirmative stories, more than half of the narratives present skeptical treatments of faltering relationships, and even most of the ostensibly "hopeful" stories portray disintegrating, if not moribund, marriages. The gaps or breaks between these stories reflect—no less insistently than in *What We Talk About*—a pervasive sense of detachment and dissociation. The relationships that Carver portrays in *Cathedral* typically unfold as fleeting encounters in lives still largely devoid of communal attachments.

If the collection closes on a note of apparent affirmation, it opens with three stories that portray the demise of relationships. "Feathers" recounts the odd details of a dinner at Bud and Olla's house to explain how the narrator, Jack, and his wife Fran have become parents. The couple has pursued a life of exclusive togetherness, and the narrator bluntly remarks: "One thing we didn't wish for was kids" (5). But the casual dinner party, which features dull conversation and television, inexorably alters their lives. The unlikely agent of change is Olla's grotesque baby, Harold, about whom the narrator says "Even calling it ugly does it credit" (20). Affected by the sight of this baby playing with a peacock allowed to roam the house, Jack later admits that "that evening at Bud and Olla's was special"; but it also marks the beginning of "bad luck." Carrying home peacock feathers, tokens of that family life, Fran later begs her husband: "Fill me up with your seed!" (25). The last paragraphs of "Feathers" comprise an ironic coda in which we learn that Fran has quit her job at the creamery, had a baby, gotten fat, and cut her hair. "We don't talk about it," Jack explains, "What's to say?" This breakdown of communication signals deeper family tensions: "The truth is, my kid has a conniving streak in him. But I don't talk about it. Not even with his mother. Especially her. She and I talk less and less as it is. Mostly it's just the TV" (26). In a few sentences, Carver sketches a disintegrating marriage. The narrator experiences the new family arrangement as a loss of trust and intimacy.

The second story, "Chef's House," invites comparison with "Where I'm Calling From" insofar as it depicts a chronic drinker's struggle to reorder his life and to achieve a reconciliation with his estranged wife, Edna, who narrates the story. When Wes invites Edna to spend the summer at a house rented from "a recovering alcoholic named Chef," he suggests that the couple can "start over." Ultimately, however, the story questions the possibility of beginning anew, that quintessentially American project. In a single paragraph, Carver outlines a fragile summer idyll of Tuesday movies, fishing, lovemaking, and "Don't Drink meetings." But when Chef arrives to reclaim the house to care for his daughter (whose husband has disappeared), Wes immediately senses that his dream of starting over has been dashed. "I'm glad we had us this time together," he tells Edna. He recognizes the inescapability of his alcoholism and accepts the inevitability of more drinking problems ahead. Wes acts out his despair in the closing scene by pulling the drapes to close off the view of the ocean. Edna heads into the kitchen, now anticipating a second breakup: "I went in to start supper. We still had some fish in the icebox. There wasn't much else. We'll clean it up tonight, I thought, and that will be the end of it" (33). The ambiguous final phrase, reminiscent of Hemingway's "The End of Something" (another story of a doomed relationship), signals the powerlessness of Carver's characters to reverse the processes of personal and marital dissolution.

Breakdown poses both a literal and figurative problem in "Preservation," the third story in *Cathedral*. Here Carver depicts the dysfunctional condition of an unemployed husband who installs himself on the living room sofa where he dozes, watches television, and reads sporadically in a book called *Mysteries of the Past*. His helplessness becomes appalling when his wife, Sandy, comes home to find the refrigerator in a state of terminal meltdown with her husband – oblivious to the smell and mess – gazing mindlessly at the TV. When she proposes to go to the "Auction Barn" to find a new refrigerator, the husband's reluctance to accompany her confirms his psychic paralysis. Her plan is both practical and symbolic: Sandy must replace the appliance, and the auction recalls the farm auctions she once attended with her father. If the desire to go to the "Auction Barn" betrays her yearning for her father's support (she is said to be "missing her dad"), the object of her quest, the refrigerator, simultaneously reminds her of what cannot be preserved or recovered.[19] The closing image – of her husband, standing in a puddle of water dripping from the thawing food – perhaps reflects Sandy's consciousness that nothing can preserve human lives or relationships against the action of time. The only permanent preservation (as suggested in *Mysteries of the Past* by the man exhumed from a peat bog) is death itself.

These three opening stories, which variously treat the disintegration of marital relationships, precede six stories that comprise the interior of Carver's *Cathedral*. Two dissonant narratives about solitary railroad journeys – "The Compartment" and "The Train" – bracket the middle of the collection. Immediately within these framing stories, in fifth and eighth positions, respectively, are two generally affirmative tales of sharing and understanding, "A Small, Good Thing" and "Where I'm Calling From," while at the center of the sequence Carver puts a brace of stories that thematize escapism and deception: "Vitamins" and "Careful." Without undertaking here a detailed analysis of the general form or details of these interior texts, we may note that this arrangement implies Carver's fastidious attention to the architectural scheme of *Cathedral* in its deliberate pairing of consonant elements within a contrastive progression. The juxtaposition of contradictory themes and types recalls the narrator's comment (in the title story) about Gothic architecture: "Sometimes the cathedrals have devils and such carved into the front. Sometimes lords and ladies. Don't ask me why this is" (224–5). Just as builders of cathedrals carved perverse, demonic forms alongside figures of nobility or faith, so Carver seems determined to produce contrapuntal effects in the sequence, balancing pity against cruelty, compassion against indifference, kindness against malice. In this cathedral of one dozen stories, the total effect is precariously uncertain.

This ambiguity deeply informs the closing stories. In each, as we have noted, an act of sympathy briefly links two characters, producing a moment of heightened consciousness. But this momentary illumination occurs, as we see, in narratives so pervaded by what Carver has called "disease" that the insights seem ironic and unconvincing.[20] Mrs. Webster's sensitivity in "Fever" allows Carlyle to say "all he knew to say" about his failed marriage and achieve a sense of acceptance. But her attentiveness stands in contrast to his awkward telephone conversations with Eileen, who calls from California to report her happiness with Richard (the man with whom she is living) and to assure Carlyle that "her head was in the right place" (165). Although she talks about the need to "keep all lines of communication open," her philosophizing about "karma" and creativity baffles her erstwhile mate.

When she calls during his sickness, urging him to "translate that [fever] into something usable" (181), Carlyle reacts in a way that underscores the linguistic abyss:

> He pressed his fingertips against his temple and shut his eyes. But she was still on the line, waiting for him to say something. What could he say? It was clear to him that she was insane.
> "Jesus," he said. "Jesus, Eileen. I don't know what to say to that. I really don't. I have to go now. Thanks for calling," he said.
> "It's all right," she said. "We have to be able to communicate. Kiss

the kids for me. Tell them I love them. And Richard sends his hellos to you." (181–2)

Despite Eileen's repeated emphasis, Carver shows that between Carlyle and his estranged wife communication has ceased, just as the relationship itself has "come to an end." And the departure of the sympathetic Mrs. Webster leaves Carlyle without a dependable babysitter for his two children. The absence of other family relations, civic or religious ties, or significant friendships – apart from his casual affair with Carol, the school secretary – leaves Carlyle precisely where he was in the story's opening line: "in a spot." His consciousness that he has let go of Eileen implies a certain resolution of conflict, but the indeterminacy of the story's ending underscores the blank uncertainty of a life devoid of communal connections.

A sense of despair similarly informs "The Bridle," despite the temporary bond between the narrator and Mrs. Holits. While the story focuses on the minimal existence of the Holits clan, Carver hints that the narrator confronts the empty banality of her own life. When Betty Holits voices her unhappiness, Marge decides to confess her secret discontent: "I pull the stool right up next to her legs. I'm starting to tell her how it was before we moved here, and how it's still like that" (201). Elsewhere she alludes to her husband's annoying habits: when Harley is not mowing the lawn, he watches television mindlessly, ignoring Marge as he slumps in his chair, a straw hat "glued" to his head. She notes the thoughtlessness of his washing his dirty hands in the kitchen sink: "It's something I don't like him to do. But he goes ahead and does it anyway" (192). At a party, when a tenant's lawyer-boyfriend offers as a door prize "one free uncontested divorce," Marge and Harley decline to participate in the drawing but exchange ambiguous glances.

The most telling sign of Marge's alienation appears, though, when she takes out the fifty-dollar bills (the "U. S. Grants") that Holits has used to pay his rent and security deposit. Musing on the circulation of money she reveals her fantasies of travel and excitement: "I can imagine one of the Grants finding its way out to Waikiki Beach, or some other place. Miami or New York City. New Orleans. I think about one of those bills changing hands during Mardi Gras. They could go anyplace, and anything could happen because of them" (192). As if to achieve a symbolic escape, Marge prints her name across Grant's forehead on each of the bills. This longing explains her curious response, in the story's closing lines, to the horse's bridle that Holits has left behind in the empty apartment. She thinks: "If you had to wear this thing between your teeth, I guess you'd catch on in a hurry. When you felt it pull, you'd know it was time. You'd know you were going somewhere" (208). Rather than connoting freedom, however, the bridle implies controlled movement; for Betty and Marge, maintaining a marriage is finally a matter of staying in harness.[21]

Despite an apparently euphoric conclusion, marital discontent also underlies the narrative action in "Cathedral." When his wife asks him to treat Robert as a friend, the narrator insists, "I don't have any blind friends," a remark that prompts her retort: "You don't have *any* friends. . . . Period" (212). Suspicion contributes to his alienation, and from the outset, his prejudices about blind people betray ignorance and insecurity. The stereotypical notions of blindness "from the movies" fuel his anxieties, and his uneasiness even takes the form of irrational sexual jealousy. When the guest arrives, the narrator imagines himself the victim of invidious comparisons to the blind man; after dinner, his wife glances at him "with irritation" when he turns on the television and later gives him "a savage look" (218, 220) when he suggests smoking marijuana. Significantly, during the drawing exercise, he refuses to answer the last question his wife poses: "What are you doing? Tell me, I want to know" (227). Carver indicates through such details that beneath the surface pleasantries and social gestures of "Cathedral" lurks a vicious domestic tension.

This undercurrent complicates our reading of the story's last pages, in which an apparent rapport develops between Robert and the narrator. From one perspective we may conclude that the physical touching between the two men discloses the primal basis of intersubjectivity and implies the possibility of community. Accepting the presence of Robert's hand upon his own, the narrator overcomes his irrational aversion to blind people and experiences the world as Robert does. For the first time, it would seem, he achieves a sense of identification with another person; his sense of being no longer "inside anything" perhaps signals a transcendence of his neurotic preoccupations. It would be comforting to think that this is the ultimate implication of "Cathedral" and that, as the tailpiece in the sequence, it sums up Carver's optimism about the cultural recovery of such communal virtues as kindness, compassion, and fellowship. But the story's outcome is by no means so clear, and the gestures of sympathy that briefly connect characters throughout the collection stand in contrast to scenes of misunderstanding that produce various ruptures and divisions. If in its closing pages "Cathedral" portrays the importance of caring relationships in a postmodern world, this emphasis runs counter to the patterns of escape and evasion that pervade the sequence.

Carver depicts three cultural practices, all loosely reflective of contemporary life, that work against the formation of personal relationships or communal ties. The most obvious of these – an authorial obsession – is the chronic, self-abusive drinking that has already wrecked relationships in "Chef's House" and "Where I'm Calling From" and that has prompted the separation of Inez and Lloyd in "Careful.". Without obvious moralizing, Carver shows how deceit and alienation typically accompany compulsive drinking. For Inez and the bibulous Lloyd, communication has also become a major problem – a point literalized by the ear obstruction that impairs Lloyd's hearing. Even when the wax dissolves, however, he refuses to listen to his wife (123) and sends her away so that he can resume his secretive tippling.

Although Carver (a recovered alcoholic) portrays dipsomania as self-inflicted rather than socially induced, he links it suggestively with the vacuousness of postmodern life in "Vitamins," where the narrator's drinking seems a response to his "nothing job" at the hospital and his hollow relationship with Patti, whose vitamin business has collapsed. After an abortive fling with Donna, Patti's "best friend," the narrator returns from a racial confrontation at the Off-Broadway bar, pours himself a Scotch, and ransacks the bathroom for aspirin: "I knocked some stuff out of the medicine chest. Things rolled into the sink. . . . I knocked down some more things. I didn't care. Things kept falling" (109). This final action effectively metaphorizes the recklessness of his existence; aspirin and alcohol temporarily kill the pain of everyday life.

In "Vitamins" Carver also locates a second source of malaise – rootlessness – which he associates with the great American myth that going west, or simply somewhere else, may open up a new life. First we learn that Sheila, the lesbian salesgirl rebuffed by Patti, has packed up and "gone to Portland"; then, Patti and the narrator talk about relocating: "We got to talking about how we'd be better off if we moved to Arizona, someplace like that" (96). Finally, after the narrator loses his interest in her, Donna thinks about moving: "Portland's on everybody's mind these days. Portland's a drawing card. Portland this. Portland that. Portland's as good a place as any. It's all the same" (108). For Carver's characters, real life is always elsewhere, even though – as Donna suspects – all postmodern places may be finally alike. He comments briefly on the psychic effects of rootlessness in "Cathedral" when the narrator alludes to his wife's nomadic life with her first husband, an Air Force officer: "One night she got to feeling lonely and cut off from people she kept losing in that moving-around life. She got to feeling she couldn't go it another step. She went in and swallowed all the pills and capsules in the medicine chest and washed them down with a bottle of gin" (211). For Carver, the "moving-around life" works against the experience of community, intensifying the vulnerability of his transients.

The third sign of postmodern sickness figures in the inveterate television watching in *Cathedral*. Bud has the TV on when the guests in "Feathers" arrive for dinner: "On the screen stock cars were tearing around a track" (11). Television provides an escape from conversation, a distraction from the process of getting acquainted – and indeed we later learn that the couples never see each other again. In "Preservation," television anesthetizes the unemployed husband, providing a simulation of life and movement in the figures that cross the screen. Lloyd, the similarly inert husband in "Careful" also leaves his television on "all day and all night" (113), and after his uncomfortable encounter with Inez (who insists, "we need to talk"), he automatically reaches over to turn on the TV as he opens his champagne. In "Where I'm Calling From," the narrator's friend J. P. tells how he liked to drink "beer at night while he watched TV" or sometimes consume "gin-and-tonic after dinner, sitting in front of the TV" (133). Marge's half-alive husband in "The Bridle" likewise sits moronically in front of the television watching baseball or anything else that may be on. In "Cathedral" a television program indirectly brings characters closer together, but the connection develops through a drawing exercise so absorbing that no one notices when "the TV station went off the air" (227).

As Bellah and his associates acutely observe, television is not merely a symptom of our contemporary "culture of separation": it contributes to alienation by encouraging a facile skepticism; modeling absurd, superficial versions of personal relationships; and fostering an expectation of "extraordinary discontinuity" in lived experience.[22] Television moreover encourages withdrawal by creating the mere illusion of human connection and community – the electronic "host" is always happy to "see" the unseen viewer, who thus "joins" other viewers – while undermining actual relationships and obviating participation in real communal activities. Television may indeed figure as the comprehensive sign of postmodern life in its flattening of experience into meaningless, illusory images as it sucks human energy out of passive viewers.

Significantly the narrator of "Cathedral" confirms this function by admitting his indifference to Gothic churches: "The truth is, cathedrals don't mean anything special to me. Nothing. Cathedrals. They're something to look at on late-night TV. That's all they are" (226). While the architecture briefly evokes a signifying power – when the narrator explains that men built great churches because they "wanted to be close to God" – his superficial characterization of the cathedral as a visual distraction, an electronic phantasm, betrays the insubstantiality of postmodern culture itself. No longer a sign that God is "an important part of everyone's life," the cathedral has become little more than "something to look at on late-night TV."[23] The narrator frankly admits: "I guess I don't believe in . . . anything." Rather, the blind man – who cannot see the television – exemplifies a capacity for faith. When Robert urges the narrator to "put some people" in his drawing, he asks: "What's a cathedral without people?" (227). His rhetorical question pertains both to the drawing and to the sequence itself – to Carver's *Cathedral* – with its ironic, fugitive rituals and shallow communal ties.

With his title story (the first to be composed), Carver sets the tone for the entire sequence, sounding a more hopeful note consonant with the positive changes in his "post-drinking life." Such narratives as "A Small, Good Thing" and "Fever" (the last story in order of composition) show an unexpected regard – some would say a sentimental weakness – for sympathy, understanding, and emotional growth. In several stories, characters actually share meals and break bread together, implying an apparent desire to be connected to others, to discover common commitments that might break down the alienation so often associated in Carver's fiction with violence or escapism.

But like the author himself, we also recognize signs of an earlier, self-destructive life and symptoms of a "certain sense of pessimism." Although he liked to tout the more optimistic tone of the sequence, Carver admitted: "If you look closely at *Cathedral,* you'll find that many of those stories have to do with that other life, which is still very much with me."[24] Traces of engrained "pessimism" persist in the brokenness of lives and relationships; although characters want to create or to reestablish connections, such efforts (as we see in "Chef's House") seem doomed from the outset. Even in stories that portray temporary or tentative bonds, the framing circumstances reflect broader, prevailing patterns of mistrust, indifference, or betrayal. In *Cathedral* characters socialize with and occasionally help each other, but nowhere do we witness communal action or collective praxis. The question "What's a cathedral without people?" indeed cuts to the heart of Carver's critique of postmodern experience, which, in its preoccupation with television and other modes of escape, is exposed as superficial, spectatorial, and solipsistic. By titling the sequence itself after the concluding story, Carver patently invites a comparison between medieval and postmodern culture, juxtaposing the Gothic cathedral (as a sign of faith, purpose, and communal cohesiveness) against the skepticism and estrangement inscribed in his own latter-day *Cathedral.*

Using the short story sequence to expose the absence of community – a critique all the more searing because it teases us with moments of connection – Carver links his work with Anderson's *Winesburg* and other twentieth-century collections that implicitly represent the atomistic tendencies of modern, technological culture. The arranged collection lends itself to this cultural work perhaps because the short story form – with its inevitable circumscription of relations – isolates characters from a larger social order, whereas the sequence, with its inevitable breaks between stories, mirrors the gaps or barriers that partition social reality along lines of class, gender, religion, education, or ethnicity. Rejecting the novelistic illusion of a continuous experiential world, the sequence constructs instead a segmented fiction of separate lives and seemingly discrete problems. Yet such collections also reveal the commonalities – the shared predicaments, desires, and anxieties – that allow us to glimpse the possibilities of community inherent in the text.

Like other sequences, Carver's *Cathedral* portrays individuals sunk in the immediacy of their own predicaments; but it also allows us to imagine encounters between characters who never meet – between the grieving parents in "A Small, Good Thing" and the obdurate father in "Feathers"; between the abandoned husband in "Fever" and the frustrated wife in "Preservation"; between the cautiously hopeful narrator of "Where I'm Calling From" and the despairing Wes in "Chef's House." Although the textual autonomy of each story precludes such interactions, the recent Robert Altman film, *Short Cuts,* captures just this potentiality in the tangential encounters that connect the multiple story lines developed there. Altman's use of gratuitous coincidence accentuates the underlying absence of collective obligations; preoccupied by their private pleasures and miseries, his angry Angelenos lack any sense of belonging to a community. If the situation is not quite so bleak in *Cathedral,* only a few extemporized rituals bear witness to the persistence of civic relations in the middle-class, mainstream, postmodern world that Carver portrays. Against the pervasive self-absorption that conduces to isolation, he projects here and there a tug of compassion or fellow feeling that briefly illuminates a broader ground of being. In stories like "Where I'm Calling From," "Fever," and "The Bridle," Carver suggests that we recover a sense of connection only when we attend to each other's narratives and affirm the communal desire of storytelling. In this sense *Cathedral* tacitly manifests that nostalgia for community that, at least since Turgenev, has shadowed the writing of short stories and the modern literary ascendancy of the story sequence.

NOTES

1. Philip Selznick, *The Moral Commonwealth: Social Theory and the Promise of Community* (Berkeley and Los Angeles: University of California Press, 1992), 362.
2. M. M. Bakhtin's discussions of polyvocal and dialogic narratives seem peculiarly relevant to the story sequence, in which stories are played off against each other. See *The Dialogic Imagination: Four Essays* (Austin: University of Texas Press, 1981). Sandra A. Zagarell has introduced the phrase "narrative of community." Using a loose theory of genre, she includes story sequences and novels among those works she regards as fundamentally concerned with representing communal life. See her "Narrative of Community: The Identification of a Genre," *Signs* 13 (Spring 1988): 498–527.
3. See Walter Benjamin, "The Storyteller," *Illuminations*, ed. Hannah Arendt (New York: Schocken, 1969), 93.
4. "Bezhin Lea" first appeared in the Russian journal, *The Contemporary*, No. 2, 1851.
5. See Frank O'Connor, *The Lonely Voice: A Study of the Short Story* (1963; rpt. New York: HarperCollins, 1985), 15, 19.
6. See Susan Garland Mann, *The Short Story Cycle: A Genre Companion and Reference Guide* (New York: Greenwood, 1989), 12.
7. See, for example, the New Critical emphasis on "bonds of unity" and "integral wholeness" in Forrest Ingram's important study, *Representative Short Story Cycles of the Twentieth Century* (The Hague: Mouton, 1971), 19, 25. More recently Robert M. Luscher has asserted the primacy of formal unity in "The Short Story Sequence: An Open Book" in *Short Story Theory at a Crossroads*, ed. Susan Lohafer and JoEllen Clary (Baton Rouge: Louisiana State University Press, 1989), 148–67.
8. Sherwood Anderson, *Winesburg, Ohio* (1919; rpt. New York: Viking, 1968), 148. Subsequent parenthetical references to *Winesburg* will correspond in pagination to this edition.
9. Many readers have perceived the time problem inherent in the cited paragraph, which finds Hartman reacting to the frustration Kate manifests after her encounter with George. Yet George says that he has been holding the woman "only a moment before" the minister's arrival. Conceivably Kate was pounding her fists into the pillow *prior* to the scene with George, but Anderson seems to rule out that possibility when he writes: "On the night of the storm and *while the minister sat in the church waiting for her* [my emphasis], Kate Swift went to the office of the *Winesburg Eagle*, intending to have another talk with the boy" (164).
10. Edwin Fussell, "*Winesburg, Ohio*: Art and Isolation," in *The Achievement of Sherwood*

Anderson: Essays in Criticism, ed. Ray Lewis White (Chapel Hill: University of North Carolina Press, 1966), 113.

11. Thomas Yingling, *"Winesburg, Ohio* and the End of Collective Experience," in *New Essays on "Winesburg, Ohio,"* ed. John W. Crowley (New York: Cambridge University Press, 1990), 107.

12. Yingling, "The End of Collective Experience," 125.

13. Robert N. Bellah, Richard Madsen, William M. Sullivan, Ann Swidler, and Stephen M. Tipton, *Habits of the Heart: Individualism in American Life* (New York: Harper & Row, 1986), 50.

14. This designation assumes that Carver's last volume of fiction, *Where I'm Calling From: New and Selected Stories* (New York: Vintage, 1988), is more properly regarded as a miscellaneous collection. The seven new stories appeared, however, in England as *Elephant and Other Stories* (London: Collins Harvill, 1988), a fact that argues for seeing this book as Carver's last sequence. But the palpable absence of any conceptual matrix or principle of arrangement suggests the largely commercial motive for separate publication.

15. Carver used this phrase in at least five different interviews. See *Conversations with Raymond Carver,* ed. Marshall Bruce Gentry and William L. Stull (Jackson: University Press of Mississippi, 1990), 56, 70, 125, 199, 210.

16. William L. Stull, "Beyond Hopelessville: Another Side of Raymond Carver," *Philological Quarterly* 64 (Winter 1985): 2.

17. Ewing Campbell, *Raymond Carver: A Study of the Short Fiction* (New York: Twayne, 1992), 48.

18. Stull, "Beyond Hopelessville," 11. Another index of the difference between the stories is Carver's treatment of the mother's brief hospital conversation with an African-American family awaiting word on the condition of *their* son, who has been slashed in a knife fight. In "The Bath" the brief scene ends in confusion, without any recognition of a mutual predicament. In "A Small, Good Thing" the mother and the family commiserate with each other, understanding what they have in common, and the mother later checks on the condition of the young black man.

19. Randolph Paul Runyon links the "awful smell" from the broken refrigerator with Sandy's painful memory of her father's asphyxiation and partial decomposition in a car bought at auction. See Runyon, *Reading Raymond Carver* (Syracuse, NY: Syracuse University Press, 1992), 143–4.

20. Carver defined "dis-ease" as "a kind of terrible domesticity." Quoted in William L. Stull, "Raymond Carver," in *Dictionary of Literary Biography Yearbook: 1984,* ed. Jean W. Ross (Detroit: Gale Research, 1985), 235.

21. Runyon rightly infers that the insinuated pun — bridle and bridal — holds the key to the title image. See *Reading Raymond Carver,* 179–81.

22. Bellah, *Habits of the Heart,* 277–81.

23. Fredric Jameson, in his chapter on "Video," pronounces the "extinction of the sacred and the 'spiritual'" in postmodern culture, a circumstance said to expose "the deep underlying materiality of all things." See Jameson, *Postmodernism, or the Cultural Logic of Late Capitalism* (Durham, NC: Duke University Press, 1991), 67.

24. Larry McCaffery and Sinda Gregory, "An Interview with Raymond Carver," in Gentry and Stull, *Conversations with Raymond Carver,* 100, 101.

Index

Page numbers in boldface indicate principal discussions.